THE WITENAGEMOT
IN THE REIGN OF
EDWARD THE CONFESSOR

THE WITENAGEMOT
IN THE REIGN OF
EDWARD THE CONFESSOR

*A Study in the Constitutional History
of Eleventh-Century England*

BY

TRYGGVI J. OLESON

London: Geoffrey Cumberlege
OXFORD UNIVERSITY PRESS
TORONTO: UNIVERSITY OF TORONTO PRESS

1955

PRINTED IN GREAT BRITAIN

PREFACE

THIS monograph was begun as a doctoral dissertation under the patient guidance of Professor Bertie Wilkinson at the University of Toronto. It has been very considerably altered in many details but the main conclusions of the original remain. Dr. Wilkinson's influence will be apparent throughout to anyone familiar with his work, although in some matters we do not see eye to eye. His encouragement has been at all times of the utmost help to me.

I am also greatly indebted to Dr. F. E. Harmer of the University of Manchester who read my original dissertation and parts of the revised work. For her many and invaluable suggestions I am most grateful.

To the Canadian Social Science Research Council I am in debt for both a pre-doctoral fellowship and a grant-in-aid toward publication of this book. The University of Manitoba aided me in many ways. It has made both a grant-in-aid toward publication and other grants during the course of the preparation of the revised version of this work. The librarian of the university, Miss Elizabeth Dafoe, and the library staff have shown the utmost courtesy and goodwill in response to my unending demands on their time and energies. The Editorial Office of the University of Toronto Press, in particular Miss M. Jean Houston, merit my thanks for gracious and valuable contributions.

CONTENTS

ABBREVIATIONS

(a) *Abbreviations of Some Works Cited*

The figure in brackets indicates the number of the work in the bibliography.

AfU: *Archiv für Urkundenforschung*

AHR: *American Historical Review*

ASC: *Anglo-Saxon Charters* (ed. Robertson) [51]

ASChr: *Anglo-Saxon Chronicle* (ed. Thorpe) [4]

ASEng: F. M. Stenton, *Anglo-Saxon England* [202]

ASW: *Anglo-Saxon Wills* (ed. Whitelock) [52]

BJRL: *Bulletin of the John Rylands Library*

BKN: W. G. Searle, *Anglo-Saxon Bishops, Kings and Nobles* [194]

CD: *Codex diplomaticus aevi Saxonici* (ed. Kemble) [56]

CH: W. Stubbs, *The Constitutional History of England* [215]

CHJ: *Cambridge Historical Journal*

CHMed: J. E. A. Jolliffe, *The Constitutional History of Medieval England* [140]

CH1216: W. A. Morris, *The Constitutional History of England to 1216* [167]

Chron Abingdon: *Chronicon Monasterii de Abingdon* [9]

Chron Evesham: *Chronicon abbatiæ de Evesham* [7]

Chron Rameseiensis: *Chronicon abbatiæ Rameseiensis* [8]

CrawCol: *The Crawford Collection of Early Charters and Documents* (ed. Napier and Stevenson) [57]

CS: *Cartularium Saxonicum* (ed. Birch) [55]

DB: *Domesday Book* (ed. Farley and Ellis) [60]

DEPN: E. Ekwall, *Oxford Dictionary of English Place Names* [108]

EHR: *English Historical Review*

Encomium: *Encomium Emmae reginae* (ed. Campbell) [11]

FAC: *Facsimiles of Ancient Charters in the British Museum* [61]

FASM: *Facsimiles of Anglo-Saxon Manuscripts* (ed. Sanders) [62]

FlWig: *Florentii Wigorniensis monachi chronicon ex chronicis* (ed. Thorpe) [15]

GP: *Willelmi Malmesbiriensis de gestis pontificum Anglorum libri quinque* (ed. Hamilton) [41]

GR: *Willelmi Malmesbiriensis monachi de gestis regum Anglorum libri quinque* (ed. Stubbs) [42]

HLC: *A Hand-Book to the Land-Charters and Other Saxonic Documents* (ed. Earle) [64]

ÍF: *Íslenzk fornrit* [23]

LD: *The Lincolnshire Domesday and the Lindsey Survey* (ed. Foster and Longley) [66]

MGH: *Monumenta Germaniae Historica*

MHB: *Monumenta Historica Britannica*

NA: F. Liebermann, *The National Assembly in the Anglo-Saxon Period* [156]

NC: E. A. Freeman, *The History of the Norman Conquest of England* [114]

Peter Chron: *The Chronicle of Hugh Candidus* (ed. Mellows) [22]

PL: *Patrologia Latina*

PNDB: O. von Feilitzen, *The Pre-Conquest Personal Names of Domesday Book* [112]

RAS: W. Stubbs, *Registrum sacrum Anglicanum* [215]

RB: *Revue Bénédictine*

RS: *Rolls Series* (*The Chronicles and Memorials of Great Britain and Ireland*)

TCPB: *Two Chartularies of the Priory of St. Peter at Bath* (ed. Hunt) [72]

TRHS: *Transactions of the Royal Historical Society* (4th series)

TSCP: *Two of the Saxon Chronicles Parallel* (ed. Earle and Plummer) [36]

VCH: *The Victoria History of the Counties of England* [225]

Vita Wulfstani: *The Vita Wulfstani of William of Malmesbury* (ed. Darlington) [40]

Writs: *Anglo-Saxon Writs* (ed. Harmer) [53]

(b) Other Abbreviations

Bd	Bedfordshire	He	Herefordshire	O	Oxfordshire
Bk	Buckinghamshire	Ht	Hertfordshire	OIcel	Old Icelandic
Br	Berkshire	Hu	Huntingdonshire	Sa	Shropshire
C	Cambridgeshire	K	Kent	Sf	Suffolk
Ch	Cheshire	L	Lincolnshire	So	Somerset
Co	Cornwall, Cornish	La	Lancashire	Sr	Surrey
D	Devonshire	Lei	Leicestershire	St	Staffordshire
Db	Derbyshire	Mx	Middlesex	Sx	Sussex
Do	Dorset	Nb	Northumberland	W	Wiltshire
E	Essex	Nf	Norfolk	Wa	Warwickshire
EA	East Anglia	Nt	Nottinghamshire	Wo	Worcestershire
Gl	Gloucestershire	Nth	Northamptonshire	Y	Yorkshire
Ha	Hampshire				

CHAPTER ONE

The Reign of Edward the Confessor

FEW problems in English constitutional history have had less serious attention paid to them than has that of the Anglo-Saxon witenagemot. Apart from Liebermann's study of the witenagemot during the whole of the Anglo-Saxon period, and Purlitz's of the relations of king and witan, all recent discussions of the assembly appear as parts of larger works. On the whole it may be said that the witenagemot is generally regarded as the successor of the tribal assemblies of the ancient Germans and/or as the direct or indirect ancestor of the English parliament.

No attempt has been made, in the past, to study the composition and function of the assembly at a given moment. It seems worth while to make such an attempt, although, admittedly, the character of the witenagemot may not have been the same throughout the entire Anglo-Saxon period. This study will in the main be confined to the reign of Edward the Confessor, both because materials for such a study exist in some abundance and because the reign is in many ways a period of transition. An attempt will be made especially to determine the personnel of the witenagemot, how far it was a representative assembly and how far it is correct to call it national. It is also hoped that some light will be thrown on the question of the extent to which the witenagemot is to be considered one of the "lineal ancestors of the British Parliament."[1]

In Professor Wilkinson's penetrating analysis of the Northumbrian revolt of 1065 the following statement occurs: "The treaty of Olney shows that, only fifty years before the Conquest, ancient ideas of dividing England into two could be revived, under terrible stress. But those fifty years had been years of rapid change, in which national unity had become much more secure. *The danger now was that of the ambition of the Earls acting within the framework of the national state.*"[2] The italicized words supply a key to an understanding of the reign of Edward the Confessor. One might even qualify them and substitute for "Earls" the words "family of Godwin." The ambitions of this house, which stopped at nothing, explain the turbulence of much of the Confessor's reign and the failure of the Anglo-Saxon monarchy to maintain itself against foreign powers. Again, although

---

[1] *NA*, § 1; cf. § 71. All references to this work are to the sections (designated §) into which it is divided.

[2] B. Wilkinson, "Northumbrian Separatism," p. 505. Italics mine.

paradoxical, it may be true that the ambitions of Godwin and his sons enabled the best in the administrative structure of the Anglo-Saxon state to survive the Conquest. It is interesting to speculate how the Conqueror would have acted had he triumphed over Harold, not as over one who had "usurped" the Crown of England, but as over the champion of the last of the line of Cerdic, the young Ætheling Edgar.

It is indeed true that by the time of the Confessor "national unity had become much more secure."[1] All the inhabitants of England, or at least the overwhelming majority of them, felt it right and natural that they should have a common king. Racial antagonism between Dane and Anglo-Saxon may be said to have been a thing of the past.[2] This is best shown by the Northumbrian revolt of 1065. Never does it seem to have entered the minds of the Northumbrians to renounce their allegiance to Edward or to set up a separate kingdom.[3] An efficient administrative system, as far as justice and local government are concerned, had been worked out and was to survive the Conquest. The royal writs, used so extensively by the Confessor, made for an extension of royal power. It is true that the system allowed great local diversity in many fields, but this is not to be regarded as a sign of weakness. The principle of co-operation between monarch and folk was firmly maintained.[4]

The great, if not sole, weakness of the Anglo-Saxon state in the middle of the eleventh century lay in the possibility which the earldoms offered to men greedy for power. In the family of Godwin were men ready and eager to avail themselves of this. Even the panegyrist of the family, E. A.

---

[1] Cf. *ASEng*, p. 537: ". . . the ideal of political unity was accepted in every part of pre-Conquest England. . . ."

[2] It is true that in the early years of Edward's reign there was some danger that certain influential people would support either Magnus Olafsson or Sveinn Ulfsson (Estrithson) in claiming the English throne. But it seems that any attempt on the part of these monarchs would have received little support even in the Danelaw. Cnut's widow, the mother of Edward, appears to have been the most prominent of those favouring a Scandinavian succession (*TSCP*, II, 222–3). Among others of like mind may have been Osbeorn, brother of king Sveinn (*NC*, II, 41); Osgod Clapa (*ASChr*, C 1046; *FlWig*, 1046); Gunnhild, the niece of Cnut (*ASChr*, D 1045; *FlWig*, 1044). Godwin no doubt was prepared to support the man he thought he could most easily control. On the whole matter see *NC*, II, 38–41; *ASEng*, pp. 420–1.

[3] On this see especially Wilkinson, "Northumbrian Separatism." F. M. Stenton (*ASEng*, p. 582) rightly emphasizes that it was not a desire to make themselves independent of Harold, but the defeat at Fulford, that accounts for the failure of Edwin and Morcar to support Harold at Hastings. Cf. in this connection also F. M. Stenton, "The Scandinavian Colonies in England and Normandy," p. 11.

[4] Cf. F. M. Stenton, "English Families and the Norman Conquest," pp. 11–12: "One of the cardinal features of English medieval history is the extent to which men of all ranks above serfdom in normal times co-operated with the crown in the work of government. To this co-operation the English administrative system in the middle ages owed the solidarity which enabled it to survive the recurrent shocks of rebellion and foreign war."

Freeman, cannot hide their ambition by the patriotic motives which he ascribed to all their acts.[1]

It is difficult to avoid the conclusion that the ambitions of the house of Godwin were the greatest disruptive forces in the last years of the Anglo-Saxon state.[2] None of the other earls seems to have aspired to rule more than his own earldom or a portion of the kingdom. Godwin and Harold must control the king. Upon the death of Edward, Harold seized the Crown with unseemly haste. Throughout their lives the father and his sons fought against everything which might limit their power. They supported Edward at first and forced him to marry Godwin's daughter. They attempted to break any other earl who might be an obstacle to their ambition.[3] They acquired earldom after earldom for the family.[4] They may have been responsible for the dismissal of the permanent navy. They ran foul of the standing army composed of the huscarles. They opposed reform in the church,[5] seized its lands,[6] and thrust their favourites into church offices.[7] They fought desperately against the king's Norman friends and finally expelled them after a crisis that brought the country to the verge of civil war. From 1052 until the end of the reign of Edward the government was dominated by Harold, and the king apparently resigned himself to a secondary position.[8] Some time after that date Harold began to aim at the Crown, although he may at first have been satisfied to remain the power behind the throne. His share in the return of the Ætheling Edward is obscure. This may have been his work, but on the other hand he may have worked to prevent the ætheling's succession.[9] However that may be,

[1] Cf. for example *NC*, II, 21: "Again, it is hardly possible to acquit Godwine of being, like most fathers who have the chance, too anxious for the advancement of his own family."

[2] Cf. *ASEng*, pp. 410–11: ". . . the career of aggrandizement which he [Godwin] opened to his family accounts in great part for the sense of strain and unrest which colours the reign of Edward the Confessor."

[3] I can find no other explanation, for example, for the twice repeated outlawing of Ælfgar, 1055 and 1058. [4] See *NC*, II, 374–83.

[5] I infer this from Godwin's antagonism to the Norman prelates and his support of Stigand. This is not to say that Godwin and Harold were opposed to reforms as such, but only to reforms which would place the church in an independent position and dissolve the close ties existing between church and state in Anglo-Saxon England.

[6] *ASChr*, C 1052. The Domesday entries dealing with property of the church seized by Godwin and Harold were collected by Sir Henry Ellis (*Introd. to Domesday*, I, 313). Freeman's discussion of the whole question is in *NC*, II, 363–71. I am of course not suggesting that Godwin and Harold were the only magnates to seize church property (cf. *Vita Wulfstani*, p. xxiv). [7] E.g., Ælfric and Stigand.

[8] I am not suggesting that Edward was a weak, incompetent monarch or too other-worldly to handle the government efficiently. On the contrary I agree with F. M. Stenton (*ASEng*, p. 418) that he has probably been underestimated and that he had greater ability than is generally ascribed to him. But I think that after 1052 he recognized defeat and to a very great extent withdrew from an active share in the government.

[9] For reasons I will later discuss I rather incline to the former view. Sir Francis Palgrave (cited in *NC*, II, 276) inclined to the latter. Freeman (*ibid.*) indignantly rejected this

Harold steadily increased his hold on the government, so that when Edward died, he easily acquired the Crown.

I do not wish to suggest that Harold's path to the throne was easy. He had many obstacles to overcome, the greatest probably being the antagonism of his fellow earls—an antagonism shown in the alliance of those earls with the king in 1051 which almost brought the career of Godwin and Harold to a catastrophic end.[1] Another opposing force was the reforming party in the church. This was no mean opposition. While in Normandy Edward had probably imbibed some of the Cluniac-Papal spirit. His Norman clerics no doubt regarded the Anglo-Saxon church as corrupt and many of its practices as obsolete; yet at the same time they desired preferment in that church. But they met opposition not only from Godwin and Harold but also from the majority of English churchmen.[2] Edward was on the side of the reformers until 1052. After that time he seems to have acquiesced in that union of church and state which English ecclesiastics and laymen both seem to have been striving for. The result was that in 1066 the English church, of all the *Landeskirchen* in Europe, was "die am stärkesten gesunkene und reformbedürftige".[3]

Other hostile forces, at least during a part of the reign of Edward, were the standing army and, until its dissolution, the permanent navy. As long as the king possessed these forces, loyal to himself, it would be difficult to coerce him unless the whole nation turned against him. The hand of Godwin is probably, as mentioned above, to be seen in the dismissal of the navy.[4] There can be no doubt that the huscarles, offended by Swegen, were arrayed against Godwin in 1051. When or why their hostility disappeared it is difficult to say, but they fought loyally for Harold at Hastings and perished heroically about the royal standard.

charge against "the West Saxon Earl, ambitious no doubt and impetuous, but ever frank, generous, and conciliatory. . . ."

[1] On this see B. Wilkinson, "Freeman and the Crisis of 1051," pp. 368–87.

[2] It must always be remembered that by this time a very large part of the landed wealth of England had passed into the hands of the monasteries and churches of England. Harold, and Godwin before him, had therefore very practical reasons for opposing any movement, such as the Cluniac reform, which tended to free the church from lay control, and for supporting native churchmen who were satisfied with the close interdependence of church and state which existed in England. (See Dom David Knowles, *The Monastic Order*, pp. 59, 100–1.) On the rapacity of Godwin and Harold see *ASChr*, C 1052; Ellis, *Introd. to Domesday*, I, 313; the so-called autobiography of Giso of Wells (*Ecclesiastical Documents: I. A Brief History of the Bishoprick of Somerset*, pp. 15–20); and the authorities cited in *TSCP*, II, 241).

[3] H. Böhmer, *Kirche und Staat*, p. 79. Böhmer in this work paints a dark, but on the whole, probably true, picture of the state of the English church on the eve of the Conquest. See Appendix R.

[4] On the lithsmen and the huscarles see L. M. Larson, *King's Household*, pp. 152–71; J. C. N. R. Steenstrup, *Danelag*, pp. 127–66; F. M. Stenton, *The First Century of English Feudalism*, pp. 119–21; *ASEng*, pp. 406, 424, 574.

The various Norman or French laymen who accompanied Edward to England were also a threat to the family of Godwin. It is to their influence (and to that of the Norman prelates) that we must ascribe the promise of the Crown which was made to William by Edward and possibly his witan, in 1051 or 1052. But with the return, in 1052, of Godwin to power, the ability of these men to oppose Harold was greatly weakened if not wholly destroyed.

Harold's problem was perhaps further complicated by the personality of the Confessor himself. Of the latter Freeman has said:

His heart was French. His delight was to surround himself with companions who came from the beloved land and who spoke the beloved tongue, to enrich them with English estates, to invest them with the highest of offices of the English kingdom . . . his real affections were lavished on the Norman priests and gentlemen who flocked to his Court as the land of promise. These strangers were placed in important offices about the royal person, and before long they were set to rule as Earls and Bishops over the already half-conquered soil of England . . . these were again only the first instalment of the larger gang who were to win for themselves a more lasting settlement four and twenty years later. In all this the seeds of the Conquest were sowing, or rather . . . it is now that the Conquest actually begins. The reign of Edward is a period of struggle between natives and foreigners for dominion in England.[1]

This is the famous description given by the great historian of the Norman Conquest. Perhaps the dominance of the foreigners is exaggerated. If this were not the case we might expect to find Normans or Frenchmen as the chief advisors of Edward, his most trusted witan, outnumbering by far native Englishmen, a situation which does not occur at any time during the reign.[2] But the picture nevertheless contains an element of truth.

Is the reign, then, not so much a period of a "struggle between natives and foreigners," as of a struggle between a monarch striving to retain some of his powers, and a set of powerful magnates bent upon usurping them? Has the England of the Confessor, while possessing a highly developed sense of unity, nevertheless become the field of battle between great and discordant forces? It would seem so. Magnate was arrayed against Crown, great subject against great subject, native ideas against foreign ideas in the realm of both church and state. In the midst, however, of all these forces—abnormal, violent, and almost revolutionary—the ancient political and legal concepts of the Germanic peoples maintained themselves and were paid more than lip service. It is possible that the failure to understand these conditions explains to a large extent the confusion of ideas which marks the opinions of contemporary observers as well as those of modern historians.

[1] *NC*, II, 18–19.
[2] In a footnote to the passage quoted above, Freeman himself marvels at how seldom foreigners sign charters in the early years of the reign.

CHAPTER TWO

Opinions of Some Historians on the Witenagemot

To deal with the history of any institution over a period of some four or five centuries is a difficult undertaking. There is always the danger of making generalizations which, while they may contain much truth, will never fit the facts at a specific moment. In that length of time, and in a society subject to such great convulsions as was the Anglo-Saxon, a variety of circumstances might alter the character of an institution from time to time. Moreover the influx of a large number of people, speaking a more or less alien tongue and exercising a tremendous influence on all aspects of national life,[1] might lead to changes in nomenclature or in the meaning of words—changes of which a later age might be unaware. It is to be remembered, however, that, although in the Anglo-Saxon period there were obvious and sweeping changes in social and economic life, there was no great transformation in political thought and ideas. Both Danes and Anglo-Saxons accepted the principle of law, an eternal and unchanging law.

Another danger that has beset most historians of the witenagemot is that of reading back into Anglo-Saxon times ideas that did not arise until much later. The witenagemot has been viewed from the standpoint of nineteenth-century parliamentary and representative government or, when this has been avoided, from the standpoint of the later Middle Ages when specialization and bureaucracy had developed. Into these pitfalls even Liebermann in his work *The National Assembly in the Anglo-Saxon Period*, which is the only recent and detailed study of the witenagemot, seems to have fallen at times. To say that the witenagemot is one of the "lineal ancestors of the British Parliament"[2] is to say a great deal. To say that in the eleventh century "monarchy, meaning the government by king and court council, gradually came to dispose of crown lands arbitrarily,"[3] is to read back into the Anglo-Saxon period ideas which only came to

---

[1] The most detailed analysis of the impact of the Danes on English ideas and institutions is Steenstrup, *Danelag*.

[2] *NA*, § 1; cf. § 71.

[3] *Ibid.*, § 29. In the following chapters I hope to show that the conception of a royal court council distinct from the witenagemot in the Anglo-Saxon period is untenable.

birth at least a century or two later. On the whole, however, these are only occasions on which Liebermann, like Homer, may be said to have nodded.

F. M. Stenton recently summed up well the attitude of late nineteenth-century historians to the witenagemot:

In dealing with politics as with society, the scholars of this generation [before 1890] emphasized the freedom of the individual. They were compelled to recognize the development of private lordship and the over-riding authority of the king. But to them the king in the exercise of his power was narrowly restricted by the existence of a Council—the *witena gemot* of the Anglo-Saxon documents—which had an existence independent of the king himself and without which no king could take any major decision. The Council, in their opinion, was a large body, and Freeman, in particular, believed that there was a popular element in its composition. In any case, it was held that the Council was at liberty to speak its mind against the king's declared opinion, and that in the formation of its mind every member was free to make his own contribution. It is not unfair to say that the history of the *witena gemot* put forward in this age was at least highly coloured by the example of the parliamentary institutions which all these historians admired. Freeman was even prepared to attribute modern procedure to the feudal assemblies which William the Conqueror summoned in Normandy.

... each of ... [these historians] believed in a primitive constitutionalism which survived the Norman Conquest itself and after a time of suppression under autocratic foreign kings, re-appeared in the medieval English parliament.[1]

How much has been done to modify this viewpoint? To answer this question I propose to summarize here the viewpoints of representative nineteenth- and twentieth-century historians. My own conclusions may then be compared with these. The subject may be conveniently handled under the headings of function, personnel, and time and place of meetings. As the first is such a large topic I have in Appendix A printed Kemble's canons one by one and then placed under them a list of passages wherein other historians have discussed the witenagemot. In this chapter I have indicated only the general standpoint of various scholars.

J. M. Kemble may be said to have been the first to make a systematic study of the functions of the witan.[2] Briefly his view was that the witan

---

[1] F. M. Stenton, "Early English history, 1895–1920," pp. 10–11. On the influence of German historians on English historians in the nineteenth century see Klaus Dockhorn, *Der deutsche Historismus in England*, pp. 123–88; and Alfons Dopsch, *The Economic and Social Foundations of European Civilization*, pp. 1–29.

[2] In his *The Saxons in England*, London, 1849. The second edition appeared in 1876 and all my references are to it. There were, of course, earlier studies in the nineteenth century, but without much influence. One of these was Sharon Turner, *History of the Anglo-Saxons*, London, 1799–1805. Turner believed that members of the witenagemot attended as representatives and were chosen by "classes analogous to those who now possess the elective franchise" (p. 186). John Lingard on the other hand regarded the witan as an aristocratic body whose functions may never have been fully defined (*The History of England*, 6th ed., London, 1878, I, 203–4; the first edition appeared 1819–30). Among other works that may be mentioned are Francis Palgrave, *The Rise and Progress*

"possessed a consultative voice, and the right to consider every public act, which could be authorised by the king";[1] that they with the king made and promulgated new laws, but that the former had the greater share in this; that they made alliances and treaties of peace; that they elected the king and on occasion deposed him; that they with the king appointed prelates to vacant sees and dealt with all ecclesiastical matters; that they levied taxes and raised land and sea forces; that they converted folkland into bookland and *vice versa*; that they adjudged lands forfeit to the king on occasion and formed a supreme court of justice.[2]

Kemble's approach is still the standard one, and historians, on the whole, have tended to ascribe the same functions to a witenagemot as he did. F. Purlitz in a brief monograph, *König und Witenagemot bei den Angelsachsen*, concluded[3] that the Anglo-Saxon state was 'kein Wahlkönigreich sondern ein Erbkönigreich"; that the witan did not have a constitutional right to depose a king; that the king and not the witan had the greatest part in the election of prelates and earls; that the right of the witan to legislate was not greater than that of the king; that it is doubtful that the witan had much share in levying taxes, although they did at times act with the king; that the conversion of folkland into bookland required an act of the witan; that the witan acted as a high court of justice; and that the witan shared in the formulation of foreign policy and constituted a war council.

Liebermann agreed with Kemble on the great majority of the functions of the witan. Freeman indicated such full agreement with Kemble that I have not felt it necessary to include his views in Appendix A,[4] especially as they do not differ in any essentials from those of Stubbs, although the latter usually employed more guarded language than Freeman.[5] Morris

---

of the English Commonwealth, London, 1832, and J. M. Lappenburg and R. Pauli, *Geschichte von England*, Hamburg, 1834–58.

[1] Kemble, *Saxons*, II, 204.

[2] *Ibid.*, pp. 213, 214, 219, 221, 222, 223–5, 228, 229.   [3] Pp. 32–64.

[4] *NC*, I, 67–78, 399–404. Freeman writes: "I conceive that my notions about the Witenagemot do not differ essentially from those of Mr. Kemble" (p. 399). Freeman, however, probably went further than anyone in his identification of witenagemot and parliament. Speaking of Westminster he made the following statement: "And by the minster still stands the palace; no longer indeed the dwelling-place of kings, but more than ever the true home of the nation; where the Witan of all England still meet for judgment and for legislation, as they did in the days when Eadward wore his Crown at that last Midwinter Feast" (*NC*, II, 336–7). He believed the witenagemot to be, at least in the days of the Confessor, a regular meeting of the witan of all England at fixed places on the high feasts of the church. He even argues that a certain gemot did not take place at Easter at Gloucester on the ground that "it was not the Easter but the Christmas festival which was commonly held at Gloucester" (*ibid.*, p. 452).

[5] *CH*, I, 133–57. Stubbs seems to have regarded the witenagemot as something akin to the House of Lords, and spoke of the king's power of increasing the number of his dependants in the witenagemot by nomination so that he could "at any time command

gives qualified agreement,[1] and Stenton says: "It was the duty of the council to advise the king on any problems which he *might* choose to bring to its notice. . . . There are few matters of importance to the state on which an Anglo-Saxon king cannot be shown to have consulted his council."[2] Jolliffe is very cautious and observes:

As between two authorities, king and witan, each felt deeply if obscurely to bear the person of the race, there could be no conflict of powers. Where the first function of both is not to make law but to apply an unchanging custom, neither king nor witan have reason to assert a superiority over the other, and we cannot force upon these primitive assemblies the monarchy, aristocracy, or democracy of which it is so hard to rid our minds. For this reason our authorities show neither king nor witan superior in making dooms or decisions of policy, or in executive enactments.[3]

As for modern textbooks (for example, those of Adams, Hodgkin, Larson, Maitland, Marcham, and White) the first thing that strikes one is the extremely cursory treatment of the subject.

Probably the most pronounced deviation from the commonly accepted viewpoint is that of Chadwick: "I have not thought it necessary to discuss at length the nature of the powers possessed by the council, for in spite of all that has been said there can be little hope of arriving at any definite conclusions on this subject. Indeed it seems at least doubtful whether the functions of the council were ever properly defined. . . . it is very difficult to point to cases of concerted action on the part of the council."[4] R. H. Hodgkin has little to say on the witan but he minimizes the importance of the witenagemot: "In the nineteenth century much—certainly too much—used to be written about the functions of the 'Witenagemots,' or of the local courts or 'folk-moots.' Now having acknowledged that the principle of popular assent existed, we need only recognize what is sufficiently obvious, that its application varied with time and circumstance, that is, with the size of the kingdom and with the character of the king and of his great men."[5] I will later on deal with one difficulty confronting all who write on the witenagemot, viz., the nature of the body, its self-awareness, if any, or conception of itself as anything beyond a gathering of individuals whose opinion the king wished to ascertain. In Chadwick's words: "But of combined action on the part of the council as against the king we have, so far as I am aware, no example."[6]

It is possibly premature to advance here any criticism of the views set

a majority in favour of his policy." Thus, he said, "the witenagemot was verging towards a condition in which it would become simply the council of the king instead of the council of the nation" (p. 157). He does not question the validity of this distinction in the Anglo-Saxon period.   [1] *CH1216*, pp. 59–69.

[2] *ASEng*, p. 544. Italics mine.   [3] *CHMed*, p. 26; see also pp. 25–32.

[4] H. M. Chadwick, *Studies on Anglo-Saxon Institutions*, p. 355.

[5] *A History of the Anglo-Saxons*, I, 211.   [6] *Studies*, p. 356.

out above, but it may be permissible to note the air of vagueness characterizing most discussions of the functions of the witenagemot. This is, of course, hardly surprising, for both the Anglo-Saxon society, and the institutions of which the witenagemot is an example, were possibly never defined as to function in the minds of even the witan.[1] It may well be that it is impossible to go beyond Chadwick's conclusions. Perhaps all that can be done is to examine every instance of a so-called witenagemot and attempt to assess the share of the witan in the matters dealt with therein. One learns little about the functions of the witan from such a statement as: "Every landbook was made in a witenagemot." What precisely did the witan do? Did the king cause the landbook to be read and did the witan then affix their crosses? Or did they then proceed to debate the advisability of alienating whatever was alienated by the particular landbook? Even such a statement as Freeman's, "The King could do nothing without the Witan"[2] is meaningless unless concretely illustrated. How was the government saved from paralysis, or did king and witan never disagree? Would the king have to bow to the will of the majority? How is this illustrated in the crisis of 1051? It may be that only by examining each particular case in the light of all evidence available can one hope to arrive at any satisfactory conclusion, and that that conclusion may hold only for the particular case. Any other method may only cloud the issue instead of clarifying it, for, while in certain matters there may be a customary method of procedure, there is always, in a society governed by the principles the Anglo-Saxon recognized, great freedom for departure from even the customary. But more on this below.

As to the personnel of the witenagemot, there seems to be fairly substantial agreement. The only detailed list, however, is that supplied by Liebermann. The witness lists of the Anglo-Saxon landbooks are his only important source. In addition to the king, he mentions such classes as the king's family, bishops (including archbishops), other ecclesiastics (abbots "in their character as powerful landowners," priests who, he says, were probably court chaplains, archdeacons, priors, and even deacons), kings of Scotland and Wales, underkings of mediated heptarchic states, noblemen with various titles (*duces*, ealdormen, etc.), household officers, earls and thegns (these occur late and of them the former are usually called *duces*, the latter *ministri*), king's reeves, warriors (huscarles, lithsmen) in the last days of the Anglo-Saxon state, Londoners (who play an important part in the later days of Anglo-Saxon England), commoners ("to the commoners may have belonged some of the clerks in lower orders, reeves, warriors and Londoners . . . as well as some of the witan learned in

---

[1] K. Feiling speaks of the "Witan, which in name and fact was vague and shifting" (*A History of England*, p. 71).   [2] *NC*, I, 76.

ecclesiastical knowledge and secular law") including witan with no special title, although these might not have been life members. Ordinary citizens, however, were not integral members of the witenagemot, although they may at times have been present at meetings. The minimum or maximum number of members seems, he says, never to have been fixed, at least legally. The maximum was probably a hundred and the minimum eight or ten.[1]

Kemble failed to deal adequately with the personnel. He made no attempt to examine the extent to which the witan were mere creatures of the king or free agents. Nor did he ask how truly representative of the folk they were, or how numerous. Indeed he never discussed how real the concept of representation (if known at all) was to an Anglo-Saxon.

Other historians who treat of the witan have contented themselves with mentioning only the principal classes such as bishops, earls, thegns, and household officers. Neither these writers nor Liebermann himself have made any serious attempt to show the weight of the various classes in the witenagemot. Stubbs is typical of most historians in this matter:

> The members of the assembly were the wise men, the sapientes, witan;[2] the king, sometimes accompanied by his wife and sons; the bishops of the kingdom, the ealdormen of the shires or provinces, and a number of the king's friends and dependents. These last generally describe themselves as *ministri*, king's thegns, and numbered among themselves no doubt the chief officers of the household, and the most eminent of the persons who, in the relation of gesith or *comes* to the king, held portions of folkland or of royal demesne, and were bound to him by an oath of fealty. . . . Occasionally a *praefectus* or *gerefa* appears in the early charters. . . . Under the later kings, a considerable number of abbots attest the charters . . . as the feudal principle grew stronger the number of king's thegns must have largely increased, and, as their power became preponderant in the assembly, the royal authority became supreme in the country at large. . . .[3]

Stubbs regarded thirty as the average number of witan present at meetings.

Stenton concludes that "the bishops, abbots, and earls attended in virtue of offices which they held by a royal grant; the priests belonged to the king's household; the thegns were present in obedience to a royal summons."[4] He ascribes great weight to the thegns. "It was in men of his

---

[1] *NA*, §§ 32–44. The minimum figure would seem to provide a very strong argument against equating the witenagemot with crown-wearings, and also against regarding it as an invariably summoned assembly. Liebermann's account, of which the above is a very bald summary, is detailed and amply documented. It would be going outside the limits of this work to discuss it in detail, but I will deal with the relevant portions when I treat of the personnel of the witenagemot in the reign of the Confessor.

[2] A *wita*, of course, is "one who knows" and only in that sense can he be called "a wise man" (cf. *NA*, § 10). *CH*, I, 138–40.

[3] *CH*, I, 138–40. In the last assertion, Stubbs seems, however, to be referring to only the tenth century. What his authority is, I do not know.

[4] *ASEng*, p. 545. He is discussing why the council would be unlikely to oppose the king.

type [i.e. Wulfric Spot, a thegn who disposed of more than seventy villages], who were much more numerous than would be gathered from narrative history, that the potential independence of the *witan* lay." Although the ecclesiastical element was dominant during part of the tenth century, yet "at the recorded councils of Edward the Confessor, though the ecclesiastical order was always powerful, the earls and thegns generally outnumber the bishops, abbots, and priests." In the tenth century witenagemots were attended by numerous witan. He refers to one attended by eighty-four witan in addition to the king and queen.[1]

Morris mentions the usual classes of witan and, while stating that "the exact number of *witan* who were present on any occasion is not known," gives fifty as the average number and cites an instance on which a hundred were present. He quotes Liebermann, apparently with approval, as concluding "that the clerical element in the *witan* when weighed against the lay element was decidedly preponderant in influence." He also says: "A majority of the *witan* in attendance in the tenth century were the king's thegns, and among these were included various royal household officials," but he does not indicate the significance of this.[2]

Böhmer, speaking of the period immediately preceding the Conquest, holds that the prelates were "die wichtigste und einflußreichste Klasse der königlichen Ratgeber."[3]

Jolliffe has little to say on the composition of the witenagemot, but he does make an interesting comment on what he calls imperial councils:

The normal governing force of the tenth century is the witenagemot of the real English of the South and Midlands, the bishops of the southern province, the five or six ealdormen who survive south of the Trent, and lesser thegns and churchmen whom we may guess to have been southerners also. . . . Beginning, however, with Eadward's Bakewell council of 924, the full extension of the empire is at times exemplified in a witenagemot which can fairly be called imperial. [Two examples are then cited, 931 and 934.] To them, in addition to the English witan of the South, came Welsh kings . . . the archbishop of York and the Northumbrian bishops, the northerners Ealdred and Uhtred, with Osuulf, later high-reeve of Bamborough, and many *duces* who by their names must have been the Danish eorls of Yorkshire and the Five Boroughs. . . . [There were other such assemblies in 942, 946, and 973.] These great witenagemots are special and occasional demonstrations of the *Imperium Britanniae*. The attendance of the northern archbishop at more ordinary meetings, which becomes common from the last years of Eadmund, is, perhaps, a better test of its reality.[4]

[1] *Ibid.*, pp. 542, 543.
[2] *CH1216*, p. 58.
[3] Böhmer, *Kirche und Staat*, p. 54.
[4] *CHMed*, p. 103. Stenton also draws attention to these gatherings and says: "They were national assemblies, in which every local interest was represented, and they did much to break down the provincial separatism which was the chief obstacle to the political unification of England" (*ASEng*, p. 348).

So much for the composition of a witenagemot. Where and when did it meet? On this scholars are by no means agreed. Liebermann states: "No place was fixed for the witan's meeting, neither by custom nor theory." Some kings had a preference for one place or another but none became fixed by custom. From the tenth century, Liebermann says, "Winchester and Gloucester saw indeed several gemots, but not so very often that the Conqueror's choice of these towns for two of his three annual courts could be called a continuation of an old rule. Tradition may have influenced him only with regard to the third place he favoured: in London no less than 22 witenagemots are recorded from 811 to 1066, nine of which from 1044."[1] He lists 116 places where Anglo-Saxon gemots were held. Those from the Confessor's reign I will examine later.

As to when gemots were held Liebermann writes: ". . . no rule seems to have existed on which day or how often the witan were to meet."[2] However, there was, he says, at least one meeting a year. Referring to the statement that the Conqueror kept court with his barons and wore his crown at Christmas, Easter, and Whitsuntide, he states: "If that periodicity had existed before 1066 in real life or in theory, the Anglo-Saxon annalist would not have noted it among William's characteristic features." Yet he does admit that "we find those three highest church festivals to be by far the most frequent on which gemots can at all be dated."[3]

Kemble held that Christmas and Easter were the "usual periods for holding the gemot."[4] Freeman maintained that the witan usually met at Gloucester for a midwinter gemot and at Winchester for an Easter gemot.[5] Stubbs saw no regular meetings in the early Anglo-Saxon period, but "as we approach the Conquest, it seems more probable that the great courts were held as they were by William the Conqueror, at Easter, Whitsuntide, and Christmas; and that the deliberations of the witan took place in them."[6] In the tenth century, he thought, gemots were held "at fixed times and places," but he did not specify these.[7]

[1] *NA*, § 45.

[2] *Ibid.*, § 46. In some years, he says, there may have been three meetings on the three high church festivals "but it is not likely that this occurred often." He states again: "The Conqueror's rule of keeping court on the three high festivals of the year was a French novelty." This opinion that there were one, two, or possibly three meetings a year, which is found in so many studies of the witenagemot, can mean only that the writers equate the witenagemot with crown wearings or other similar ceremonial gatherings or emergency meetings. The latter, however, would seem to have been rare indeed!

[3] *Ibid.*

[4] *Saxons*, II, 192. Kemble attempted a list of Anglo-Saxon witenagemots but this, at least for the eleventh century, is sadly deficient, and the confused chronology of the *ASChr* for the reign of the Confessor led him astray (*ibid.*, pp. 257–61).

[5] *NC*, II, 8, 40, 231, 233, 452.

[6] *CH*, I, 138. The documents he cites for these dates are, however, all from early centuries.

[7] *Ibid.*, p. 140. He bases his views only on the attestations of charters.

Stenton claims that "so far as can be seen, the Conqueror's practice of meeting the great lords of England at Christmas, Easter, and Whitsuntide was an innovation."[1] Morris says: "There seems usually to have been at least one meeting a year, and in a few known instances two, three or even four within a space of twelve months. Meetings occurred more frequently at Christmas, Easter or Whitsuntide than at other seasons."[2]

Larson holds that there was considerable regularity in the Confessor's witenagemots: "An examination of the sources dealing with Edward's reign will show that the royal court met in festive gatherings with considerable regularity on the great church festivals in the boroughs of Gloucester and Winchester. . . . William was certainly violating no English precedent when he celebrated Christmas at Gloucester and Easter at Winchester. We hear nothing of Whitsuntide celebration in Edward's time."[3]

Jolliffe seems to believe that the Conqueror made no innovation: "The crown-wearings continued at the three annual feasts, and were held at Gloucester, Winchester, and Westminster."[4]

It must, I think, be evident that these conceptions of the witenagemot have about them an air of indefiniteness and at the same time of great rigidity. At one time in the same work the witenagemot is a body of one kind, at another a vastly different body. But then these differences are forgotten and the gemot is spoken of as if it were something very definite. What Baldwin calls "the extreme flexibility of institutions in a formative state"[5] seems often to be imperfectly realized.

The point may be illustrated by some of Liebermann's remarks on the witenagemot:[6]

Wherever the counsel, consent, witness or license of several aristocrats is in any way expressed, all scholars agree that this was given in a witenagemot.

The ambiguity of names (assigned to the institution by contemporaries) discloses the vagueness of the notion itself. Even Alfred did not discern between the

---

[1] *ASEng*, p. 633. See the map in this work (p. 346) showing meeting-places of the Old English Council. On it only six witenagemots held in five places are listed for the years 1042–66: Sutton 1042 (? from Hardecnut's reign), Gloucester 1051, London 1052, 1055, Oxford 1065, and Northampton 1065, but the list is probably not intended to be exhaustive. For reasons which will appear below I am unable to regard the assemblies at Gloucester, Oxford, and Northampton as witenagemots.

[2] *CH1216*, p. 58. He also says: "The *witan* formed a regular assembly summoned by the king, and was not merely a chance assemblage" (p. 57). Just what "regular" means in this context, I am uncertain.

[3] Larson, *King's Household*, pp. 200–1. Larson also observes: "It also appears that London was a favourite place for holding national assemblies and that these might be called for any date" (p. 201).

[4] *CHMed*, p. 176.

[5] J. F. Baldwin, *King's Council*, p. 1.

[6] The following quotations are from *NA*, §§ 9, 17, 18, 21, 45, 46.

ecclesiastical council, common to Christian countries, and the secular national assembly legislating on English criminal law.[1]

There are three criteria which authorize us to assume a witena gemot: the secular object, layman's cooperation, and the date.

. . . whenever we meet more than, say, a dozen bishops or magnates with the king in his vill or huntingseat, we cannot but suppose that a previous summons has called them there. . . .

. . . to a witena gemot . . . ought to be referred all those records that bear the same year and the identical witnesses. . . .

Not every royal document comes from an assembly. A small permanent court council must necessarily be discerned from the large number of bishops and magnates, who had purposely to be summoned for a future term and met scarcely oftener than three times a year.

When the army was gathered with its leaders, king, bishops, ealdormen, king's thanes, and reeves, these noblemen, though summoned for the military purpose only, might constitute a witena gemot, legislating, settling suits, or conveying bookland.

Considering the number of undateable records and the amount of material that has perished, we may safely conclude that a witena gemot was held at least once a year and probably oftener.

Some questions suggest themselves. What differentiates a witenagemot such as is meant in the first extract from the small court council of the sixth? The summons? Yet the first statement is in no way qualified. Again, have Cnut's laws (e.g., I Cnut 1–2) concerning the church a secular object, or are they to be considered the work not of a witenagemot but of a church synod? When the army is gathered have we not a folkmoot (*heregemot*) rather than a witenagemot, even though only a small number of magnates deliberated? With the first extract in mind, one might ask: Was an Anglo-Saxon king ever without counsel? Is it to be seriously contended that there were years in which "the counsel, consent, witness or license of several aristocrats was in any way expressed" on only one, two, three, or four occasions?

[1] As I can find no trace of church synods as independent assemblies in the eleventh century (and certainly not in the reign of the Confessor) there will be no need for me to discuss the relation of church synods and witenagemots. Attention should, however, be drawn to R. R. Darlington's suggestion that synodical councils may have been held as late as the reign of Edward the Confessor ("Ecclesiastical Reform in the Late Old English Period," pp. 414–16). The evidence he cites seems not entirely convincing. In fact the passage: "De qua re interrogati sunt senes et aetate provecti, quid vel ipsi vidissent, vel a majoribus atque antiquioribus veraciter ac probabiliter ipsi audissent" rather suggests that the "retro multis annis" should be understood liberally and not conservatively, for the men consulted were "senes et aetate provecti," yet they could not wholly rely on what they themselves had seen but had to base their judgment on what their seniors had told them. Again, the seating arrangement referred to may have been that of the clergy in a witenagemot and not in a synod.

To sum up: Are we to consider almost any occasion on which the king is given advice, counsel, licence, etc., a witenagemot, or are we to confine our definition of a witenagemot, as Kemble, Stubbs, Freeman, and many recent historians[1] certainly do, to emergency meetings at a time of crisis and to occasions which we may call festive or ceremonial such as crown-wearings?

[1] Not all, however. Cf. the definition of a witenagemot by F. M. S. in the *Encyclopaedia Britannica*, 14th ed., *s.v.*, and *CHMed*, pp. 25–26. Cf. also Feiling, *A History of England*, p. 71.

CHAPTER THREE

Observations on the Nature of a Witenagemot

As has been pointed out no really satisfactory definition of the Anglo-Saxon witenagemot exists. This is perhaps not unfortunate, for in dealing with judicial and political practices in the Middle Ages there is danger that whenever one lays down a hard and fast rule or attempts an exact definition one may be doing violence to the spirit of the Middle Ages and to historical accuracy. However, in the case of an institution as often mentioned as the witenagemot, it would seem futile to attempt a discussion of, say, its functions without having at least tried to define its nature and composition. Was it a body with a fixed membership, meeting at regular intervals, or was it an indeterminate body, meeting only irregularly? As we have seen, there is no agreement on this matter.

It is especially, I think, lack of definition on this point that accounts for the many differing views on the nature and functions of a witenagemot. What, for example, is one to make of Liebermann's statement that: "Wherever the counsel, consent, witness or license of several aristocrats is in any way expressed, all scholars agree that this was given in a witena gemot"?[1] Does this not indicate a body whose composition is extremely fluid, the presence of whose members is often the result of accident rather than plan, and whose meetings might take place anywhere and at any time? Yet the same writer tells us:

> Not every royal document comes from an assembly. A small permanent court council must necessarily be discerned from the large number of bishops and magnates, who had purposely to be summoned for a future term and met scarcely oftener than three times a year. This council, most likely guided by the king's bishop or "handpriest," issued all those governmental writs which appear from Ethelred II's time. As the king did not write himself, and these records also bear as a rule a few witnesses' names,[2] they are not private royal letters. Other court council documents may possibly be those issued under the king's name, which betray no trace of an assembly and show a very small list of witnesses (without the possibility of its having been curtailed by some lazy copyist), and are undated. If on the other hand place and day are given, and especially if they coincide with

---

[1] *NA*, § 9.

[2] Dr. Harmer has pointed out to me that, as a generalization, this is, of course, not true. They are generally unwitnessed.

B 4133   C

a favourite assembly locality and with christmas, easter or whitsuntide, the presumption speaks rather for the origin of such documents in a witena gemot.[1]

From this certain conclusions emerge. The witenagemot is a body whose
members are summoned to meetings. It meets with some regularity, occasionally as often as three times a year, at certain favoured meeting places.
It is thus a formal assembly. In other words, the witenagemot here seems
to be conceived of as an assembly similar to the formal crown-wearings
of the Norman kings.[2] How is such a conception of the witenagemot to be
reconciled with that of the former quotation which, as I understand it,
must mean that whenever the king consults, or acts with the counsel of,
a few lay and/or clerical magnates, the occasion should be regarded as
a witenagemot?

Moreover in another passage Liebermann largely qualifies the formal
and ceremonial character ascribed to the assembly in the second quotation:

> . . . whenever we meet more than, say, a dozen bishops or magnates with the
> king in his vill or huntingseat, we cannot but suppose that a previous summons
> has called them there, since without preparations a mere village would have been
> unable to feed the royal court and noble guests, each with a couple of persons
> as retinue and with several horses.[3]

Here the summons seems to be the determinant of whether the assembly
is to be considered a witenagemot. Time and place seem of little importance.

What, again, is to be made of the "small permanent court council"?
Liebermann cites a homilist of the eleventh century as "admonishing the

---

[1] *NA*, § 21. F. M. Stenton seems to make a similar distinction between what he calls
the *curia regis* and the *commune concilium* of the Conqueror. He calls the latter "the Anglo-
Norman equivalent of the Anglo-Saxon *witena gemot*." It met three times a year (*ASEng*,
pp. 632–3). As I understand it Professor Stenton implies that the witenagemot handled
the business which after the Conquest was dealt with by both the *curia regis* and the
commune concilium: "But the business of the *Commune Concilium*, though equal in range, was
certainly less in volume than that with which the *witan* had dealt" (*ibid.*, p. 633). He
would, however, probably agree that the distinction is a modern one, hardly perceived
by contemporaries. Cf. Baldwin, *King's Council*, pp. 3–4; W. A. Morris, "The Lesser
Curia Regis under the First Two Norman Kings of England," pp. 772–8. G. O. Sayles
makes a distinction between the formal meetings of the witan, attended by about thirty
or forty persons, at least once and frequently three times a year, and meetings of an
administrative group which was in continuous existence (*The Medieval Foundations of
England*, pp. 175–6). There is, he says, "more than the presumption . . . that the king
and his intimate advisors formed a small body, constantly supervising the work of government and controlling the administration of justice as they journeyed through the country"
(*ibid.*, p. 175). This myth of a small court council, distinct from the king and his witan,
dies hard.
[2] *ASChr*, E 1087. According to J. C. H. R. Steenstrup (*Normandiets Historie*, p. 231)
the Norman dukes were accustomed to hold such gatherings in the duchy before the
Conquest: "Herredage blev altsaa holdte. Det var vel især ved de tre store Kirkefester,
at Hertugen samledes med Stormendene."   [3] *NA*, § 18.

king often to mediate wisdom with his *witan*," and then goes on to say that the homilist "seems rather to send him to the council chamber than to lay stress on frequent witena gemots."[1] On what grounds the homilist made a distinction between the council chamber and a witenagemot one is not told. Nor is it clear just what Liebermann means by this small council "likely guided by the king's bishop or 'handpriest,' " which "issued all those governmental writs which appear from Ethelred II's time."[2] It seems that this council might far better be called the writing office of the Anglo-Saxon kings,[3] for its chief function would seem to have been that of issuing documents not made, presumably, in a witenagemot. In any case there appears to be no justification for regarding the king's intimate advisors as counsellors distinct from the witan, unless a witenagemot is defined as a summoned gathering of large numbers of witan.

Thus, even the foremost authority on the Anglo-Saxon witenagemot fails to make clear just what kind of gathering is to be considered a witenagemot. This confusion arises in many cases, perhaps, from the assumption, conscious or unconscious, that the witenagemot was a much more clearly defined body than it actually was, that it consisted of a group of men who represented the folk and every local interest in much the same way as parliament does in a later age, that it was a national assembly in the modern sense of that term. Such conceptions cannot, however, be reconciled with the sources, any more than can the conception that only a large gathering of witan deserves the name of witenagemot. Smaller gatherings must also be given this designation, and indeed this is admitted by Liebermann.[4] Hence, it seems impossible to agree with Professor

[1] *Ibid.*, § 21.

[2] His footnote (*NA*, § 21), "Harold I. at Oxford in 1039–40 was accompanied by one bishop. Stigand was in 1051 the king's handpriest and counsellor," is not enlightening.

[3] There is little doubt, I think, that there was a writing office, if not a chancery, in existence in Anglo-Saxon England in the tenth and eleventh centuries. Both Stenton (*ASEng*, p. 349) and H. W. C. Davis (*Regesta regum Anglo-Normannorum 1066–1154*, p. xi) affirm that the tenth-century English kings had a staff of clerks who accompanied them and issued their charters and ordinances. R. Drögereit has shown that from the time of Ethelstan to *ca.* 973 charters were being produced by the royal clerks ("Gab es eine angelsächsische Königskanzlei?" pp. 335–436). In the eighth and ninth centuries there may have been no royal writing office. Mary Prescott Parsons has shown that in these centuries some charters were produced by the beneficiaries themselves ("Some Scribal Memoranda for Anglo-Saxon Charters of the 8th and 9th Centuries," pp. 13–32). I may add here a few further references on the subject of the writing office: J. R. Green, *The Conquest of England*; J. H. Round, *Feudal England*, pp. 421–30, and "The Officers of Edward the Confessor," p. 92; W. H. Stevenson, "An Old English Charter of William the Conqueror," pp. 731–44; Larson, *King's Household*, pp. 140–4; Hall, *Studies*, pp. 205–7; *Feudal Documents*, ed. Douglas, p. xxxii; Harmer, "Anglo-Saxon Charters," pp. 339–67, and *Anglo-Saxon Writs*, pp. 57–61; S. B. Chrimes, *An Introduction to the Administrative History of Mediaeval England*, pp. 11–17. For further references see Drögereit, "Gab es eine angelsächsische Königskanzlei?"

[4] *NA*, § 9: "Charters signed by 1–3 bishops, 2–5 earls are inscribed as 'witena gemot.' "

Morris: "The *witan* formed a regular assembly summoned by the king, and was [*sic*] not merely a chance assemblage as was once believed."[1] Only by defining a witenagemot as a national assembly and then confining the definition of a national assembly to large, ceremonial gatherings to which the witan have been summoned on the high church feasts can such a statement be justified. There is nothing to show either that an informal meeting of the king and a few witan might not be called a witenagemot, or that in such a meeting the same business might not be handled as in a large, formal meeting.

It must be emphasized that in the Anglo-Saxon period the state, as we know it, scarcely existed. To speak of an act of an Anglo-Saxon king as unconstitutional has no meaning in the modern sense of that term. There is no such thing as a constitution in the early Middle Ages; there is only the "eternal law" which it is the duty of the king and every member of the community to maintain. An act of the king must be either legal or illegal. If it conforms to the law, maintains it, or executes it, it is legal. If it goes against the law, does violence to it, it is illegal, and in that sense only is it unconstitutional.[2] It must, of course, be remembered that the principle of consent is fundamental in the early Middle Ages, but there is no hard and fast rule as to how the ruler is to obtain consent. If his action is in accord with the law,[3] consent on the part of the community may be assumed, and failure to consult the community or those deemed to represent it does not make the act of the king unconstitutional. If in doubt the king *may* consult the community or those who speak for it. Thus at one time consent or counsel may be explicitly sought; at another (in exactly similar circumstances) the king may act alone. It is true that certain lines of procedure often become customary, but at all times there is great freedom in the method of assuring supremacy of law.[4]

---

[1] *CH1216*, pp. 57–58. He gives no adequate reasons for his statement. I shall have much to say below on the matter of summons. The important question is, of course, whether only such things as are done at meetings to which the king has summoned his witan are to be considered as acts of the king and witan, or whether the day-to-day acts of the king which he does after consulting a few magnates who happen to be with him are also to be reckoned as acts of the king and his witan.

[2] Jolliffe brings this out clearly when speaking of a case in which the witan deemed that a bishop had been unjustly deprived of land by the king. He sees in this "a practical application of the supremacy of law," and says that the verdict "reflects no constitutional subordination of the king to the witan" (*CHMed*, pp. 27–28). Of all the accounts of the witan, Jolliffe's seems to me to show the clearest perception of the fundamental principles of the society in which the witan existed.

[3] There is, of course, no question of the law being in the bosom of the king in the sense that he declares what is law. It is here that the principle of consent becomes operative. The king and the witan (those who know and are felt to represent the nation) declare what is law. There is no conflict between the supremacy of law and the principle of consent or counsel. Cf. *CHMed*, p. 25.

[4] Fritz Kern, *Kingship and Law in the Middle Ages*, pp. 187–94.

It follows from this that the ruler may consult whom he wishes, within limits, for usually custom decrees who are the proper men to consult. But the king does not have to consult all for his acts to have full validity. He decides whom he is to consult and they may be many or few or none at all. Thus an Anglo-Saxon king may consult all his witan or only a few of them, but the meeting, whether large or small, will, according to the ideas of the Anglo-Saxons, rank as a witenagemot. For the important matter is consent or counsel, not the number consulted or counselling.

It is impossible to hold that "wherever the counsel, consent, witness or license of several aristocrats is in any way expressed . . . this was given in a witena gemot," and then deny the competence of a witenagemot to any but meetings to which the witan have been summoned in fair numbers and with some regularity or at a time of grave crisis. It is, of course, possible to define arbitrarily only such large meetings as witenagemots, but one must then be prepared to show that the Anglo-Saxons distinguished between them and less formal and smaller gatherings. The chroniclers, indeed, seem to speak chiefly of large and formal witenagemots, but this should not be taken to mean that they deemed only such assemblies witenagemots, for they record only the outstanding and not the everyday business of the realm.

That an eleventh-century Anglo-Saxon king was never without the presence of a dozen or more great churchmen and lay magnates at his court goes without saying.[1] Then there were always in attendance the members of the king's household.[2] Are they to be considered witan? Are they, together with the great churchmen and lay magnates present at court, the witan whom the king as a rule consults, the men on whose advice he relies as he progresses throughout the country? Are they the witan who witness various transactions which, to give them greater validity or for some other reason, are performed in the presence of the king and his entourage?[3] Did this body, presided over by the king, differ in organization and function from the larger body which may have met on festive occasions or at a time of grave crisis or are the two one and the same institution, differing only in size and magnificence? Could one do what the other could?[4]

---

[1] Cf. Steenstrup, *Normandiets Historie*, p. 231: "Raadgivere og Fortrolige have Hertugerne altid omkring sig, deres Medvirkning ved hans Beslutninger omtales ved hver en Lejlighed."

[2] The most detailed examination of the household of the Anglo-Saxon kings is Larson, *King's Household*. Cf. Steenstrup, *Danelag*, p. 125: "Omkring den angelsaksiske Konge færdedes i övrigt en Mængde *cyninges þegnas* med forskjelligt Hverv. Saaledes nævnes Skatmesteren (hordere), Drosten (discþegn), Skjænken (pincerna), Hrægelþegn, som har med Kongens Klæder at gjöre, Horsþegn, som vilde svare til Marsken eller Stalleren andensteds, Bannerföreren (vexillifer) osv."

[3] I am thinking particularly of such things as grants of land made by private individuals and bequests and wills.

[4] Cf. Baldwin's discussion of the Anglo-Norman *curia regis* (*King's Council*, pp. 1–6).

The small body of those who happened to be in attendance on the king would seem to be what Liebermann calls the "small permanent court council," although his use of the word "permanent" might suggest that he believed its membership to be confined to individuals who were permanently attached to the court; in this case its members would be the royal chaplains, the personnel of the king's writing office, and such magnates as held household offices and were resident at court. Even such a body, although Liebermann seems to assign little importance to it, might when reinforced with such lay magnates and churchmen as happened to be with the king at any given time and place be competent to do all that a larger witenagemot could do. It might correspond to what Stenton calls the *curia regis* of the Conqueror.[1] If its members were witan, did they, when they met to consider any question the king submitted, form a witenagemot? Did contemporaries make any distinction except that of numbers—which in mediaeval times was of no consequence—between these meetings and larger assemblies? All these questions demand answers.

A further query may be made: Would it be correct to call such a gathering a national assembly? To this question one may reply with another: Is there any evidence that our conception of what constitutes a national assembly was known to the Anglo-Saxons? Kern has pointed out that "certainly, in point of law we have to distinguish between rules of folk-right and royal law, between popular courts and royal courts in, for example, the Frankish period. But the period itself, in theory, did not and could not know this difference."[2] In the same way a modern historian may distinguish between the king's meeting with the few witan who happened to be at court and his meeting with numerous witan in more formal, more ceremonial, and possibly specially summoned gemots. But would it be safe to assume that contemporaries saw any basic differences between the larger and smaller assembly?

The function of the state, if such a term may be employed when speaking of the early Middle Ages, was simply the maintenance of law, i.e., the securing of his subjective rights to every individual. The king and every individual in the state are bound to uphold the law. The way in which this is done is of no consequence. A few witan acting with the king (if not the king alone) may be as representative of the nation, provided their actions are in conformity with the law, as the whole nation acting as one.[3]

The above remarks are simply to be taken as a *caveat* against reading the present into the past; against making distinctions which, although

---

[1] *ASEng*, p. 632.
[2] Kern, *Kingship and Law*, p. 190; cf. also Geo. L. Haskins, *The Growth of English Representative Government*, pp. 95–96.
[3] Cf. Kern, *Kingship and Law*, pp. 70–71.

they may seem natural to us and necessary for the understanding of the growth of institutions, may have been unknown or meaningless in the past.[1] To attempt to confine the definition of a witenagemot to gatherings which are, for all essential purposes, crown-wearings, or to gatherings of most of the leading lay and ecclesiastical personages on the occasion of some great emergency, is, possibly, to neglect the ideas and concepts of the time. To call such meetings national assemblies is, possibly, also misleading. It may be that only in the sense that the king is the centre of the government, and the assembly with which he meets the central assembly, can the witenagemot be called a national assembly.[2] In the mind of the Anglo-Saxon the hundred and shire moots, i.e., the real folkmoots, in which the folk or nation participated directly, were, possibly, more truly national assemblies than the gathering of the witan about the king.[3]

The very "ambiguity of names," to use Liebermann's phrase, seems to betray the lack of any definition or distinction in the Anglo-Saxon period. It is true that Liebermann asserts that about the year 1000 the name *witenagemot* "begins to bear the technical sense for the English institution" and that "by the middle of the eleventh century it . . . constitutes the official name."[4] He does not explain what makes a name official, and he admits that, although it is the "official" name, it "retains several other meanings even in the twelfth century," e.g., county court in 1124. The great number of names used to designate meetings of the witan to the very last is interesting.[5] It is also noteworthy that as late as the end of the tenth century a shire court is referred to as "on ealles heres ge mote on hamtone."[6] This is, of course, the same word as the OIcel *alsherjarþing*. How often do we find such an all-inclusive term used for a witenagemot? Liebermann sees a national and republican meaning, independent of monarchy in certain cases, e.g., *þeodwitan*.[7] However, at least one of the examples he cites as conveying this meaning, *Angelcynnes witan*,[8] seems to mean nothing more than "the witan of the Angle race" as contrasted to those of the Danish race. This certainly seems the sense in version F (1016) of the *Chronicle*, for the other versions (C, D, E) speak only of

---

[1] An example of what I mean is found in a statement of L. M. Larson made in the process of attempting to establish a date: "With fresh legislation in mind the king would hardly have fallen back on the authority of 'ancient law' " ("The Political Policies of Cnut as King of England," p. 741). This statement introduces the concept of enacted law into an age which knew no other law than the "ancient law." Cf. Kern, *Kingship and Law*, pp. 70–75; Geo. L. Haskins, *English Representative Government*, pp. 100–1.

[2] See chap. VII.

[3] Jolliffe is instructive here (*CHMed*, pp. 23–25).

[4] *NA*, § 15.

[5] Cf. *ibid.*

[6] See *CS*, 1130.

[7] *NA*, § 10.

[8] *ASChr*, 978.

"all the witan that were in London." But the function of these various gemots is the same, the maintenance of the rights of the individual, the preservation of the supremacy of law.

Let us now examine what the evidence from the reign of the Confessor has to tell about the nature of a witenagemot.

CHAPTER FOUR

Direct and Indirect Information on Witenagemots in the Reign of the Confessor

To a certain extent we are, when dealing with the witenagemot, arguing in a circle. We usually start with the assumption that a witenagemot is an assembly competent to do certain things. Then, when we find our sources telling us that these certain things were done, we treat this as proof that a witenagemot was held. For example, we start with some such a premise as: "Bishops are appointed by the king and witan." Then we find in the sources: "*Anno* 1044 a bishop was appointed." *Ergo*, we conclude: "In 1044 a witenagemot was held." But how do we know that our original premise is true? Very often our only reason for thinking so is that our sources have recorded, to use our example, the appointment of a bishop in such terms that the co-operation of king and witan in the appointment may be inferred. It is true that in certain cases the sources are explicit in their statement that king and witan acted jointly, but this is the exception and not the rule.[1] Nor does it follow that, even in matters which are explicitly mentioned as having been handled jointly by king and witan, the two co-operated on every occasion when problems of a similar nature demanded attention.

Unfortunately the sources for the Confessor's reign very seldom contain

---

[1] All the entries in the *Anglo-Saxon Chronicle* which, in my opinion, contain explicit references to witenagemots in the reign of the Confessor are cited on the following pages. How few they are! But this is not all. In many cases where the sources seem to speak explicitly we are by no means on sure ground. For example, the laws *II Cnut* begin: "This is further the secular ordinance which, by the advice of my councillors [mid minan witenan ræde], I desire should be observed over all England" (*The Laws of the Kings of England from Edmund to Henry I*, ed. A. J. Robertson, pp. 174–5). This seems clear enough until we ask: What exactly do the words *witenan* and *ræde* mean? As for the first, almost our whole knowledge of the personnel of the witan comes from the witness lists of the landbooks, and there is no agreement on the question of how many of those present at a witenagemot had their names inscribed on the landbooks made in the gemot. As to the second, even if we admit that the witan had some share in the declaration of law, there is no agreement as to whether the part they played was active or passive. Similarly varied opinions exist as to the meaning of the word "consent" in the phrase which occurs so often in the landbooks, *his testibus consentientibus* (see e.g., Drögereit, "Gab es eine angel-sächsische Königskanzlei," p. 430).

explicit information on the holding of witenagemots. Usually one can only infer meetings from the accounts of the events of the reign. It is true that the *Anglo-Saxon Chronicle* and histories of monastic foundations do sometimes definitely state that a witenagemot or a *concilium* was held, but such instances are few. It is also true that genuine charters must be presumed to have originated in a witenagemot,[1] but it is often difficult to determine the authenticity of a charter, and even when it is possible to do so the charter may carry no date and place.

What has the *Anglo-Saxon Chronicle* to offer in the way of definite information on witenagemots? It is well known that the word "witenagemot" does not occur in Anglo-Saxon laws or charters, but it does occur in the *Chronicle.* As we have seen, it is Liebermann's opinion that around the year 1000 it begins "to bear the technical sense for the English institution," and that "By the middle of the eleventh century it is used freely in the Anglo-Saxon annals (A 1048, 1050, 1052, 1055) and constitutes the official name."[2] An examination of the *Chronicle,* however, hardly bears out this statement of Liebermann. The word is used in the entries dealing with the Confessor's reign only seven times, in connection with four gemots in four versions of the *Chronicle.*[3]

On the other hand the words "mycel gemot" occur four times for three gemots in three versions of the *Chronicle.*[4] In addition to these meetings referred to by name, there are two instances in the *Chronicle* where Edward is said to have sent for his witan. Both refer to the same incident, the assembly at Gloucester in 1051.[5] Another entry reports that the king and witan acted.[6] It should also be mentioned that the witenagemot which outlawed Godwin is referred to as a *stefna* in one version of the *Chronicle.*[7]

The Latin historians and monastic chroniclers add very little definite

---

[1] Cf. *NA*, §§ 9, 18.   [2] *Ibid.*, § 15.

[3] C 1050 (*recte* 1051), F 1050 (*recte* 1051), D 1052 (*recte* 1051), E 1048 (*recte* 1051), C 1052, D 1052 *bis*, and C 1055. Of these the second, third, and fourth all refer to the same gemot, and the fifth and sixth to a single gemot. In the entries *s.a.* 1000–42 I have found the word used only once, E 1036 (*recte* 1035). This can hardly be said to justify the designation "used freely."

[4] E 1047 (*recte* 1050), E 1052, F 1051 (*recte* 1052), and C 1065. Of these the second and third refer to the same gemot, the one which versions C and D 1052 call a witenagemot. These words are also used for an assembly once *s.a.* 1000–42, but in three versions, C, D, E, 1020.

[5] F 1050 (*recte* 1051) and E 1048 (*recte* 1051): "Ða sende se cyng æfter eallon his witan."

[6] E 1052: "gerædde se cyng 7 his witan."

[7] D 1052 (*recte* 1051): "7 setton stefna ut to Lundene . . . 7 sceolde Godwine eorl 7 his suna þær cuman to wiþermale." It may, of course, be argued that the *stefna* refers, not to a witenagemot, but to the *húskarlastefna* which joined with the witan in outlawing Godwin, but I think it more likely that Godwin was summoned to defend himself before the witan rather than the huscarles when the case was transferred from Gloucester to London, and the subsequent account in the *Chronicle* supports this view. We have here, I believe, an example of how loose is the terminology of the *Chronicle.*

information on witenagemots. Florence of Worcester may be taken as representative of them. In his account of the reign of the Confessor we meet with specific mention of five witenagemots under such terms as: *in generali concilio, rex in suo concilio, concilium rex habuit, habito Lundoniæ concilio,* and *coram rege et regni optimatibus*.[1] The majority of these are the same assemblies as those specifically mentioned in the *Anglo-Saxon Chronicle*.

What do these specific references tell us as to the nature of a witenagemot? Not very much, it must be admitted. The gemots mentioned above were held on the following occasions and did the following things:

1. 1044: *In generali concilio* at London, Manni was elected abbot of Evesham. Nothing is told about the composition of the assembly except that it was, presumably, a large gathering. It is stated that the gemot was held about the time of the death of Bishop Ælfweard of London which occurred on July 25. One may, therefore, assume that the meeting took place at Lammas. There is no indication as to whether this was a regular or extraordinary meeting.[2]

2. 1050: There was a "mycel gemot on Lundene to midfestene," in which nine ships of lithsmen were discharged. Again, except that the word "mycel" indicates a large gathering, we learn nothing as to its composition, nor whether it was a regular or extraordinary meeting.[3]

3. 1051: A "witenagemot [met] on Lunden to Midlencten," in which church appointments were made. Once again this tells little except that one might conjecture, from the fact that Midlent is again the time of meeting, that it was a favoured time for gemots.[4]

4. 1051: "Ða sende se cyng æfter eallon his witan 7 bead heom cuman to Gleaweceastre" to deal with the affair of Eustace.[5] This meeting is discussed at some length below.[6]

5. 1051: "Se cyng hæfde þæs on morgen witenagemot 7 cwæð hine [Godwin] utlage 7 eall here hine 7 ealle his suna."[7] This is the meeting which had been determined on at Gloucester (the *stefna* mentioned above).[8] There can be no doubt that this assembly at London (September 21–22) was an extraordinary gathering of the witan, but there is no such certainty as to what the words "eall here" mean. In another chapter[9] I have set forth my reasons for believing that they refer to a separate

---

[1] *FlWig*, 1044, 1051, 1052, 1055, 1062.   [2] *Ibid.*, 1044.

[3] *ASChr*, E 1047.   [4] *Ibid.*, C 1050.

[5] *Ibid.*, E 1048. Cf. F 1050, which is much the same, and D 1052, which says the king sent for earls Leofric and Siward.

[6] Chapter xv.   [7] *ASChr*, D 1052.

[8] The loose terminology of the *Chronicle* may again be seen in that version E 1048 states that Godwin was ordered to "comen mid XII mannum into þæs cynges ræde," a reference to this assembly at London.

[9] P. 106.

meeting of the huscarles who formed the standing army, and that the word "here" should not, in this passage, be understood to have the old meaning of the whole nation or folk.[1]

6. 1052: "On þam sylfan geare geirædde se cyng 7 his witan þ̄ man sceolde forðian ut to Sandwic scipu." This must refer to a witenagemot held early in 1052, possibly in Midlent, but it reveals nothing further about the nature of the assembly.[2]

7. 1052: With reference to the attempt on the part of Godwin and his sons to return to England, we find: "Ða wiðlæg se cing sume hwile. ac Stigand (þe was þes cinges rædgifa 7 his handprest) 7 ða oðre wise men geiræddan þ̄ man getrymde gislas on ægðræ healfe. . . ."[3] The *Chronicle* then goes on to say that when this was decided Archbishop Robert fled and "ða cwæð man mycel gemot wiðuton Lundene 7 on þam gemote wæran ða betstan men þe wæran on ðysan lande," and Godwin was inlawed. This is an extremely important entry. From it one may infer a discussion in the witenagemot of the question of inlawing Godwin. One may also infer that the debate was bitter and that the king took the side of Archbishop Robert. It is the only passage I have found that may be taken as meaning that the witan enforced their will on Edward. What seems to have happened is this. The king summoned the witan to London to aid him in resisting Godwin's invasion. A heated debate ensued at the gemot. Stigand, possibly supported by the English earls, favoured reconciliation with Godwin. Archbishop Robert, supported by the king and possibly by Earl Ralph, opposed his re-entry. Stigand carried the day and the *mycel gemot* outside London followed. It is true that version E of the *Chronicle* implies that, when the king would not yield, Stigand and others acted on their own and met Godwin to arrange terms: "þa ferde Stigand biscop to mid Godes fultume 7 þa wise menn ægðær ge binnan burh ge buton 7 geiræddon þ̄ man tremede gislas on ægðer healfe 7 man swa dyde."[4] It then implies that Robert heard of this and fled. But version D tends to support F's account: "Geiræddan þa þ̄ man sende wyse men betweonan 7 setton grið on ægðre halfe."[5] Version C uses much the same language.[6]

8. 1052: The witenagemot is the one held without London which was decreed in the last-mentioned one. Freeman has drawn a rhetorical

---

[1] See Jón Dúason, *Rjettarstaða Grænlands*, pp. 60–61, for examples of this usage of the word; and cf. H. Brunner, *Deutsche Rechtsgeshichte*, I, 163.

[2] *ASChr*, E 1052.   [3] *Ibid.*, F 1051.

[4] *Ibid.*, E 1052.   [5] *Ibid.*, D 1052 *bis*.

[6] *Ibid.*, C 1052. It is true that one might understand the words of C and D to mean much the same as Florence of Worcester (1052): "Unde sapientiores quique ex utraque parte, inter regem et ducem redintegrantes, exercitum ab armis discedere jusserunt." But it seems that a necessary prerequisite for such action would be a decision to open negotiations made in a witenagemot and finally acquiesced in by the king.

picture of this assembly, which he considered to be almost unique.[1] In his account Godwin emerges as the "great deliverer." Beside Freeman's highly coloured version should be set the sober judgment of Stenton in his recent history of the Anglo-Saxons.[2] Indeed there is nothing wonderful or constitutionally significant in the fact that the assembly should be held in sight of the armed forces of the two sides. It was natural, considering the passions that had been aroused, that the reconciliation should be carried out in public. But it can be only a gross exaggeration to say, as Freeman does, that the king was "driven at last to deal face to face with a free assembly of his people," as if for years the people had been clamouring to be heard, only to have their clamours stilled by "Norman knights and Norman churchmen." If the object desired was the recognition of the right of the people to settle the affairs of the realm in "free assemblies of the people," why did not those who gained this victory and humbled the king take care that in the future such assemblies should become the rule?

9. 1055: "Ða ðæræfter binnan lyttlan fyrste wæs witenagemot on Lundene," in which Earl Ælfgar was outlawed.[3] Version E of the *Chronicle* records that it was held in Midlent.[4] Nothing is revealed as to the composition of the assembly, but the reference to Midlent strengthens the view that it was customary to hold important gemots at that season.

10. 1062: "Coram rege et regni optimatibus," Archbishop Ealdred of York had to declare that his consecration of Wulfstan as bishop of Worcester should not be regarded as a precedent.[5] This, however, tells nothing of importance about the composition of the meeting.

11-12. 1065: "Þa wel raðe þaræfter wæs mycel gemot æt Norðhamtune 7 swa on Oxenaforda on þon dæig Simonis 7 Iude," in connection with the Northumbrian revolt.[6] This passage is an excellent example of the loose terminology of the *Chronicle*. Obviously what is meant here is simply a large gathering and not a witenagemot in the sense of the king meeting with the witan. A meeting of witan—unless the business be that of deposing or electing a king—is not technically a witenagemot unless the king is present. The words "mycel gemot" here, as often, are used loosely of a gathering other than a witenagemot in the sense of the king being offered counsel or given consent. None of our sources record the presence of the king at either Northampton or Oxford. It is Harold who carries out the negotiations there.[7] The king was and remained at Britford

---

[1] *NC*, II, 219-24. [2] *ASEng*, pp. 559-61.
[3] *ASChr*, C 1055. [4] *Ibid.*, E 1055.
[5] *FlWig*, 1062. [6] *ASChr*, C 1065.
[7] *Ibid.*, C, D 1065; *FlWig*, 1065. I owe to Professor Wilkinson the suggestion that Harold may have been Edward's deputy or lieutenant at these gemots (comparable to John of Gaunt in 1376). An acceptance of this view would hinge upon the interpretation

near Salisbury.[1] There can be no doubt that here the king held his witenagemot to decide the question of what to do with the Northumbrians, and that the author of the *Vita Æduuardi* is, at least here, to be believed when he says: "Accitisque undique regni primatibus, habebat ibi consilium quid super tali negotio esset opus."[2] It stands to reason that the king would not act in such a serious crisis without consulting the great men of the land. Where, then, did he consult them? Not at Northampton, not at Oxford, but at Britford. Thence Harold went out, after the discussions, to negotiate with the rebels. At Northampton and at Oxford (he may have returned to Britford in the interval between the two meetings) he treated with the rebels and finally agreed to their demands. At Oxford, acting no doubt with the consent of the king, he settled the trouble on the terms outlined in the *Chronicle*.[3] The assemblies at Northampton and Oxford cannot, therefore, be classified as witenagemots.[4]

one places on Florence of Worcester's statement (1065) that Harold was viceregent, and upon the comparability of a witenagemot and a parliament. My interpretation of these matters prevents me from entertaining this interesting suggestion.

[1] *ASChr*, C 1065; *Vita Æduuardi*, in *Lives of Edward the Confessor*, ed. Luard, p. 422; cf. *ASEng*, p. 570. I may say that I regard the *Vita Æduuardi* as of very little worth for the reign of the Confessor, although I do not deny that it may be a contemporary work. For its genuineness there are very strong arguments. See Eleanor K. Heningham, "The Genuineness of the *Vita Æduuardi Regis*," pp. 419–56. Her article contains a very good bibliography.

[2] *Vita Æduuardi*, p. 422. I am unable to understand why Professor Wilkinson denies the character of a witenagemot to the assembly at Britford, and thinks that *consilium* may mean something else in this context ("Northumbrian Separatism," p. 515).

[3] *ASChr*, D 1065.

[4] The views of earlier historians on the Northumbrian crisis have been examined by Professor Wilkinson in his "Northumbrian Separatism" carefully and thoroughly. I think he is correct in saying that it was felt that the election of an earl was a matter, not for a local gemot, but for the king and witan, although of these two the approval of the king was the more important. Again I agree that the action of the rebels points to the conclusion that they themselves felt that to guard against future revocation of their act they must gain the consent of the king and witan, although I am inclined to feel that they placed more emphasis than Professor Wilkinson is prepared to allow on their right to depose an unjust earl and to be consulted as to the choice of a successor. They did not wish to sever their connection with the rest of the kingdom, but were, I think, prepared to do this if their wishes were not granted. Their behaviour is, therefore, not a sign of separatism at work but rather, as Professor Wilkinson emphasizes, the opposite. It shows that in this period of the history of the Anglo-Saxons it was recognized that the appointment of earls needed at least the confirmation of the king. To secure this was, I believe, the chief purpose of the assembly at Oxford, although here the king acted through agents who were carrying out the instructions they had received in the witenagemot at Britford. Furthermore, in my opinion, there can be no question of identifying the army as such with a witenagemot, and herein I agree with Professor Wilkinson, but my reasons for this opinion are not entirely the same as his. The army *qua* army is the nation in arms or the folk in arms (cf. Brunner, *Deutsche Rechtsgeschichte*, I, 163); the witan are always a small, select, aristocratic body (cf. *NA*, § 23). It may well be true that when the army was assembled the leading men might meet in a witenagemot, but only in this sense is Liebermann's statement (*NA*, § 45) acceptable. That the army as a whole constituted a witenagemot is to me inconceivable.

Although the above references to witenagemots do not give very much information about the composition of these assemblies, they supply other information of value. The business done in the above-mentioned witenagemots may be summarized as follows:

1044: Election of an abbot.
1050: Dismissal of the lithsmen.
1051: 1. Ecclesiastical appointments.
      2. Outlawry of Godwin.
1052: 1. Defence of the realm.
      2. Discussion of the invasion of Godwin.
      3. Inlawing of Godwin and outlawing of the Frenchmen.
1055: Outlawry of Earl Elfgar.
1062: Ecclesiastical business.
1065. Northumbrian revolt.

Thus during a reign of twenty-three years the principal sources mention specifically only ten witenagemots held in seven of the years. In them only very serious secular business and ecclesiastical questions occupy the attention of the witan. It is indeed a slim list for as eventful a reign as that of Edward the Confessor, and it indicates that the chroniclers recorded only the weightiest business transacted by the king and witan. A major crisis, the defence of the realm, matters affecting the greatest subjects, and the affairs of the church found a place in their pages. Few will consider that only such matters were discussed by the king and his witan. I am not suggesting that other meetings of the witan cannot be inferred from the chronicles. These will be dealt with below. All that I wish to suggest is that if a witenagemot was a large, summoned gathering, in which all the major business of the kingdom was handled, and which assembled two or three times a year—a meeting whose functions were as well defined and varied as Kemble and others hold—direct reference to it would have been made oftener. Is it not permissible to infer from the terminology of the chronicles that large gatherings very seldom took place, the ordinary affairs of the realm being decided normally by the king and those about him? Had the chroniclers felt that there was a difference between the acts of the king and a few counsellors on the one hand, and those of the king and numerous counsellors on the other, might we not expect to find some trace of this feeling in the chronicles? But, as I have said, there is no evidence for the existence of a small court council distinct from the witenagemot.

Again, it seems evident from the language of the chroniclers that the Anglo-Saxons had no single "official" term to designate gatherings of the king and numerous witan. The same term is employed for a gathering of the king and his witan, for a gathering of a large number of magnates, and for a gathering of the people in arms (as in 1065) or in the county court (as in 1124). "Gemot," "mycel gemot," "witenagemot," all are used very indiscriminately in the *Anglo-Saxon Chronicle*. Even the word *stefna* (possibly Old Icelandic) seems to be used in one version of the *Chronicle* for an assembly that in another version is a witenagemot.

Even the word "witan," which we meet most frequently, can scarcely be said to have a strictly technical meaning, but only to describe men whom the king consults. (In *CD*, 693, it is used of those attending a Berkshire shire court.) In the pages of the *Anglo-Saxon Chronicle* it is found several times denoting the feudal baronage and high churchmen who formed the *curia regis* of the Norman kings.[1] In the mind of the chronicler the Conqueror had his witan. Had the word "witenagemot" been the official name of the national assembly in the Anglo-Saxon period, one might expect that when the Conqueror gathered his witan about him the meeting would be recorded as a witenagemot in the *Chronicle*, but this is not so. The entry for the year 1085 tells us that William was at Gloucester "mid his witan 7 heold þær his hired v. dagas. . . ." Again of 1086 we read: "Her se cyng bær his corona 7 heold his hired on Winceastre. . . ." In the entry for the same year the chronicler distinguishes witan and "landsittende men." This one would hardly expect if the important thegns of England had been wont to attend witenagemots in considerable numbers in the reign of the Confessor.[2] I cannot conceive that it was not the normal practice to discuss the business of the realm at the Conqueror's crown-wearings, or that contemporaries made such a fine distinction as appears in the following: "The Chronicler of Peterborough, writing in English, calls them [the crown-wearings] *hyreds*, households, and says that some of them at least were accompanied by a witenagemot."[3] Actually the chronicler does not use the word "witenagemot," but I presume that the author infers the witenagemot from such a phrase as "mid his witan."

If one's list of witenagemots were confined to those specifically mentioned in the principal sources for the reign of the Confessor it would be short. But, as is not surprising, the chroniclers were not interested in mentioning explicitly every occasion on which the king consulted his witan. It was the nature of the business, not the fact of consultation between king and witan, which interested the chroniclers. Therefore only incidental mention is usually made of a meeting of king and witan. But what the chroniclers do record supports the view that the constitution of

[1] *ASChr*, E 1085, 1086.
[2] Cf. *CHMed*, p. 176, where attention is drawn to the fact that *Domesday Book* calls Edward's *hyreds*, *curiae*.
[3] *Ibid.*

a witenagemot was "arbitrary and undefined."[1] A witenagemot was, in other words, any occasion when "the counsel, consent, witness or license of several aristocrats"[2] was in any way offered to the king.

The scarcity of explicit references mentioned above may not be as serious as it seems at first sight. If we keep steadily before our minds the fundamental ideas and concepts of the age with which we are dealing, we may feel justified in arriving at certain conclusions. In the Anglo-Saxon period the principles of the supremacy of law and of the necessity of consent are basic. Operating within that framework the king has considerable freedom in the methods he uses. The king, in theory, is not and cannot be a despot. Nor can he be a figurehead. The "divinity which hedges a king" was a very real thing in the Germanic concept of throne-worthiness and in the sacred nature of monarchy taught by the church.[3] Co-operation between king and people is the normal state of affairs in the Middle Ages, and especially so in a society such as the Anglo-Saxon, in which, from the earliest times, kingship was of the greatest importance and, at the same time, local government was highly developed. Normally, therefore, we may expect to find close co-operation between king and people, the latter finding a vehicle for expression in the witan, and, possibly, more particularly in the lay witan or the leading magnates of the various subdivisions of the country.[4] The churchmen, however, are also the spokesmen of the folk, and by reason of their venerated office and their great wealth exercise tremendous influence. In the last phase of Anglo-Saxon society the great earls dominate the lay witan, but at least until 1060 they speak with no common voice, and this may have given the king considerable power and freedom.[5]

---

[1] Wilkinson, "Freeman and the Crisis," p. 379. He goes on to say that "there were probably some rough and ready standards to be applied," but beyond the act of consultation I see no evidence for this.

[2] *NA*, § 9.

[3] Cf. Kern, *Kingship and Law*, pp. 27–61.

[4] Professor Stenton has emphasized (*ASEng*, p. 545) the importance of the thegns in the witenagemot in the late Anglo-Saxon period.

[5] It may be well to emphasize again that in the Middle Ages every royal servant had in common with the king the function of maintaining the law. He was the king's servant to further this, and ceased to owe allegiance to a king who did not pursue righteousness (cf. Kern, *Kingship and Law*, p. 195). Speaking of the duties of a courtier, an anonymous Norwegian, who wrote in the thirteenth century, and who firmly believed that kingship was superior to the *sacerdotium*, says (*The King's Mirror—Speculum regale*, trans. Larson, p. 205): "This should be the first principle of all your conduct, never to let your heart be wanting in reverence and fear of God, to love him above everything else, and next to him to love righteousness." On the duties of a king he comments: "It surely is his bounden duty to seek knowledge and understanding, and he ought to be well informed as to what has occurred in the past, for in that way he will gain insight for all the business that pertains to his kingship" (p. 247). ". . . he is after all merely a servant of God" (p. 249).

For all practical purposes we may, then, expect to find that Edward the Confessor ruled with the counsel of his witan—that all important questions were settled by the king and few or numerous witan. Whenever the sources record that an important decision has been taken, we may assume, in the absence of an explicit denial, that it was made with the advice, counsel, consent, or witness of several aristocrats, i.e., in a witenagemot. This would be the normal procedure.

It would be repetitious to discuss here every reference in the sources which allows us to infer a witenagemot, for such entries will be dealt with in the chapters devoted to a discussion of the various functions of the witan. Here I content myself with listing the various matters and occasions which, when mentioned in our sources, allow us to infer that the king may have consulted his witan in large or small numbers.[1]

1. Large ceremonial gatherings (e.g., consecration of a king, visits of high foreign potentates, consecration of an important ecclesiastical foundation or of a high prelate, crown-wearings).[2]

2. The despoiling or outlawing of prominent subjects.

3. Ecclesiastical appointments and important ecclesiastical business.

4. Defence of the realm.

5. Relations with foreign powers.

6. Taxation.

7. Revolt or rebellion.

8. Bestowal of earldoms.

9. Booking of land. One might add assemblies which came together to elect or depose a king. I deal with these matters in the chapters on the various functions of the witan.

In Appendix O are listed all the occasions on which I think Edward the Confessor may have consulted his witan, as far as our sources reveal. I would hesitate to state that all the matters mentioned in this list were dealt with in a witenagemot, but in view of my understanding of what a witenagemot meant to an Anglo-Saxon I would be even more loath to name a single instance in which an Anglo-Saxon may have felt that the king acted without counsel.

[1] I may emphasize again that I regard number as in no way a determinant of whether a meeting is to be considered a witenagemot or not. When Freeman says that Ealdred had to declare "perhaps before the assembled Witan" that he claimed no authority over the bishop of Worcester, although he had consecrated Wulfstan, he adds in a footnote: "Or, as Florence, when he speaks of the Witan, is rather fond of using popular language, this may mean some smaller council" (*NC*, II, 310). Yet Freeman has nowhere established the existence of any small council, distinct in organization and functions from a witenagemot.

[2] I give no references here as they are fully given in Appendix O.

CHAPTER FIVE

Information on Witenagemots in Anglo-Saxon Diplomas

What J. L. Goebel calls "the miserable state of English diplomatics"[1] must be acutely felt by anyone studying the reign of Edward the Confessor. A great number of diplomas exist from the reign,[2] but their authenticity is often open to grave doubt, and there do not seem to be commonly accepted standards for determining their genuineness.[3] The result is that these sources must be used with extreme care.

The matter is complicated by the fact that forgeries cannot in all cases be dismissed outright, for the statements made therein may often be true. This arises from the nature of mediaeval forgeries. In many cases the forger, confronted with a situation for which he had no written confirmation, but plenty of oral support in tradition, proceeded to supply the want. Again, charters were often lost or destroyed and the forger obligingly supplied fresh ones, which more or less faithfully reflect the original. Alistair Campbell, in trying to establish the status of Queen Emma, says of the witness lists to the charters he uses for this purpose:

. . . forgers and modifiers of charters usually had documents before them, which provided models for lists of signatures, and, although they often produce impossible lists, if chronological details are considered, their products, considered in

[1] *Felony and Misdemeanor* (1937), p. 339. His statement is true in spite of the fact that the last half century has seen the publication of several admirable editions of Anglo-Saxon documents. In addition to such older works as *Land Charters and Other Saxonic Documents*, ed. Earle (1888), and *The Crawford Collection of Early Charters and Documents*, ed. Napier and Crawford (1895), the latter of which is especially valuable, one may mention such recent works as *Anglo-Saxon Wills*, ed. Whitelock (1930), and *Anglo-Saxon Charters*, ed. Robertson (1939). But neither of these latter contains more than a few documents from the Confessor's reign. All known Anglo-Saxon writs have been published recently by Dr. F. E. Harmer (1952). This is an extremely valuable addition to the literature on diplomatic of the reign. The only relatively complete collection of the diplomas from the reign is still *Codex diplomaticus aevi Saxonici*, ed. Kemble (1839–48, 6 vols.), a work whose shortcomings are well known. *Cartularium Saxonicum*, ed. Birch (1885–93, 3 vols.), covers only the period previous to the late tenth century, and *Select English Historical Documents*, ed. Harmer (1914), the ninth and tenth centuries.

[2] Goebel speaks of "Edward's fifty odd writs and 60 or more charters" (*Felony and Misdemeanor*, p. 355). I use the word "diploma" here in its general sense; for the various technical terms see *ASC*, pp. xiv–xv.

[3] Cf. Goebel, *Felony and Misdemeanor*, p. 339: "By some occult process never disclosed most scholars test and brand documents as forgeries and the lawyer has to accept the *ipse dixit*."

bulk, are not likely to be misleading on broad questions such as, Did the queen usually sign immediately after the king in a given period? In deciding such a question, quantity rather than quality of evidence is called for: one document, though extant in a fine contemporary copy, may be abnormal, but the agreement of ten, even if they are known only from chartularies, and include some forgeries, provided they are derived from a variety of sources, will point to a norm.[1]

In short, although forgeries cannot be considered original sources in the strict sense, they may sometimes be regarded as secondary historical material and judged by the same criteria. They are often confirmatory.[2]

In dealing with the diplomas which I have used from the Confessor's reign, I have adopted the following method. I have divided the charters into three classes or groups. In the first I have put those documents which, after examination, I have come to regard as authentic; in the second group those whose authenticity I regard as not above suspicion; and in the third group those which I deem unquestionably spurious. My conclusions, based on this material, have then been drawn primarily from the evidence supplied by the first group, and only secondarily by that supplied by the second group. The third group I account as almost, if not wholly, worthless.

It would be idle to suggest that in my grouping of the charters I have succeeded in placing each charter in the correct group, but the margin of error should not be large enough to invalidate the conclusions I have drawn from this material. There are many reasons why it is extremely difficult to establish the authenticity or spuriousness of a charter. In many cases the charters exist only in copies and not in the original. Allowance must then be made for scribal errors, and indeed these cannot be wholly discounted even in the case where the original exists. The following observations are apposite:

. . . it does not follow that because a charter, as we have it, exhibits some inaccuracy, it is valueless. . . . We have to make allowance for the possibility of inaccuracy on the part of the original copyist (where the original does not exist). What, for example, is more likely than that a copyist having accurately set down the description of one witness as "archiepiscopus" should append the same to the name of the next witness, who was only "episcopus"? Or that not being familiar with the persons whose names he was writing, he should sometimes make a mistake, and give us the name of some man who could not have been present at the grant, in place perhaps of another man's name. . . . Even in charters which have evidently been fabricated, there is often historic truth; for some of them appear

---

[1] *Encomium*, p. 62.

[2] On mediaeval forgeries see Kern, *Kingship and Law*, pp. 171–4. I have included among my list of occasions on which Edward may have consulted his witan (Appendix O) one referred to in a charter (*CD*, 791) whose genuineness is not above doubt, although its witness list seems authentic, and Professor Stenton (*ASEng*, p. 461) cites it as the authority for his statement that the consent of the pope was sought before the see of Crediton was transferred to Exeter.

to have been written to supply the place of originals that were lost; and they at least show us that at the time they were written the monastery was either possessed of, or laid claim to, the land to which they refer.[1]

Again, it must be remembered here that information regarding the dates of many Anglo-Saxon bishops and abbots, not to mention earls, is often indefinite and the dates assigned are sometimes only approximate.[2] Our knowledge of the whole history of the Anglo-Saxons in the eleventh century before the Conquest is very incomplete.

The matter is further complicated by the whole question of the nature of the Anglo-Saxon landbook. Was it both dispositive and evidentiary or was it only the latter? This is a subject which cannot be dealt with here.[3] It must suffice to say that I incline to the view that it was only evidentiary,[4] from which it may follow that the witnesses to the *donatio* may not always have been the same as those who attest the document, and that the charter may not always have been drawn up at the time that the *donatio* was made. A confusion in dating may result, i.e., a confusion of the date of the gift with that of the charter. At least in the case of foundation charters[5] this would seem to be true, whatever may be the case as far as landbooks in general are concerned. Witnesses may, therefore, appear on a charter at a seemingly impossible date, if we assume that the clerk who drew up the charter sometimes composed his witness list from those who were present at the original donation.[6]

There is, moreover, little information as to whether individuals attesting charters did so personally (i.e., themselves made the sign of the cross) or

[1] *TCPB*, p. xxxiii.

[2] Cf. the remarks on Leofsige of Ely, *ASC*, p. 467. For an interesting example of the difficulties of establishing the authenticity or otherwise of a document see *Feudal Documents*, ed. Douglas, pp. xxxii–xxxiv. At first sight this diploma appears to be a forgery, but on examining it Douglas began to doubt that this was so and left the question open. Now Dr. Harmer has suggested that the document, if it is not authentic, may have been confected with the purpose of supporting the authenticity of the charters of earlier kings cited in the text (*Writs*, pp. 143–5).

[3] On this see Galbraith, "Monastic Foundation Charters," pp. 205–14; *ASW*, pp. vii–xl; Stenton, *Transcripts*, pp. xvi–xvii; G. J. Turner, "Bookland and Folkland"; Brunner, *Deutsche Rechtsgeschichte*, I, 563–75; Mary Prescott Parsons, "Some Scribal Memoranda for Anglo-Saxon Charters of the 8th and 9th Centuries," pp. 31–32.

[4] In 1948 V. H. Galbraith felt able to write: "No-one any longer believes with Brunner that these [the landbooks] belong to the sphere of private diplomatic, still less that they are 'dispositive' documents, marking the exact moment of conveyance" (*Studies in the Public Records*, p. 31). See also T. F. T. Plucknett, "Deeds and Seals," pp. 143–4.

[5] Cf. Galbraith, "Monastic Foundation Charters," pp. 214–22. For what it is worth it may be mentioned that Holy Cross, Waltham, was consecrated in 1060, but the charter (*CD*, 813), whose witness list I regard as spurious, and whose authenticity is also doubted by Dr. Harmer ("Anglo-Saxon Charters," p. 342), and by Goebel (*Felony and Misdemeanor*, p. 362), purports to be made in 1062 (cf. *NC*, II, 453–4). I have ventured to suggest that *CD*, 810, was made some years after the gift it records.

[6] Cf. *NC*, II, 453–4.

whether both the cross and the name were inserted by the clerk who drew up the document. In both cases there is, of course, room for error, but especially in the latter, which is a more likely method in a comparatively illiterate age.[1] I do not, however, think that there can be much doubt that in the reign of the Confessor the witnesses attesting were actually present, in most cases, at the reading of the landbook, whatever may have been the case with private charters which were not read in the presence of king and witan.[2]

All these factors should be kept in mind when judging the grouping I have made of the Confessor's charters and the use I have made of the information they contain or which I think they contain. My reasons for assigning them to the various groups I have set out in Appendix M.[3]

In the past all historians have agreed that "charters commuting folcland into bookland or exempting from political duties"[4] come from a witenagemot. Even Hubert Hall, who held that there was very little evidence for a chancery, much less a chancellor, in the Anglo-Saxon period, and who, in speaking of the landbooks, said: "The handwriting is local, the language is local, the formulas are adapted by local scribes from academic models," admitted that "the attestation . . . is official, inasmuch as the court by which it is ratified followed the king into the locality."[5] These charters are thus of primary importance to any study of the witenagemot.

It must, however, be admitted that there is little in the body of the charters from the reign of the Confessor that throws light on the composition and function of the witenagemot. In the great majority of cases not even the date of the instrument is given or the place at which it was made. In fact, forged charters seem to bear place and date much more

[1] V. H. Galbraith is strongly of the opinion that the crosses on the charters are in no case autograph ("The Literacy of the Mediaeval English Kings," p. 217); cf. also his "Monastic Foundation Charters," p. 210; and M. Deanesly, "The Court of King Æthelberht of Kent," p. 104.

[2] Cf. *Feudal Documents*, ed. Douglas, pp. xli–xliii; *Transcripts*, ed. Stenton, p. xxxi; *ASW*, pp. xvii–xviii. It might be urged that actually the scribe recorded the names, not of persons who were present, but of such individuals as he knew would be willing to subscribe to whatever the attestation of a charter implied. This would, for example, explain the almost constant appearance of the signature of the archbishop of York on the witness lists from the Confessor's reign—an occurrence which might imply a more constant attendance on the king than the location of the archiepiscopal see would seem to allow. It would be futile to argue this point for which little positive evidence can be offered on either side, but it would seem to have been the normal practice, in the matter of private charters in the Anglo-Saxon period, for the scribe to enter the names of those witnesses who were actually present. Nor am I aware that this has been seriously questioned.

[3] While attempting to assess the authenticity of these documents, I (no expert in these matters) have often been reminded of Galbraith's words: "The honest diplomatist asked to distinguish the true from the false is often tempted to answer in the famous words of a Bury abbot: *Deus scit, ego autem ignoro*" (*Studies in the Public Records*, p. 49).

[4] *NA*, § 45.

[5] *Studies in English Official Historical Documents*, p. 177.

often than genuine ones. For example, the following carry the date and/or the place, but only the last, which carries only the date, seems to be above suspicion: *CD*, 779, 786, 815, 816, 824, 825, 1332. *CD*, 956, seems genuine and was made at Lincoln, but the place is not explicitly stated and no date is given. Similarly in the case of *CD*, 768, 773, the place where the document was made may be inferred but neither it nor the date is explicitly stated. It would not be going too far to say that a charter which carries both place and date (especially if it include the day and month) should be suspect.[1] It cannot, of course, be denied that a forger may have given a date and place at which an actual gemot took place. I have, however, preferred to omit witenagemots which are found only in suspicious charters and are not supported by other evidence. In any case this is, in my opinion, a matter of slight importance, for, as I have indicated throughout this work, I regard a witenagemot as any meeting at which many or few witan offered the king counsel. Any list of meetings must therefore be incomplete, as only the more important meetings would be recorded. The most that can be hoped for is a list large enough to enable some conclusions to be drawn.

The value of the witness lists of the charters in supplying information about the composition of a witenagemot is another question. Did all those present at a gemot sign or only a few? To this there can, probably, be no definite answer. Professor Stenton warns against placing too much faith in these lists:

The only documents which show a council in session are the royal charters attested by its members.[2] So far as they go, the lists of witnesses with which the charters end are good evidence for the composition of the assembly. But the length of a list of witnesses was determined by the size of the parchment on which the charter was written. Few lists can be relied on for a full enumeration of the less important thegns who attended the meeting, and a description of the *witena gemot* which took this evidence at its face value would certainly over-emphasize the official element in the assembly.[3]

This is a salutary *caveat*, but one or two observations must be made. It is difficult to accept the statement that the size of the parchment determined the length of the list of witnesses. Parchment was not scarce in Anglo-Saxon England, and it would seem reasonable to assume that the scribe would first inscribe the charter and only then cut the parchment.

---

[1] *CD*, 779, professes to be made at London on August 1, 1045; *CD*, 816, at Windsor on May 4 (Kemble's May 20 is an error, *RB*, LII, 98), 1065; *CD*, 815, at Winchester on December 31, 1065; *CD*, 824 and 825, at Westminster on December 28, 1065. *CD*, 809, gives no place, but is dated on November 30 with no mention of the year. *CD*, 853, purports to be made at Windsor eleven days before Easter with no mention of the year, but it is a writ.

[2] To these documents may be added private charters and wills witnessed in a witenagemot, and, if there are any such, witnessed writs.

[3] *ASEng*, p. 543.

Thus the length of the charter with its witness list would determine the size of the parchment. It is true that many charters occupy the whole piece of parchment on which they are written, but this in no way weakens the argument that the parchment was cut only after the charter was inscribed and attested. It is true, also, that numerous charters are extant with ample space for additional names on the parchment on which they are written.[1]

That the names of the less important thegns attending a gemot of the witan might often be missing from the witness lists of the charters seems, at first sight, a reasonable enough statement. But, unfortunately, we are not even in a position to assert that thegns were in the habit of attending meetings. One might go so far as to say that there is little evidence to enable us to conclude that even important thegns were in the habit of attending. If they were, it would be reasonable to assume that the names of the more important ones would be found on the charters. But the names of some of the most important thegns of the Confessor's day are not to be found on any of the extant charters of the reign.[2] To say that the witness lists are incomplete because of the absence of names is, therefore, to beg the question. When names of important thegns do occur, they seem, in most cases, to be those of household officers or royal agents[3]—men one would expect to find attending gemots. No doubt a number of thegns from the neighbourhood of the meeting place might also be expected to be present. The earls might be attended by a few of their thegns or retainers, but whether they were deemed witan cannot be easily determined. At a time of crisis, such as 1051, thegns were no doubt with the king, but even then, their inclusion among the witan may by no means be taken for granted. To assert that they normally attended gemots seems a gratuitous assumption. I suspect, on the contrary, that thegns were not in the habit of attending gemots in large numbers.

---

[1] A cursory examination of the charters reproduced in *FASM*, II, revealed plenty of space in the following cases: Westminster, iii (Eadwig 957); Exeter, i (Eadgar 967), vi d (Eadgar 969), vii (Eadward 976), ix (Cnut 1018), xii (Eadward 1044); Winchester, i (Æthelwulf 854), ii (Eadwig 857); Earl of Ilchester, ii (Cnut 1024), iii (Eadward 1044); Winchester College, iii (Eadmun 940). On one charter, Worcester (Uhtred of the Hwiccas 770), the scribe has written some of the signatures on the back of the document. Many of these charters carry long witness lists, e.g., Exeter, ix, 28 witnesses, xii, 52 witnesses. Again, *FAC*, IV, revealed several charters on which there was space for more names, e.g., charters 10 (Eadweard 909), 18 (Cnut 1031), 31 (Eadweard 1045), and 38 (Bishop Ealdred 1058). Furthermore, B. M. Cott. MS. Aug. No. 25 (reproduced in *Feudal Documents*), an alleged charter of William I, has ample space for more names.

[2] E.g., that of Brichtulf, whose extensive possessions are discussed in *Feudal Documents*, p. xcvi.

[3] E.g., that of Eltstan, discussed in *ASEng*, p. 480, who signs half a dozen charters and seems to have been a sheriff and staller. This subject is dealt with more fully in subsequent chapters and in Appendix B.

Whether thegns did or did not attend witenagemots in large numbers does not, of course, diminish their importance in the country. That would not be determined solely by their membership in the witenagemot. But it seems extremely doubtful that they had much voice in the council.[1] Nor would their influence, if any, necessarily depend on their numbers in the assembly. The earls would be the natural spokesmen for the thegns, and would have to take into account the wishes of the thegns of their earldoms if any matter touching the interests of the latter arose. Professor Stenton writes: ". . . it is important to remember that in the lower ranges of the council, among thegns whose names end witness-lists, there were men whom the king could not easily coerce, and whose influence in the shires could not be ignored."[2] It is well to bring out the importance of these thegns and the difficulty the king would find in attempting to coerce them. On the other hand, however, it must not be assumed that the kings normally had any great desire to coerce such men. If they had, there would be evidence of occasions on which the interests of king and thegns would seem to conflict, and, possibly, evidence of a growing sense of solidarity among the latter. However, in a state such as eleventh-century England, there would normally be few occasions which would lead to a conflict between the king and the average thegn. In what way, or for what purpose, would, for example, Edward the Confessor wish to coerce the thegns? Conflict between king and subject arises normally only when one or the other is abusing his power. Misgovernment and heavy exactions, such as practised by Hardecnut, might lead to such a clash. Unjust deprivation of his property might force a thegn to oppose the king. But in eleventh-century England the only tax, with the exception of the customary *geld*, was the *heregeld*[3] and it was not levied after 1051. The king was supported by the *geld* and customary rents and produce from the estates belonging to him.[4] Only when the king ceased to be able to live on his customary income would serious conflict arise, and the lesser nobility feel it necessary to resist him. Such a state of affairs was later to contribute to the rise of parliament.

The absence of such occasion for conflict between the king and the lesser magnates does not necessarily mean that certain thegns may not have been ambitious, but their ambitions, which would largely consist in

[1] See chaps. VI and VII.
[2] *ASEng*, p. 545.
[3] On these taxes see *Writs*, pp. 439, 513; *ASEng*, pp. 406, 636.
[4] It is not necessary for my argument to discuss whether folkland, which Professor Stenton (*ASEng*, p. 308) says "meant land from which the king drew food-rents and customary services," included all the land of the country except that especially exempted, or only the estates of the Crown, as G. J. Turner maintains ("Bookland and Folkland," pp. 357–86). In either case the revenue of the king would be customary and no extraordinary demands need be made.

increasing their holdings, were such that they could be satisfied without serious conflict with the Crown. There is nothing to show that the lands with which Edward endowed his foreign favourites were taken unjustly from English thegns. Nor is there any evidence to show that the earls treated unjustly the thegns in their earldoms or laid on them illegal exactions. Indeed, the balance of forces in the England of the Confessor would seem to have been such as to favour the thegns. Any encroachment on the part of the earls would tend to drive the thegns into the arms of the king or of another earl. Moreover, the earls, who were seeking not only economic aggrandizement but in some cases political power, would not wish to alienate possible supporters. They would, again, be prepared to lend support, for the same reason, to any thegns in their earldoms who were being dealt with unjustly by the king. In short, there seems to be no reason to believe that thegns felt insecure or unjustly treated by the king during the reign of Edward the Confessor, whatever may have been the case in earlier reigns. There is no evidence for any coercion which would have the effect of welding the thegns into a self-conscious body wishing to avail itself of representation in the witenagemot in order to strengthen its hand against the king. It may well be that certain sheriffs did on occasion act highhandedly, but this cannot have been serious in the reign of the Confessor.[1] The only examples of confiscation of lands and encroachment on rights seem to involve church lands[2] and these did not implicate Edward but the earls. The very fact that the reign was regarded as a sort of golden age by succeeding generations is an argument against assuming any desire on the part of the king to coerce. The situation at other times in the Anglo-Saxon period is not within the scope of this work.

The question of the participation of the thegns in witenagemots is complicated by the very imperfect information we possess as to what a thegn really was.[3] Some of them, no doubt, were independent and large landowners. Others, probably, were wholly or almost dependent on the king. Many of the names found on the witness lists of the Confessor's charters are those of thegns dependent on the king by virtue of personal tie or office.[4] And on *a priori* grounds this is exactly what one would expect to find. Attendance at court on the part of the lesser nobility in the Middle Ages was not regarded as a privilege, but as a burden which was to be evaded if at all possible. It is well known that it was difficult to get the knights of the shire and the burgesses to attend parliament. Unless

---

[1] Cf. W. A. Morris, *The Mediaeval English Sheriff to 1300*, p. 36.

[2] Cf. *NC*, II, 554–67, 698–705, where Freeman seeks with little success to minimize such acts.

[3] On the Anglo-Saxon thegn see Stenton, *First Century*, chap. IV, *CHMed*, pp. 87–97; Turner, "Bookland and Folkland," pp. 381–5; *ASEng*, pp. 479–81.

[4] See chaps. VI and VII.

it can be shown that the Anglo-Saxon thegn had better reasons for wishing to attend witenagemots and to undergo the expense and trouble involved in attendance, it must be presumed that he exhibited no greater willingness than did his brethren two or three centuries later.

On *a priori* grounds it would, therefore, seem rash to assume that the witness lists as they stand are incomplete in the case of the thegns. The completeness of the listing of other classes of witan, even to the extent of including, on occasion, the names of such unimportant classes as priests and deacons, seems to argue against any such assumption. If thegns had normally been summoned in large numbers to witenagemots, it would be strange to find this nowhere as much as hinted at, in all the hundreds of documents we possess. On the contrary, as will be shown below, the evidence of the witness lists strengthens the view that the "official element in the assembly" can scarcely be overemphasized as far as thegns are concerned.[1]

In addition to the royal land charters there exist, from the Confessor's reign, a number of landbooks of private individuals, which have been witnessed by the king and a number of ecclesiastics and laymen. There can be little doubt that these documents were attested in a witenagemot, that is to say that their makers availed themselves of the opportunity of strengthening these books by having them witnessed by the king and his witan. This was usually, no doubt, done when the king came into a district during his peregrinations, although some may have been attested in larger witenagemots, possibly held on one of the high feasts of the church. For convenience I have listed these charters and one bequest separately in Appendix Q.

The wording of the witness lists on some of these private documents might lead one to think that it was not customary to include on the lists the names of all the witan. Thus the list of witnesses on several of these charters is followed by such words as: "and many good men," "and all the thegns in Essex," "and many other worthy men," or "and with the cognisance of all the citizens of Lincoln and of all the men who attend the yearly market at Stow."[2] But it is not necessary to hold that those whose names are omitted were witan. Wherever the king stopped during his progress throughout the country the inhabitants of the town or of the

---

[1] Cf. H. M. Chadwick, *The Heroic Age*, p. 369: "The latter [the royal councils of the Anglo-Saxon kingdoms] however were nothing more than meetings of the court from the earliest times to which our records go back. When important questions were discussed care may have been taken to summon all the leading men; and no doubt age and high rank ensured priority of hearing, as in the assemblies of Tacitus' day. But still they remained essentially meetings of the king's personal dependents."

[2] *CD*, 768, 788, 822, and 956 (Miss Robertson's translation of *CD*, 956, *ASC*, pp. 215, 217).

neighbourhood would no doubt flock to the court, and any business which the king might transact would often be done in the open. Thus a charter brought in by a local landowner might be attested in the presence of a considerable number of local people. The scribe would indicate this in the words above cited, without meaning to imply that these people were also witan in spite of the fact that their names were not given.[1] Certainly few would contend that "all the citizens of Lincoln" are to be considered as the king's witan, or that the term can apply to "all the men who attend the yearly market at Stow." It might more reasonably be maintained that "all the thegns in Essex" could be considered witan, but in view of the evidence supplied by the witness lists, dealt with in a subsequent chapter, this does not seem tenable. It is, however, difficult to rule them out entirely, as at least potential witan. On the whole it seems more reasonable to assume that the clerk inscribed only the names of those who formed the king's entourage, together with the names of the thegns of the locality who were royal officials or had some interest in the business of the moment. Allowance must also be made for inexact use of the word "all" so often met with in mediaeval writings.[2] It is unsafe, in such matters as these, to draw fine distinctions, yet it would seem to be going too far to say that contemporaries did not consider that such attestations were made by the king and his witan—that they thought them made simply in a meeting of the king with some prelates, nobles, and local freemen. On the contrary there is considerable justification for believing that contemporaries deemed the document to be attested by the king and his witan in the presence of the people of the neighbourhood.[3]

Witnessed writs from the Confessor's reign are generally regarded with suspicion,[4] and I have hesitated to use them. They are in any case few,[5] and the witnesses range in number from two to five, in addition to the king. They are usually the queen, an archbishop, an earl, and a household

---

[1] The very fact that such phrases as those cited above exist might be taken to suggest that in the minds of contemporaries there was no such body as a witenagemot, but only the king, his witan, and the other folk, or, perhaps, only the king, his court, members of which were witan, and the folk in general.

[2] Dr. Harmer has drawn my attention to what may originally have been an endorsement, but is now in the body of *CD*, 797: "Her swutelað on ðissere boc . . . on þæs cyncges gehwitnesse and on ealra his hwitena." This is followed by the signatures of one archbishop, three bishops, four earls, four abbots, one deacon, four monks, and two thegns (styled monks in error).

[3] A will from 997–9 (*ASW*, XVI) purports to be witnessed by king and witan. Attention may also be called to *CD*, 745, which, after giving the names of Cnut and several other witnesses, ends with "and all the king's advisers" (*rædesmen*).

[4] See Harmer, "Anglo-Saxon Charters," pp. 339–67. Dr. Harmer writes me that after preparing her edition of Anglo-Saxon writs for the press, she has not "anything to modify or add to what I wrote in my article about writs that are witnessed."

[5] *CD*, 839, 847, 853, 891, 904, 908.

official or two (staller, *cubicularius*, chancellor). In one instance the witnesses seem to be solely ecclesiastics. If genuine, these lists might be held to supply some evidence for a small court council in the reign of the Confessor, but their authenticity is much too doubtful to support any speculation on this.[1]

Let us now turn our attention to a detailed study of the charters we possess from the reign of the Confessor, and examine what evidence they offer for the holding of witenagemots, reserving for a later chapter the problem of the personnel of the witenagemot.

Genuine royal charters exist from nine years of the reign.[2] From 1042 there is extant one charter.[3] It carries the date and records the grant of land in Wiltshire to *meo ministro* Ordgar. Four charters[4] are found from the year 1044. Of these, the first two are Winchester charters recording grants of land in Somerset and Oxfordshire to the Old Minster. Both carry the date and were evidently made at the same time (possibly at Winchester), for the witnesses attesting are the same for both charters. The third one is dated and records a grant of land in Devonshire. Its witness list contains eighteen more names than the above two charters; there are fewer ecclesiastics but twenty-five more thegns. It is not possible to deduce much about the peregrinations of the king from these charters, but it is not unreasonable to suppose that, if the first two charters were made at Winchester, some of the ecclesiastical witan returned to their sees after attending the king there, while he himself toured the south and was joined on his progress by local thegns. The fourth charter from 1044 records a grant of land in Worcestershire, and would seem to reveal that the king visited that district either before or after his tour of the south. This charter is not dated.

[1] *Ibid.*, 1319, a writ of Cnut, has a long witness list, but its authenticity is very doubtful. *ASC*, CXVIII, a charter of the Confessor confirming a grant made by his mother, has a witness list of the same type as that found on the above-mentioned writs, but it is very likely spurious and I have set it aside along with the writs.

[2] That is to say, charters which can be assigned to specific years. There are also two private charters which allow of such assignation. I have not included the few charters which contain no witness lists.

[3] *CD*, 1332. Liebermann (*NA*, § 45) cites three witenagemots from 1042—one at East Horstead (*Quadripartitus*, Arg. 9), one at Sutton (*CD*, 762, 765 sq.), and the last at Gillingham (*CD*, 1332). I think, however, that the *Quadripartitus* reference, if any faith is to be placed in it (*Die Gesetze der Angelsachsen*, I, 533), must concern a witenagemot held in 1041 when Edward returned to England. The charters from the Sutton meeting belong to Hardecnut's reign. The only authority Liebermann cites for the Gillingham gemot is *CD*, 1332, which, as far as I can judge, has nothing to do with that place, but deals with land at Littleham. Having cited these three meetings in 1042, Liebermann goes on to say (*NA*, § 46) that two meetings admit of proof in 1042, apparently rejecting the East Horstead meeting as unproven. Why he does not accept a witenagemot at London in this year for the election of Edward, I do not know.

[4] *CD*, 774, 775; *FASM*, II, Exeter xii; *CD*, 797.

Three royal charters and one private charter exist from 1045.[1] The royal charters are all dated and record grants of land in Hants to the Old Minster at Winchester. Two are from the same gemot for they contain identical witness lists. The third is from a later gemot, for Harold signs this as earl, while he signed the other two as thegn, and Earl Beorn's name appears on it but not on the others.[2] Are we to presume then that the king visited Winchester twice in 1045? The private charter is an agreement concerning land in Kent between Æthelric Bigga and Archbishop Eadsige. It is not dated and there is no way of knowing at what time of the year it was made. It simply argues that the king was in Kent in 1045.

From the year 1046 three charters are found.[3] The first two have identical witness lists and must have been made on the same occasion. They both record grants to the Old Minster at Winchester and carry the date. We may thus infer that the king and a few witan were at Winchester at some time in 1046. The third charter can be dated subsequent to March 23, when Bishop Lyfing died. It is signed by his successor, Leofric, and also by Bishop Ealdred of Worcester, both of whom were appointed at the same time.[4] The charter is dated and records the grant of land in Rutland. Possibly one may infer from this that the king was in Lincoln in 1046.

The next year from which a charter is extant is 1049.[5] This is a dated document which records a grant of land in Cornwall to a thegn. It testifies to the presence of the king in southwest England in 1049. A dated charter[6] is extant from the following year. It records the transference of the see of Crediton to Exeter and testifies to the presence of king and witan at Exeter in 1050.

Not until 1059 is another genuine charter to be met with. It deals with the grant of land in Cornwall to the bishop of Worcester.[7] From 1060 two charters,[8] one royal and one private, are extant. The royal charter records the grant of land in Lincolnshire to Peterborough. The other deals with land in Worcestershire. The presence of king and witan in Lincoln

---

[1] CD, 776, 780, 781, 773. Liebermann (NA, § 45) assigns the private charter, CD, 956, to 1045, but this cannot be correct. It belongs to the period 1053–5 (see ASC, p. 465).

[2] The fact that Beorn's name appears on only the third charter would seem to dispose of any possibility that all three emanate from the same gemot at which Harold and Beorn were made earls. Had this been so we should expect that his signature, as that of Harold, would appear among the *ministri* of the first two charters. Both gemots must be dated after April 22, the date of Bishop Beorhtweald's death, for his successor signs all three charters. It should be noted that I always use the term "thegn" for the Latin "minister" and for the English term.

[3] CD, 783, 784, 1335.   [4] FlWig, 1046.
[5] CD, 787.   [6] Ibid., 791.
[7] HLC, pp. 300–2.   [8] CD, 808; HLC, pp. 247–8.

may be inferred from the royal charter. The sole charter[1] extant from 1061 records a grant of land in Somerset to Wulfweald, abbot of Bath. It is dated and testifies to the presence of the king in southwest England. No genuine charters can be assigned to specific years in the last five years of the reign.

A royal charter is extant from the period 1055–60 and another from the period 1060–6.[2] They both deal with grants to the abbey of Peterborough. Of the six private charters which cannot be assigned to a particular year, one is from Winchester, one from Essex, two from the church of Worcester, one from the abbey of Bath in Somerset, and one from Lincoln.[3]

In these twenty-six royal and private charters we possess documents which were made, it may be confidently stated, in the following places: Winchester (8), Worcester (5), Lincoln (4), Devon (2), Somerset (2), Cornwall (1), Essex (1), Kent (1), Rutland (1), Wilts (1). Beyond that, the bodies of these charters reveal little on the witenagemot. It would seem that it was not customary to state in the charter the place where it was made, and that the dating was confined to the year, if the document were dated at all. Moreover, the charters are too few to enable one to draw any conclusions as to Edward's itinerary. It is when we come to the question of the personnel of the witenagemot that they become valuable.

[1] *Ibid.*, 811.
[2] *Ibid.*, 806, 819.
[3] *Ibid.*, 768, 788, 805, 807, 822, 956.

CHAPTER SIX

The Personnel of the Witenagemot

THE king is the head of the witan and, as Liebermann states,[1] often stands above them. This is abundantly proved, for the reign of the Confessor, by the royal land charters. Edward's name invariably heads the list of witnesses, and he is usually represented as the initiating power, the other witnesses simply consenting, confirming, or attesting.[2] The private charters tell the same story. The king is the most important personage in a witenagemot.

Liebermann lists as next in importance or rank the members of the royal family.[3] This is perfectly in accord with old Germanic conceptions of kin-right, but in the Confessor's reign such witan are not conspicuous. To a certain extent this may be the result of the small number of near kinsmen which the Confessor possessed. Only his mother and his queen take precedence over all other witan. Ælfgifu seems to have been almost constantly at her son's side, if we judge from the charters of the reign, until Edward married Eadgyð in January of 1045. Her place then seems to have been taken by Eadgyð and her attestations soon completely cease. Before 1045, however, out of a possible eight charters Ælfgifu attests six.[4] It cannot be as confidently asserted that Eadgyð was very frequently present at gemots. She attests seven royal charters, which originate in only five gemots. It is to be noticed, however, that she attests four private charters out of a possible six.

Of other kinsmen of the king, none rank high on the witness lists. In fact the title *regis consanguineus* is found only on a spurious charter, applied to a Robert and an Esbern.[5] The former signs other charters, but Esbern's

---

[1] *NA*, § 31.

[2] The usual terms are: "... haec regalis concessio atque donatio facta est, sub astipulatione primatum quorum nomina hic caraxata sunt" (*CD*, 774, 775, 776, 780, 781); "His testibus consentientibus quorum", etc. (*CD*, 784, 812, 813, 817); "ad notitiam principum quorum," etc. (*CD*, 783); "Huius assertionis hi testes idonei comprobantur" (*CD*, 806); "confirmatum est hoc testamentum cui testes conspicui subscribendo annotantur" (*CD*, 808); "jubente piissimo rege Anglorum" (*CD*, 791); "Ad confirmandum uero nostrae beneficiae munus hi testes affuerunt quorum nomina infra sunt carraxata" (*CD*, 811); "Huius rei testes hic subnotantur" (*CD*, 819).   [3] *NA*, § 32.

[4] This, again, supports the view which I have advanced elsewhere, that a reconciliation between Edward and his mother was soon affected after the despoiling of her in 1043. Dr. Harmer says (*Writs*, p. 547); "She attested charters after her disgrace; her last datable signature seems to occur between 26 December 1045, and 1047" (on *CD*, 773).

[5] *CD*, 813. For the identity of these men see Appendix B.

signature does not seem to occur elsewhere on royal charters. The relation-ship of these men to the king is not known. But the position of their names on the witness list is certainly not determined by their kinship with the king, for their names are found with those of their fellows near the end of the lists. Earl Ralph, the nephew of the king, signs several charters, but never with the designation of royal kinsman, and his signature occurs among those of his equals. The same is true of the Earl Odda.[1] The signature of Edward's kinsman, Bishop Rotholf, seems never to occur, but since he was given Abingdon only in 1051 and no charters are extant from 1051 and 1052, its absence is not surprising.[2] Abbot Wulfric of Ely, who was a kinsman of the king, signs a few times, but always in his character of abbot. His brother, Guðmund, seems never to have attested a charter.[3] Leofric, abbot of Peterborough, who is said to have been related to the king,[4] always signs, when he appears, as abbot.

As far, then, as the Confessor's reign is concerned the kinsmen of the king played a very small part in the witenagemot, certainly small in comparison to that of his in-laws, the family of Godwin; but then Edward had no real family—no brothers, no sisters, no uncles to assume the roles such relatives usually do.[5] He had only his mother, with whom he was not always on good terms. Earl Ralph and Robert fitz Wymarc are the only kinsmen of the king who are fairly outstanding. Godwin's family, after Edward's marriage to Eadgyð, takes the place of blood relations and is certainly important in the counsels of the king.

Liebermann has emphasized the importance of churchmen as witan in the Anglo-Saxon period.[6] Böhmer, speaking of the reign of Edward, claims that they were "die wichtigste und einflußreichste Klasse der königlichen Ratgeber".[7] Knowles stresses the importance of the abbots as the counsellors of the Confessor.[8] How far do the charters of the reign of Edward bear out these statements?

---

[1] Odda and Ralph are called *regis cognati* (*GR*, I, 243).

[2] Rotholf may, however, have reached England in 1049 or in 1050. On him see *Safn til sögu Íslands*, IV (Reykjavík, 1907–15), 823–5, and the references there given; *Diplomatarium Norvegicum*, XVII, part 1 (Christiania, 1913), 197.

[3] On Wulfric see Appendix B. His brother, Guðmund, held lands in E, Nf, Sf, and was the king's thegn (see *PNDB, s.v.*). The absence of his signature is significant.

[4] Ellis, *Introd. to Domesday*, II, 162.

[5] Edward's brother, Ælfred, was dead (murdered in 1036) and his sister, Godgifu, whose second husband was Eustace of Boulogne, no doubt spent little time in England, although she held lands there. Edward's half-sister, Gunnhildur, played no part in his life. She married the Emperor Henry III in 1036 and died in 1038. (On this see *Encomium*, pp. xliii, xlv, xlvii, xlix–l.) [6] *NA*, §§ 33, 34.

[7] *Kirche und Staat*, p. 54. He also says: ". . . in England wird dies illustriert durch die Reihenfolge der Unterschriften an den Urkunden; vgl. z. B., die Urkunden über West-minster aus Eduards Zeit (Mansi XIX, 1052, 1057): erst die Bischöfe, dann die Äbte, dann der Kanzler, darauf die Duces." By using spurious charters Böhmer has his chancel-lor, but his other remarks are true. [8] *The Monastic Order*, p. 407.

The eighteen royal and eight private charters which I have used are all signed by ecclesiastics. The total number of signatures is 592, of which 253 are those of churchmen. They represent 46·08 per cent of all signatures excepting those of the royal family, viz., the king, queen, and queen mother.

Out of a possible 36 attestations[1] by the archbishops of Canterbury and York, 33, or 91·6 per cent, are found on the royal charters. The signature of the former is missing on only one royal charter, and that of the latter on only two.[2] The signatures of both archbishops are lacking on three private charters, and on two of them only the archbishop of York appears.[3] It may be concluded from these figures that the archbishops were seldom absent from gemots and were very intimate counsellors of the king.[4] Their importance, too, may be gathered from the fact that their attestations invariably succeed those of the king and, when they are present, the queen and queen mother.[5]

The bishops are next in rank and were possibly the most important class of witan. Their diligent attendance at court is attested by their numerous signatures on the charters. They sign every charter and account for 124 of the 592 signatures on the royal and private charters. This represents 22·5 per cent of the signatures of non-royal witan. The average number of bishops signing royal charters is 5·4, and private charters 3·3. This must be considered high, when it is remembered that the number of bishops in England was small.[6] As few as one[7] and as many as thirteen[8] sign a royal charter. On the eight private charters their signatures are never missing, and range in number from one to nine. The king, therefore, seems to have been constantly surrounded by, not all the bishops, but a good number of them.

Some individuals were obviously very frequently at the side of the Confessor.[9] In the years 1042–7 Ælfwine, bishop of Winchester, signs no fewer than twelve charters. Duduc, bishop of Wells, signs fourteen charters in

---

[1] This number makes no allowance for the vacancy of one of the sees through the death of the incumbent or his absence abroad. Thus the figure is actually too high.

[2] *CD*, 797, 811, 1332. The absence of the signature on 811 (1061) can be explained by the presence of the archbishop in Rome that year.

[3] *Ibid.*, 773, 805; *HLC*, pp. 247–8; *CD*, 807, 822. One would have expected the archbishop of Canterbury to attest the last rather than the archbishop of York. Possibly because Stigand was an interested party his name is not included among the witnesses.

[4] See also Appendix D. The *Anglo-Saxon Chronicle* (F 1051) calls Stigand "þes cinges rædgifa 7 his handprest".

[5] Except on *CD*, 1332, where the queen mother signs after the archbishop of Canterbury.

[6] According to Böhmer (*Kirche und Staat*, p. 50) it was sixteen in 1050, thirteen in 1066. Professor Stenton says that there were fifteen English bishoprics in April 1070 (*ASEng*, p. 651).   [7] *CD*, 808, 819.

[8] *Ibid.*, 784.   [9] See Appendix E.

the period 1042–60, and Hereman of Ramsbury and Sherborne eleven in the years 1045–55 and 1058–66. Eight charters are attested by Æthelstan of Hereford between 1042 and 1056, and seven by Grimcytel of Selsey between 1042 and 1047. Even higher is the record of Lyfing of Worcester who signs eight charters from 1042 to 1046. Eadnoð of Dorchester attests seven charters between 1042 and 1049. Indeed, only a very few bishops seem to have come seldom into the presence of the king. The bishop of Durham's signature is not found except on spurious charters. Nor does the bishop at St. Martin's, Canterbury, attest any but spurious charters; but appointments to this office were made only exceptionally, in a case, for instance, of the infirmity of an archbishop.[1]

It must, of course, always be remembered, in estimating the importance of the various bishops and sees, that we possess many charters from the period before 1050 and only a few after that date. No doubt the man, and not the bishopric, determined the individual's importance as a wita; yet, as a general rule, the best sees would go to individuals the king trusted and favoured. On the whole it may be said, judging by the evidence of the charters and chronicles, that the archbishops and bishops of England, with the exception of the bishop of Durham and the bishop at St. Martin's, were assiduous in their attendance on Edward the Confessor and were his most trusted witan.

Along with the bishops should be placed the abbots. Liebermann held that they did not regularly attend gemots.[2] This may be true for the Anglo-Saxon period as a whole, but it is not borne out for the Confessor's reign by the evidence of the charters.[3] Here are found, spread over seventeen of our twenty-six charters, sixty-four signatures of abbots, an average of some 2·5 for all the charters. This may seem a rather small number, but it is not surprisingly so when it is remembered that the majority of the thirty-five monasteries in England in 1066 were small.[4] Only the abbots of the greater monasteries might be expected to attend gemots. It must also be noticed that during the century before the Conquest "the majority of the bishops were monks, and their presence, and that of the

---

[1] On these bishops see W. Levison, *England and the Continent in the Eighth Century*, pp. 66–68. Levison says that there is no evidence for "chorepiscopi" at St. Martin's before the eleventh century (p. 66). Miss Deanesly, on the other hand, has argued that St. Martin's was a chorepiscopate of Canterbury founded in 867 and existing until the Conquest when Lanfranc abolished it ("The Archdeacons of Canterbury under Archbishop Ceolnoth," pp. 9–10). Cf. also *ASC*, p. 451.

[2] *NA*, § 34.

[3] One reason for their absence at times in the Anglo-Saxon period would be the great setbacks monasticism suffered now and again.

[4] Eighteen had an income in 1086 of less than £100, and of these five had under £40. Only seven houses had an income of over £600. See the detailed analysis of the wealth of the monasteries in Knowles, *The Monastic Order*, pp. 100–2 and 702–3.

abbots, in the Witan . . . made the monastic body predominant in the Church."[1] Even standing alone the abbots represent some 12 per cent of the non-royal witan.

It is true that the signatures of the abbots reveal that their representation in the witenagemot was not as complete as that of the bishops.[2] At the same time many abbots were clearly in frequent attendance on the king, although not to the same extent as the bishops.[3] The abbatial witan were drawn for the most part from the great houses.[4] It may safely be concluded that in the Confessor's reign the greater abbots came regularly, though not in their full numbers, to the meetings of the witan. Their absence is the exception, not the rule.

The archbishops, bishops, and abbots—the great churchmen—sign 231 times and make up 42 per cent of the non-royal signatures. They represent, therefore, a prominent element in the witenagemot. It must also be remembered that the lower clergy, who occasionally figure on the witness lists, would be rather subservient to the bishops and abbots. There would, thus, be less division in the ranks of the ecclesiastical witan than in those of the lay.

As for these lower clergy, the list of the numbers of signatures of the various classes of witan attesting Edward's charters reveals that they are in any case of slight importance. In all, the attestations of these churchmen on the royal and private charters number only twenty-two (nine of these on the royal) of which eleven are those of priests, six those of monks, two those of deacons, and three those of deans. These signatures appear only on seven charters, four[5] of which are from Worcester and contain the signatures of local clerics: five priests who sign eleven times, one dean who signs twice, and two deacons who sign once each. A dean of Christ Church attests a Kentish charter (*CD*, 773) and it may be that a priest of the same church attests an Essex charter (*CD*, 788) which is also attested by Stigand as priest. He was probably a royal chaplain at that time. The

---

[1] *The Monastic Order*, p. 46.

[2] Sixteen houses are represented on genuine charters and five more on doubtful charters. See Appendix G.

[3] Ælfwine of Ramsey's signature occurs more frequently than that of any other abbot. Yet he signs only nine times although he held Ramsey from 1043 to 1079. We know from other sources that he was an intimate of the Confessor (cf. Knowles, *The Monastic Order*, p. 407).

[4] See Appendixes F and G. The abbots of Glastonbury (income in 1086, £827. 18s. 8d.) attest nine times, the abbot of Ramsey (income in 1086, £358. 5s.) attests nine times, the abbots of Abingdon (income in 1086, £462. 3s. 3d.) attest seven times, the abbots of St. Augustine (income in 1086, £635) attest six times. The only abbey with a small income whose abbots attest relatively frequently is Evesham (income in 1086, £129. 2s. 3d.). Its abbots attest seven times. The abbots of seven abbeys with incomes under £100 attest in all only twelve times.

[5] *CD*, 797, 807; *HLC*, pp. 247–8, 300–2.

only other attestations by royal chaplains are those found on *CD*, 791, which is attested by four priests, three of whom, Regenbald, Godmann, and Peter, certainly were chaplains of the Confessor.[1] The charters from the reign do not therefore allow us to conclude that the royal chaplains were important witan or in the habit of attesting royal documents. The single charter the royal chaplains attest is not a landbook but deals with the transfer of the see of Crediton to Exeter. It may, I think, be concluded that only the higher clergy normally attested as witan.

Nevertheless the chaplains of the king became intimate counsellors after being elevated to episcopal rank. It is true that the signature of Giso of Wells is found on only one royal charter and one private charter between 1061 and 1066, and that Wulfwig of Dorchester signs only three times between 1053 and 1066, but very few charters exist from these years so that the percentage remains rather high. Leofric of Crediton attests five times between 1046 and 1066, and Hereman of Ramsbury's name is found, as we have seen, on no fewer than eleven charters from 1045 to 1066. Ulf of Dorchester (1049–52) attests only three doubtful charters in the short time he held that see.

The secular witan are headed by the earls. They rank below the bishops, but more often than not above the abbots.[2] Their importance, moreover, is clearly attested by the number of their signatures. Like the archbishops and bishops, they attest all the royal charters, but their signatures are lacking on one private charter. In all, their signatures are found eighty-five times and represent 15·4 per cent of all non-royal attestations. The average number of earls witnessing a charter is 3·2. This must be considered high, for the number of earls in England was small. The greatest number witnessing any one charter is six, the smallest, one.[3] It is evident from these figures that the majority of the earls were present at most gemots, and that the greatest of them were most assiduous in their atten-

---

[1] I know of no instance in the reign of the Confessor where Regenbald is styled chancellor in any authentic document. I incline strongly to the view that the title was unknown in England before the Norman Conquest, but it is quite possible that Regenbald held much the same position under Edward as the chancellor did under the early Norman kings. The fact that his name precedes those of the other three priests who attest *CD*, 791, might indicate his importance in the writing office. The fourth priest attesting *CD*, 791, is Godwine. I am unable to identify him, although he must have been a royal chaplain. His attestation follows that of Regenbald.

[2] The abbots take precedence in six cases (*CD*, 773, 787, 807, 811; *HLC*, pp. 300–2; *FASM*, II, Exeter xii); the earls in ten cases (*CD*, 774, 775, 776, 780, 781, 791, 797, 822, 956, 1332). On one charter which abbots attest, no earls sign (*HLC*, pp. 247–8).

[3] *CD*, 781, 819. *HLC*, pp. 247–8, has, as we have seen, no earl's signature. The number at any one time in the Confessor's reign will probably never be known (cf. *NC*, II, 374–83). The total number of earls who attest both royal and private charters during the reign is only fourteen. Waltheof attests two doubtful charters, while Morcar's name occurs only on spurious ones.

dance on the king. Between 1042 and 1053 Godwin attests seventeen charters, and Leofric the same number during the years 1042–57. Siward attests thirteen charters from 1042 to 1055 and Harold eleven between 1045 and 1066. The number of attestations is equally impressive in the case of Swegen and Tostig. Clearly a larger percentage of the great earls than of any other class of witan, as may be seen from Appendix H, were regularly in attendance on the king although it may be a question whether their influence on royal counsels in normal times was greater than that of the less fully represented but more august archbishops and bishops.

One would expect that Edward's companions, those "who came from the beloved land and spoke the beloved tongue," and whom he delighted "to enrich with English estates, and to invest with the highest offices of the English Kingdom"[1] should be found signing the charters on most occasions. But this expectation is not fully borne out by the evidence of the witness lists. Of the two most important bishops, Robert, bishop of London (1044–51) and later archbishop of Canterbury (1051–2), signs only twice; so does William, bishop of London (1051–75). About the only one of Edward's French lay favourites who attests fairly often is the Earl Ralph.

The charters, then, must be deemed to contain full lists of the archbishops, bishops, abbots, and earls attending gemots. It would not be unreasonable, in view of this full enumeration, to assume that the witness lists of the charters would contain the names of all thegns present at witenagemots. This, however, as we have seen, is by no means certain. The participation of thegns in the business of a gemot cannot be presumed to have been as complete as that of the more influential ecclesiastics and earls. We have seen that no attendance of thegns in large numbers is *a priori* reasonable. What have the witness lists of the charters to tell us on this subject?

In all, thegns attest the charters 200 times.[2] This figure represents 36·4 per cent of all non-royal attestations—a percentage considerably higher than that of any other single class of witan. The average number signing a charter is 7·7, while the over-all average of non-royal signatures is 21·1. Thegns are thus fairly well represented on the witness lists. Under one title or another they appear on all the charters save one.[3] The greatest number signing a single charter is thirty-five, the smallest, two.[4]

From the above it may be concluded that thegns were an integral part of the witenagemot and almost invariably present at meetings of the witan.

---

[1] *NC*, II, 18.
[2] This figure includes both royal and private charters. Under the designation thegn I have included all who sign as *ministri, milites, principes, nobiles, consiliarii*, etc., as well as the untitled names that I judge to belong to thegns.
[3] *CD*, 784.
[4] *FASM*, II, Exeter xii; *CD*, 783, 1335.

They attended in as large numbers as is to be expected, when one considers that thegns were possibly not a very large body, that their influence at a meeting was likely to be small, and that the expense of attending would be considerable. The figures do not prove that it was customary to enter on the witness lists the names of all thegns who attended a gemot, but they point to that conclusion, which is strengthened when we examine the identity of the thegns whose names occur on the Confessor's charters.

It is a difficult and tedious task to identify many of these men. Almost the sole source of information for purposes of identification is *Domesday Book*, and it is not to be expected that it will contain the name of every individual thegn throughout the twenty-four years of Edward's reign. In Appendix B are set forth the results of my investigations of the identity of the witnesses on all the genuine and doubtful charters I have examined from the reign.[1] The thegns are the only class of witan that presents great difficulties in this matter. In some cases I have been unable to find any information; in others conjecture has to be resorted to; but in many, identification is certain. The most valuable result of the inquiry is the light it throws on the relation of the king and the witan of the thegn class.

The number of thegns who normally attend gemots, or—if this be saying too much—attest charters, is relatively small, and the number of individuals who seem to have been in constant attendance on the king is extremely small. In the majority of cases the signature of a thegn occurs only once. This is true of fifty-seven of the ninety-six-odd thegns[2] who attest the genuine charters of the Confessor's reign. Nineteen sign two charters apiece; eight, three apiece; one signs four times; four, five charters apiece; and three, six apiece. One thegn signs seven times; two attest nine times apiece; and one, ten times. In addition Earl Odda's signature is found on ten charters which were made before his elevation to the earldom.

Who are these individuals who attest most frequently? Earl Odda is well known, but our sources are silent as to whether he held any public office before he received his earldom. He was, however, a large landowner and a kinsman of the Confessor. He must have been often in attendance on the king, judging by the number of his attestations and the fact that

---

[1] For this task I have used principally the following works: *DB*; *VCH*; *PNDB*; *ASC*; *ASW*; *LD*; *Feudal Documents*; *CrawCol*; Morris, *Sheriff*; Larson, *King's Household*; Ellis, *Introd. to Domesday*; Searle, *Onomasticon Anglo-Saxonicum*; *BKN*; *Writs*.

[2] The total number of thegns on the witness lists is difficult to estimate accurately, for it is not always possible to establish whether a certain name is that of one and the same individual in all cases where it occurs. Thegns who later became earls are not included in the list in Appendix K.

they are found on charters dealing with Hants, Devonshire, Cornwall, Wilts, and, after he became earl, Worcester. The other thegn who attests ten times is Ordgar. He must have been a royal thegn in the south of England, but again it is not known that he was a royal official. His attestations are found on charters dealing with the same regions as do the charters attested by Odda with the exception of Worcester. Ordgar's brother, Ælfgar, attests nine times (although in two or three cases it may be a question whether he is actually the witness). His signature occurs on charters dealing with Hants, Devonshire, Cornwall, and Somerset. We know more about Osgod Clapa, who also attests nine times. He was certainly a royal official (staller). All his attestations are found on charters which deal with Hants.[1] It is, I think, not without significance that these four men, who must have been often with the king, do not attest any extant charters which deal with lands outside the regions where their interests lay.

The thegn who attests seven times is one Ælfstan, known to have been a staller and possibly a sheriff. He attests charters connected with Hants and Kent. The three thegns who attest six charters apiece are virtually unknown. The first, Carl, witnesses charters connected with Hants and Devon. The second, Beorhtric, is obscure. The third, Ordwulf, is also an obscure figure, but the name occurs frequently in the Devon and Somerset entries in *Domesday Book*. Esgar, who attests five times, was King Edward's staller. Although his lands lay in many counties, the charters he witnesses refer only to Lincolnshire and Somerset. Another thegn who attests five times is Ralph, the well-known staller of King Edward. He may have held an earldom under King William. His attestations are found on charters connected with regions in which his interests lay and not elsewhere, viz., Devon, Somerset, and Lincolnshire. Nothing much is known of the remaining two thegns who attest five times apiece. Beorhtric seems to have been a landholder in southwest England, and Dodda seems to have held land in the regions covered by the charters he attests. It may

---

[1] The case of Osgod Clapa is interesting, for we know that he was outlawed in 1046 (*ASChr*, C 1046). In the first four years of the Confessor's reign he attested nine (out of a possible fourteen) charters. The five charters he did not sign deal with land or other matters in Rutland, Wo, W, K, and E. He thus appears to have attended the king only when the latter was in a certain locality. The relatively numerous attestations he made in four years might also be taken to indicate that if a man invariably attended gemots his name would appear on witness lists, and that the more infrequently a man's signature appears on charters the more irregular his attendance is to be presumed. This is not to say that some individuals whose names appear only once or twice on the Confessor's charters may not have been fairly regular in attendance. We possess charters from a particular year for only nine years of the Confessor's reign. It is to be noticed, also, that of our twenty-six charters, sixteen are from the period 1042–50. We have thus a fairly good sample from the first part of the reign, but not from the remainder. At some future date I hope to make a similar study of the charters from the reign of Ethelred.

be mentioned that Freeman thought that Dodda was a kinsman of Earl Odda.[1] The signatures of the eight thegns who attest three times apiece are also to be found only on charters connected with regions in which their interests lay. In short, this examination of the thegns who frequently attested the Confessor's charters would seem to show that they were almost always from the shire in which the gemot was held or from the neighbouring shires; and that many of them were royal officials (perhaps many more than can now be shown to have been such).

What have the witness lists of some representative charters to tell us of the thegns who attested? The charter with the longest list, *FASM*, II, Exeter xii, made in 1044, contains the names of no less than thirty-five thegns. But an examination of what little we know of them as given in my Appendix B shows that in most instances where it has been possible to identify the thegn he is found to have landed property in Devon or in the surrounding shires.[2] This strengthens the belief that, although the king was attended on his progress throughout the country by earls, bishops, and abbots from various localities,[3] the thegns who attended him were local magnates who joined him when he came into their districts and left him when he departed.

On another witness list, this time from a Peterborough charter, *CD*, 806, almost certainly made in Lincoln, 1051–60, we find the names of only six thegns. Had the king been wont to travel in the company of many thegns who were witan, we might expect that these six thegns would be household officials. Two of the signatures are those of royal officials: the king's staller, Esgar (styled *minister regis*), and the sheriff of Lincolnshire, Mærleswegen (styled *vicecomes*).[4] The former was indeed a household official, but he held lands in the neighbouring shires; the latter was a local official, but he also held lands in many shires. Then follow the names of Ulf *filius Tofi* and Ulf *de Lincolnia* (both styled *minister*). These are well-known and large landholders in Lincolnshire. Nothing much is known of the next witness, Iadulf *Maltesune* (styled *minister*), but there is a strong presumption that he was a thegn of the shire. The last witness, Ælfnoð (styled *minister*), almost certainly held lands of Peterborough in Lincolnshire. The thegns are thus, all except one, local magnates. The other witnesses, seven in number, are the king, the archbishops of Canterbury and York, the bishops of Dorchester (here styled of Lincoln, showing that the

---

[1] *NC*, II, 381.

[2] All but some six or seven thegns (including Harold, Tostig, and Leofwine, and a couple of royal officials) may have been from the neighbourhood.

[3] In fact Ealdred of Worcester seems to be the only bishop whose see was not in the neighbourhood to attest *FASM*, II, Exeter xii.

[4] This is the only instance, on what I regard as genuine charters, that the term is used in the reign of the Confessor.

designations have been added by the copyist of the charter or translated) and Worcester, and the earls Harold and Tostig.[1]

Let us next examine two Somerset charters, one royal, *CD*, 811, and one private, *CD*, 822, made in 1061 and 1061–5. The former is signed by twelve thegns, two of whom are styled *consiliarii* and the other ten, *ministri*. Three of these witnesses cannot be positively identified, five are known to be Somerset landholders, one of whom is a steward of Queen Eadgyð in the shire, and four are the king's stallers: the above-mentioned Esgar and Ralph (who held in Cornwall and elsewhere) together with Robert (who held in Somerset and elsewhere) and Bondi (who held in Gloucestershire and elsewhere). The other witnesses are the king, the archbishop of Canterbury, the bishops of Wells, Sherborne, Exeter, and London, the abbots of Glastonbury and Evesham, and the earls Harold, Tostig, Ælfgar, and Gyrth. The private charter has fewer witnesses. The king and queen attest, the archbishop of York, the bishops of Sherborne and Wells, the earls Harold and Tostig, the abbots of Glastonbury and Abingdon, and three stallers, Esgar, Ralph, and Bondi. The thegns, thus, are only three household officials, magnates from the shire or from neighbouring shires.

A Winchester charter, *CD*, 776, made in 1045, contains a witness list of thirty-one names, headed by the king, queen, and the two archbishops. The bishops of Winchester, Crediton, Hereford, Dorchester, Ramsbury, Wells, Selsey, Lichfield, and Sherborne attest. Five of these are from Hampshire or neighbouring shires, four from regions considerably distant. Godwin, Leofric, Swegen, and Siward—all the earls who are known at this time in England[2]—follow the bishops. Then come the abbots of Ramsey, Glastonbury, Abingdon, St. Augustine, and Chertsey—two from some distance and three from the neighbourhood. Nine thegns attest. Among them are Harold, the son of Earl Godwin, Odda, later an earl, and the staller Osgod. The others are thegns from the neighbourhood.

CD, 807, is a private charter recording a grant of land to St. Mary, Worcester. It is attested by seventeen witnesses including the king and queen. The archbishop of York and the bishops of Worcester and Wells attest. Two local abbots, those of Evesham and Pershore, and two earls, Godwin and Leofric, sign next. Three members of the community—a dean and two monks—follow the earls. Finally five thegns witness the

---

[1] *CD*, 808, another Peterborough charter, is witnessed by king and queen, the two archbishops, the bishop of Dorchester (again styled of Lincoln), the earls Harold and Tostig, the two stallers, Ralph and Esgar (each styled *regis dapifer*), Mærleswegen, Ulf of Lincoln, Iadulf, and two new thegns: Godric *filius Eadgyfe* and Áskell *Tokes sune* (all five with no title). The last two are certainly Lincolnshire men. Cf. also *CD*, 819 and 956.

[2] Harold and Beorn evidently received their earldoms after the making of this charter, which Harold attests among the thegns.

document. They are all from the neighbourhood, and one of them is Cyneweard, who was sheriff of Worcestershire.

It would be possible to analyse the witness lists of the rest of the charters, but the tale they would have to tell would differ in no essentials from the above sample.[1] Analysis of the lists would seem to show that the lay witan of the thegn class were local magnates who joined the king when he visited those regions of the country in which their lands lay; and that these thegns were not in the habit of accompanying the king into districts outside their sphere of interest. It does not show that any considerable number of thegns who were household officials were constantly in attendance on the king. It rather seems that at the most two or three large landowners whose lands were widely distributed were often among his entourage. It is quite clear from the witness lists, however, that many of the local thegns who attested were royal officials, household or provincial. Others who attested were in many cases tenants or thegns of a local church, abbey, or magnate. There is nothing to indicate that even all the thegns of the neighbourhood attended on the king or, if they did, were considered witan.[2]

Admittedly the conclusions drawn here must remain tentative by reason of the small number of charters on which they are based. Yet, at least for the Confessor's reign, no other authentic sources cast grave doubts on the results which the above investigation has revealed, nor have I found reason to modify my conclusions after a cursory survey of similar material from earlier periods.[3] Indeed it seems difficult to avoid the conclusion that the lay membership of the witenagemot consisted, apart from the earls, of royal provincial administrators and household officials drawn from the immediate locality in which the king happened to be, plus a small sprinkling of non-royal thegns from the neighbourhood of the meeting place.

This conclusion is not at variance with what we might expect to find in eleventh-century England. It is not to be expected that the landowners

---

[1] Note that *CD*, 788, is analysed in *ASW*, pp. 190–2, and *CD*, 768, 773, 822, and 956 in *ASC*, pp. 433–4, 436–8, 469–70, 465–8 respectively.

[2] This conclusion is very much strengthened by the fact, to which reference has already been made, that the names of some of the most important thegns of the reign of the Confessor either never or very seldom occur on the witness lists of the period. For examples of such thegns see Appendix B, *passim*. Attention may be drawn to a few names. Burgræd, a great Northumbrian thegn, signs only one charter (*CD*, 962). On him see *VCH*, Bk. I, 240b, 241a; Nth, I, 287. Mærleswegen, who was a sheriff and held eleven manors in Y, eight in L, one in Nth, one in Gl, and ten in D, signs only two or three times (on him see *VCH*, Y, II, 172–5). Cf. also Æthelnoð, Æthelwig, Eadmær *atre* (*attile, atule*), Eadnoð, staller, and Eadric of Laxfield. Stenton ("English Families," pp. 1–12), and Douglas (*Feudal Documents*, Introduction), both mention many important thegns whose names never appear on the charters of Edward's reign.

[3] Cf. in this connection the witness lists from earlier reigns examined in *ASC* and *ASW*, *passim*.

of England would attend the court, except on rare occasions or as an escort for the earls. On the other hand the king would always have about him a few leading landholders, who would fill the various household offices. They would not be very numerous, and they might not even dwell constantly with the king. Their presence at court would, however, be required at least when the king progressed throughout the localities in which their lands lay and they would then be joined by the royal provincial administrators, the royal officers of the shires and towns the king visited. That these men—and they are by no means more than a fraction of the important landowners of the country—form, with the earls and an odd independent thegn, the lay witan, seems not an unwarranted assumption in the light of the evidence of the witness lists.

From the evidence of the sources, it may be said that a large witenagemot in the reign of the Confessor would have the following composition. The king and queen would be present. The two archbishops would be there, a good many bishops—possibly one-half of those in the country, even on occasion all of them—a number of the abbots of the great monasteries and occasionally one or two heads of the lesser houses, and sometimes, though not often, the royal chaplains, together with a priest, deacon, dean (prior), or monk of the neighbourhood of the meeting place. Heading the lay witan would be the majority, and sometimes all, of the earls. From five to twenty-five thegns would be in attendance. They would be household officers or provincial administrators, such as sheriffs, for the most part, although a few might be non-royal thegns from the neighbourhood. A more ordinary gemot would consist of the same classes, but in reduced numbers.

CHAPTER SEVEN

The National Assembly

THE great majority of those who have dealt with the witenagemot have viewed it in the light of the development of parliament. It is difficult to avoid regarding it as a body possessing certain vaguely defined functions, a body whose composition, even if loose, was to some extent determined and fixed. Liebermann and others refer to it as an assembly, a national assembly, regularly summoned, to which men from all parts of the country came once, twice, or thrice a year. The very word "assembly," however, is misleading, for it conveys to our minds something much more definite than was the case.

In our day of highly developed national states, national institutions, and all-engulfing bureaucracies, it is difficult to view correctly the early history of these states, when such concepts were both unknown and meaningless. In societies which know only positive, ever changing law it is difficult to conceive the mind of men who knew only an age-old, unchanging law. A society which conceives of a national assembly as a body which, to be national, must be based on territorial representation finds it almost impossible to envisage a society which knew neither the idea of representation (in the modern or even late mediaeval sense) nor the concept national. People who know only the omnipotent and omni-competent state find it hard to conceive of a society which knew not the concept "state," which recognized no sovereign power save that of the law, a society composed of groups and even individuals, in a sense states within the state, possessing rights which no power on earth could legally abridge or take from them.[1] A society in which custom and tradition are authorities must seem strange to one which lives under the tyranny of the printed page and the latest order-in-council.

In a very real sense, then, there is no such thing as a witenagemot, there are only witan. There is no council, there is only counsel. There is not a shred of evidence to show that the witan ever regarded themselves as a corporate assembly, having an independent, if derivative, existence apart from the king. The wita is one whom the king consults, the witena-

---

[1] Cf. Louis VII's remarks (Amy Kelly, *Eleanor of Aquitaine and the Four Kings*, 1950, p. 124): "What do I hear," he said, "a prelate subject to the judgment and condemnation of his king? How could this be? I myself am a king no doubt, yet I am bound to state that it would be beyond my royal power to degrade the humblest clerk of my realm."

gemot the occasion on which the consultation takes place, or the act of consultation or deliberation.[1] Nor is this strange. Certain things, for example the attestation of land charters, or the deeming of dooms, are done by the king with the counsel of the witan. One may, if one wishes, call the occasion a council. But to an Anglo-Saxon the distinction between council and counsel would have been meaningless. In fact, he would only recognize counsel. In his view the king would receive counsel; only in that sense does he hold a witenagemot. That this witenagemot was a body possessing certain powers or functions, or having even a vaguely defined constitution, is impossible. It is true that certain men customarily attended the king and were in a sense the natural counsellors of the king, but they offered counsel as individuals and not as members of a definite body or council possessed of certain powers and having a more or less fixed membership. It is true that they were considered representatives of the people, but an individual is as representative of the people as a hundred individuals.[2] In a society in which law is sovereign this must needs be so.

The language of the *Anglo-Saxon Chronicle* bears out this view of the witenagemot. *Sub anno* 1047 (E) we read: "on þisum geare wæs mycel gemot on Lundene", i.e. a large gathering in which certain things were done by the king and witan, not a meeting or assembly which did certain things. This is made clear by the words: "7 man sette ut." Similarly Florence of Worcester (*s.a.* 1044) states that Manni was elected abbot of Evesham "in generali concilio," not "a generali concilio."[3] It is worth emphasizing this in view of the tendency to think of the witenagemot as a body which has definite functions and definite powers as well as a more or less clearly defined membership. Such a body it was not. Rather one may think of the witenagemot simply as the occasion on which the king consults those around him or those whom he summons *ad hoc* because he desires their advice or deems it expedient to consult them. An Anglo-Saxon king ruled under God and the law, and he ruled with consent, but it is important to emphasize that this consent might be implicit or explicit. Prudence dictated that a king obtain explicit consent for all important acts and wise kings took care to do this, but, in an age in which numbers

---

[1] As Liebermann points out (*NA*, § 15), the word "witenagemot" never occurs in the laws or charters of any Anglo-Saxon state. Only in the *Anglo-Saxon Chronicle* in the eleventh century and later does it occur, and here it is used in a very loose sense. In fact, it means nothing more than the act of deliberation or consultation between king and witan, or even among a number of witan or magnates. Liebermann points out (*NA*, § 15) that the county court in 1124 is called a *gewitenemot* (*ASChr*, E 1124), and in 1065 the *Chronicle* calls the assemblies at Oxford and Northampton witenagemots.

[2] Cf. Kern, *Kingship and Law*, pp. 195, 197; T. F. Tout, *Chapters in the Administrative History of Mediaeval England*, II, 149.

[3] Examples might be multiplied, e.g., *ASChr*, C 1050: "Þa hæfde Eadwerd cing witenagemot on Lunden . . . 7 sette Hrodberd."

are of no consequence, explicit consent was obtained by consulting a few magnates who happened to be with the king, unless the matter were of such importance that it was expedient to summon all the *meliores et maiores.*[1]

English historians have tended to place far too great emphasis on a largely imaginary hostility between baronage and Crown in the Middle Ages, to the neglect of the much more customary co-operation of king and magnate.[2] The present study is not the place to treat of this, but I mention it here because it has likewise vitiated writing about the Anglo-Saxon period of English history. The great earldoms of the reign of Edward the Confessor are generally regarded as elements of weakness in the Anglo-Saxon state, forces of decentralization, hostile to the Crown. In the hands of powerful and unscrupulous men, such as the family of Godwin, they undoubtedly were dangerous. But they were dangerous in such circumstances, not because they would weaken the authority of the Crown, but because their holders, by gaining control of the king, might make of him a puppet and of the Crown an instrument of tyranny. Control of the Crown meant riches and wealth for him who gained it. It meant the control of land, offices, and emoluments. The reign of the Confessor was a troubled one because the family of Godwin had an insatiable appetite for these things. The struggle was not one between a despotic or despotically minded king on the one hand and a nation intent on preserving its liberties on the other. The conflict was rather one in which a powerful family was bent on overthrowing the equilibrium of forces in the country, was bent on triumphing over both king and fellow magnates. This attempt culminated in the crisis of 1051, which represented a victory for the forces of tradition, order, and stability.

The very elements in the Anglo-Saxon state which are usually designated as elements of weakness ensured a certain close co-operation between king and magnate. The existence of several earldoms, divided among several independent magnates, was actually a source of strength to a monarch who wished to rule legally, for it was possible to play one against the other. On the other hand any attempt by a king to flout the law or proceed to extremes could be checked by a combination of magnates. In 1051 the earls combined with the king to defeat the overweening ambitions of one of their number. In 1052 the defection of the earls from the king may be explained by their unwillingness to go to the length of civil war against one who had learned his lesson, and by their exasperation with a king

---

[1] Cf. Kern, *Kingship and Law*, pp. 74, 188–9.

[2] Bishop Stubbs is an outstanding example, but this thesis is also implicit in the whole of Tout, *Chapters*. Professor Wilkinson is one of the few who emphasize co-operation . Cf. also Professor Stenton's remarks quoted above (p. 2).

who, they felt, was advancing foreigners at the expense of natives and who stubbornly followed the advice of others than his natural counsellors.[1] But it would be a mistake to see in these troubles national opposition to the monarchy, or to think that the witenagemot played any great part in these matters. It is not the witenagemot that overrides the king. It is the individual witan, acting and deliberating under the threat of civil war. There was no constitutional conflict over the rights of the king and the rights of a national assembly in the reign. There was a conflict over the right of the Northumbrians to be rid of an earl who, through the abuse of his position, had by that very abuse ceased to be an earl. Edward, though unwilling to admit that Tostig was at fault, was persuaded, by Harold and the magnates about him, that this was the case. No formal act of deposition was necessary, nor need a witenagemot, as a national assembly, pronounce deposition.[2] Yet the Northumbrian revolt is the nearest thing in the reign of the Confessor to national resistance to a monarch who is violating the rights of his subjects. There may have been cases of individual maladministration on the part of royal officials, such as sheriffs, but this can hardly, in the reign of Edward the Confessor, be blamed on his abuse of his rights, but rather on a failure on the part of an earl to curb provincial administrators.[3] The very fact that the Confessor's reputation is what it is, proves that there was no conflict between the nation as such and the Crown. There was conflict between earl and earl, between earl and churchman, and on occasion between magnate and Crown.

Even if the powers of the Crown may have, to some extent, suffered and remained weak because of the existence of powerful earls, yet the liberty of the individual subject and his rights may well have been safeguarded by the very existence of these, so-called, agents of decentralization. The triumph of the house of Godwin was a step toward despotic government, for the family could hope to maintain itself only by the destruction of all potential rivals. It was not hedged about by a throneworthiness such as the descendants of Cerdic possessed. With the disappearance of the earls after the Conquest the shackles of a limited despotism enmeshed England, but only with the increasing scope of royal government and the king's growing need for revenue could a constitu-

---

[1] It is clear from the *Anglo-Saxon Chronicle* (E 1052) that Edward was overruled in 1052, and again from the *Vita Eduuardi* (p. 423) that he unwillingly abandoned Tostig in 1065.

[2] Cf. Kern, *Kingship and Law*, p. 195: "By a breach of the law, the monarch *ipso facto* forfeited his right to rule. He deposed himself."

[3] Morris rightly points out (*Sheriff*, p. 38) that the Anglo-Saxon sheriff "does not stand purely for central or royal power as against the local influence of the earl. Though directly representing the king in various matters, he was the judicial, it may even be the military, agent of the earl."

tional conflict emerge, which led to the birth, after much trial and error, of a body which slowly acquires self-consciousness and finally becomes parliament. Conditions in the reign of the Confessor forbade the development of any such body. There may be a difference of opinion on certain concrete issues between king and witan, between wita and wita, but there can be no constitutional conflict involving the question of the rights of the king as opposed to the rights of a body of men who, together with the king, are supposed to form the witenagemot.

It would be going beyond the limits of this work to discuss fully how far centralization had proceeded in the Anglo-Saxon state by the time of the Conquest. No doubt through the increased importance of the king resulting from the Danish invasions, through the growth of a royal writing office, and through the sheriff, the executive function of the king had increased and was increasing. Jolliffe calls our attention to the fact that the tenth and eleventh centuries appear as a time of rapid growth of royal power, but he also emphasizes that, "taking our standpoint in the twelfth century, we should be conscious of a strong contrast with the feudal and bureaucratic stability of the Angevin crown. There is the cardinal difference that the rule of the house of Ælfred was based less upon the land than upon the folk." He also points out that the Old English throne "had few positive powers, but it had access to reserves of loyalty and affection not to be explained by the legal rights of the crown."[1] Beside this we may set some earlier remarks of the same historian:

Law is not in the king's mouth, but so surely in the voice of the nation that it matters little how it finds utterance. . . . This legal popularism, elastic, practical, tolerant as to the composition of its assemblies, yet unyielding in its demand that lawful men shall pronounce right law, is the first and most far-reaching rule which united England inherited from the embryo states of the Heptarchy. It remained the prevailing current of life, strong, deep, for the most part invisible, but determining the range within which the executive power could be exerted, and in the end forcing it into avowed conformity with itself.[2]

It is true that great changes were taking place and great innovations were being made in the early Middle Ages, yet any departure from fundamental ideas and principles was avoided in various ways, and men's ideas of what we term the State, the Law, the Government, the Kingship, and so on, remained practically unaltered throughout the Anglo-Saxon period (unless the introduction of Christianity may have brought with it an emphasis on the sacral nature and dignity of Kingship). The Law, for example, remains eternal and unchanging. Recorded law is only a small part of this. In practice there may be what we call legislation; in theory there can be no such thing. From the first to the last in the Anglo-Saxon

[1] *CHMed*, pp. 136–7.　　　　　　　　　[2] *Ibid.*, p. 24.

period law remains supreme. For practical reasons the king and his witan are the ones who declare it. They do so, not because they are in any modern sense a representative national assembly, but because from the earliest historical times kings existed among the Germans in England and were accustomed to govern, if that word may be used, with the counsel and consent of the *meliores et seniores.* The words, central government or central assembly, have little meaning even in the reign of the Confessor, for the share of the king and his advisers in what we call government was very small. The business of governing, except in time of war, was largely in the hands of the folk themselves. The laws were a *pactus,* a covenant of one with all and all with one. Every man was in a sense an executive officer of the state, and the king and his court were probably until the Conquest simply *primi inter pares* in this matter.

It is a mistake to think that, because the governing body of a country is composed of royal appointees, it must necessarily be a servile or docile body, prepared to rise, stand, or sit at the regal nod. In primitive societies this is often not so. Only in a society where centralization has advanced far and where a bureaucracy exists, composed of men who would be nothing if not in the royal service, is this the case. Where old ideas and traditions are still vital, where the concepts of the state and of absolutism are unknown or weak, where bodies autonomous in their own sphere exist, royal officials are not mere instruments of the will of their creator. They will represent—if the word may be used—not only the king but various communities within the community of the realm and the latter also. In a word their task, which they share with the head of the realm, is the maintenance of the law which guarantees each his rights. They stand not powerless, because they are backed not only by divers bodies and individuals jealous of their rights, but by a living, vocal tradition teaching how things should be ordered to secure that harmony of parts which results in peace, the temporal end of man.

The foregoing pages have made it clear that only in a limited sense can the so-called witenagemot be considered a national assembly. Unless one is to abandon the idea that charters were made in a witenagemot (and that, I think, is impossible) it is necessary to recognize that the gemot was, at least for the thegns, not a national assembly. However, the earls from all parts of England seem to have been frequently with the king and so do the bishops and abbots. Yet, from the evidence of the witness lists, even the attendance of bishops was limited and by no means such as to enable us to conclude that all or even a majority of the witenagemots to which the charters bear witness may be called national as far as the attendance of churchmen is concerned. Many, too, are not national as far as the earls are concerned. Professor Stenton has recognized this fact for the eleventh-century gemots (whatever may have been the case in the tenth century) when he writes: "But so far as can be seen these later councils included very few of the magnates of northern England, and it is the range of their interests rather than their composition which entitles them to be regarded as national assemblies."[1]

Geographically the witenagemot was representative of all England only on occasion and then only as regards churchmen and the earls. The north would seem to have been as well represented as the south by these two classes of witan;[2] certainly, judging by the witness lists, the archbishop of York was regularly in attendance and so were the earls of Northumbria. However, modern ideas of national representation were unknown in Anglo-Saxon England. The earls, no doubt, in some sense represented the interests of their districts, the bishops those of their dioceses, and the abbots those of their houses, but hardly in the modern sense of representation. It is scarcely conceivable that a wita was thought of as representing any particular region; rather he was considered a depository of custom and as such represented, if anybody, the nation as a whole. To suggest, as has

---

[1] *ASEng*, p. 543. Cf. also *Transcripts*, ed. Stenton, p. xx: "With Lincolnshire, as with the north and east of England generally, the kings of the age before the Conquest had little to do." It must be admitted that all documents from the reign of the Confessor show that the north was to a great extent sharply separated from the rest of England, and no doubt enjoyed a large degree of local autonomy. I have, e.g., noted this when examining the writs from the reign that were available to me. Only one was addressed to Yorkshire. For comparative purposes I append here a list of the shires, towns, and districts to which I have found writs purporting to be directed: Berkshire 2 (*CD*, 840, 886), Dorset 2 (*CD*, 841, 871), East Anglia 4 (*CD*, 851, 852, 875, 881), Essex 3 (*CD*, 859, 869, 870), Gloucester 2 (*CD*, 829, 830), Hampshire 1 (*CD*, 845), Hereford 2 (*CD*, 833, 867), Hertford 4 (*CD*, 826, 827, 864, 866), Huntingdonshire 2 (*CD*, 903, 906), Kent 4 (*CD*, 828, 831, 847, 854), London 5 (*CD*, 856, 857, 861, 872; *EHR*, LI, 102, § 1), Middlesex 5 (*CD*, 843, 855, 860, 886; *EHR*, LI, 102, § 1), Norfolk 8 (*CD*, 853, 868, 876–80, 882), Northamptonshire 2 (*CD*, 863, 904), Oxford 4 (*CD*, 829, 862, 965; *EHR*, LI, 102, § 2), Somerset 6 (*CD*, 834–9), Stafford 1 (*CD*, 842), Suffolk 12 (*CD*, 832, 853, 868, 873, 874, 877, 879, 880, 883, 884, 905, 1342), Surrey 4 (*CD*, 846, 848, 850; *FASM*, II, Westminster xv; *CD*, 848 and 850, are, however, two copies of the same writ, and this may possibly be true in another instance or two), Worcester 3 (*CD*, 829, 830; *EHR*, LI, 102, § 3), Yorkshire 1 (*CD*, 1343). In Dr. Harmer's edition of Anglo-Saxon writs which reached me after the above list was compiled, there are additional writs addressed to Devon 1 (no. 120); Warwick 1 (no. 115, addressed also to Worcester and Gloucester); and Yorkshire 1 (no. 119, addressed also to Nottingham). Other writs of the Confessor exist but they are addressed only to shires in which certain churches hold lands, and I have not included them in the above list.

[2] On the charters I have used from the reign of the Confessor the names of bishops from all the sees of England at that time are to be found except those of Durham. Abbots of all the large abbeys attest charters from the reign with the exception of Christ Church. This omission, however, is explained by the fact that the archbishop of Canterbury stood *in loco abbatis* to Christ Church from the time of St. Augustine onwards. Its history before the Conquest is very obscure (cf. Knowles, *The Monastic Order*, pp. 50, 696–7). Monasteries in the following shires appear on the genuine charters which I have used from the reign of the Confessor: Br, C, D, Gl, Ha, Hu, K, L, Mx, Nf, Nth, So, Sr, Wo.

been done,[1] that the witenagemot was an assembly which voted as a modern parliament does is to introduce concepts which were completely unknown to eleventh-century Anglo-Saxon England. To imagine that the northern Danelaw felt the lack of representation in the supposed witenagemot which elected Harold is to endow Anglo-Saxon England with political theories and a constitution which were not known until several centuries later. There can be little doubt that the northern Danelaw was, in the reign of the Confessor, fully satisfied with its representation at court. It did not desire "representation" but local autonomy and the freedom to pursue its own distinctive way of life.[2] Its earl and its archbishop adequately looked after its interests at court.

The temporal and spiritual magnates were the natural counsellors of Edward the Confessor. He consulted such of them as he wished or was compelled to on account of their vast possessions and power (e.g., the family of Godwin). Some were more trusted than others and were more frequently with the king. Although custom decreed that he must rule with consent, political exigency, not constitutional considerations, determined whom the king would consult. Any consultation of witan was a witenagemot.

In one sense, however, the witness lists of the Confessor's charters point, if not to a national assembly, at least to national unity. They testify to the assimilation of those individuals whose ancestors, 200 years earlier, had begun a devastating attack on Anglo-Saxon society—the Northmen from the east. In estimating how far this process of assimilation had gone, it must be remembered that the majority of the witnesses whose names appear on the charters of the Confessor's reign are from the southern third of England. Yet on these witness lists many Scandinavian names are to be found—thirty-one in all belonging to some thirty-five individuals. Of these twenty-seven are those of thegns, six those of earls; one is that of a bishop and one belongs to an abbot.[3] The lands of these men were scattered throughout the country, as far as identification is possible.[4] Of course, many of them were by this time Scandinavian in name only (e.g., the sons of Godwin). Nevertheless, the names testify to the widespread permeation of Anglo-Saxon society by Scandinavian invaders.

In fact, it may be said that the witness lists of the Confessor's reign testify to the existence of a real feeling of unity in England. On the other hand, it would be erroneous to conclude from the witness lists that the sphere of action of the central government was great or that England

---

[1] *NC*, III, 37–38. Freeman is discussing the election of Harold in 1066.

[2] Cf. Stenton, "Scandinavian Colonies," p. 11. The crisis of 1065 was not of a constitutional nature. It was concerned only with the person of the earl. See *infra*.

[3] See Appendix K.

[4] Those from Lincoln seem more numerous than those from any other single shire.

possessed a strong central government. The royal charters and writs of the Confessor's reign deal with a very limited range of business—grants of land and/or jurisdiction to churches and private individuals, ecclesiastical business, and lawsuits involving land or privileges of one kind or another. But they affect many parts of England, and what little the government does, it does with the cognizance of men from those parts of the country. The England of Edward was in many ways, for example militarily, a weak state, but it was a state whose very weaknesses were, as pointed out above, not without compensation. Its monarchy was not powerful, but there was a certain balance of forces, and a certain respect for the Crown, which enabled the king, in spite of the many disruptive and discordant elements with which he had to work, to maintain his dignity and preserve political unity and internal peace. To that political unity and that internal peace the witness lists of the charters bear testimony.

CHAPTER EIGHT

Time and Place of Meetings of the King and Witan

IT follows from the view of the witenagemot suggested above that no exhaustive list of witenagemots held in the reign of the Confessor can ever be constructed. Witenagemots were held at various times and places during the progress of the king throughout the country.[1] An itinerary of the Confessor has never been worked out, and it is no doubt impossible to construct a satisfactory one, as the sources are so incomplete.[2] The following information may, however, be deduced from such an itinerary of the king as can be constructed, and from the information contained in Appendix O. Of the fifty-eight occasions, listed in the Appendix, on which the king may have consulted with his witan, thirty do not admit of localization, eleven took place in London, nine at Gloucester, three at Sandwich, two at Winchester,[3] and one at each of Exeter, Waltham, and Britford.[4] Since Sandwich knew the presence of the king only when danger

---

[1] Many early charters are dated at royal manors, e.g., Frome (So), December 16, 934 (*CD*, 1110); Dorchester (Do), Easter 934 (*CD*, 1119); but see Liebermann's list of the meeting places before the Confessor's reign (*NA*, § 45). He does not mention the above Dorchester. The date is corrected from 843 to 934 by Miss Robertson (*ASC*, p. 301).

[2] Larson made a beginning of working out Edward's itinerary (*King's Household*, p. 200). Using this and supplementing it with information I have gleaned from the sources, I have drawn up the itinerary given in Appendix T.

[3] The charters testify to three or four meetings at Winchester in 1044–6. See Appendix T for other evidence from the charters.

[4] To the list of meeting places may be added Lincoln (*CD*, 956), although the year is uncertain, and, if we accept *CD*, 816, Windsor. *CD*, 853, also purports to be made at Windsor, but it is a forgery (Earl Gyrth is addressed but Earl Godwin witnesses). Liebermann lists gemots at the following places during the reign of Edward the Confessor (I place his authority in brackets following the name and date): *Gillingham*, 1042 (*CD*, 1332). This charter, however, deals with Littleham (D) and there is no mention of Gillingham. William of Malmesbury (*GR*, I, 238) gives Gillingham as the location of a gemot in 1042, but Liebermann does not cite him. *Gloucester*, 1051 (*ASChr*). *Lincoln*, 1045 (*CD*, 956). The date is wrong; Miss Robertson (*ASC*, p. 465) correctly assigns this charter to 1053–5. *London*, 1045 (*CD*, 779). This charter is spurious. *London*, 1044 (*ASChr*). *London*, 1047 sq. (*ASChr*). Presumably "sq." means 1048, but how Liebermann concludes, from the account of the *Chronicle* for 1047–8, that London was the scene of a witenagemot in these two years, is difficult to see. It hardly seems reasonable to suppose that he erred and used *ASChr*, E 1047 and 1048, without noticing that the correct dates are 1051 and 1052. Certainly, however, the *Chronicle* makes no mention of gemots in London in 1047 and 1048. *London*, 1052 *bis* (*ASChr*). These are the Midlent and September gemots. *London*, 1055 (*ASChr*). *London*, 1065 sq. (*ASChr*). The reference would seem to be to the gemot

threatened from abroad, it is clearly the location of none but emergency gatherings. The meetings at Exeter, Waltham, and possibly Britford were also unique. London, Gloucester, and Winchester are thus the only places where witenagemots seem to recur, and all three seem to be mentioned often enough to enable us to say that the Confessor showed a preference for them. It is hardly safe to say more. Certainly it would seem rash to go as far as Freeman did in holding that the Confessor invariably met with his witan at Easter and Christmas at Winchester and Gloucester respectively.[1] Of the eleven gemots held in London, only two met at Christmas (the hallowing of Westminster Abbey and the election of Harold, i.e., both in the same Christmas season), three met at Easter or in Midlent, three in September, one at Whitsuntide, one at Lammas, and one in June. Of the nine that were held at Gloucester, two met at Christmas, three at Easter, and one in each of the months of August, September, October, and November. Of the gemots held at Winchester only two can be dated and they were held at Easter. It is, thus, impossible to discern any regularity in the meetings at these three places. At the same time it is not possible, because of our scanty information, to deny that these three cities were the favourite dwelling places of Edward, and therefore the scene of most of those occasions on which Edward took counsel with numerous witan or celebrated the high church festivals.

It may be questioned whether ceremonial witenagemots, on a scale comparable to the later crown-wearings of the Conqueror on the festivals of Easter, Whitsuntide, and Christmas, were held in the reign of Edward the Confessor. Of course it cannot be denied that this may have been the case, and it is well known that these festivals, or these seasons, were the favourite times for banqueting and feasting in both Christian and heathen days.[2]

on the occasion of the hallowing of Westminster Abbey, and the one at which Harold was elected king. *Northampton*, 1065 (*ASChr*). This, I have tried to show, was not a witenagemot. *Oxford*, 1065 (*ASChr*). This, too, I do not regard as a witenagemot. *Winchester*, 1065 (*CD*, 815). This is a spurious charter, which in any case is dated at *Wendlesore*, which is surely Windsor and not Winchester (cf. *DEPN*, *s.v.* Windsor). *Winchester*, 1043. This was the occasion of the coronation of Edward. Kemble, who was led astray by the confused chronology of the *Anglo-Saxon Chronicle* in the reign of Edward, attempted a list of witenagemots (*Saxons*, II, 260) which is inadequate also.

[1] *NC*, II, 8, 40, 231, 233, 452; cf. IV, 422: "The national Assemblies prescribed by English Law were carefully held [by the Conqueror] at the accustomed places and seasons. . . ." I do not know Freeman's authority for the statement that English law prescribed these national assemblies. Cf. also *ibid.*, V, 259: "The old Assemblies went on; and, during the reign of the Conqueror at least, they went on in the old places and at the old seasons. Three times in the year, at Winchester, at Westminster, and at Gloucester, did King William wear his Crown and gather around him the great men of his realm, as King Eadward had done before him."

[2] Cf. Larson, *King's Household*, p. 201; and G. Vigfusson, *An Icelandic-English Dictionary*, *s.v. blót*: "The feasts were, esp. the three great annual feasts, when the winter set in (Oct.), at Yule time and mid-winter (Dec. or Jan.), and when the summer began

The words of the *Chronicle*,[1] when reporting the death of Godwin at Winchester during Easter 1043, perhaps imply a festive gathering. It is, however, extremely doubtful that ceremonial gemots were held, at least with any regularity. Such a charter as *CD*, 813, reflects almost certainly a much later stage than the reign of the Confessor. The high church feasts, however, would probably see large numbers of witan at court, but such meetings in Anglo-Saxon times may have lacked the formality of the Norman gatherings.

Of the fifty-eight occasions listed in Appendix O on which a witena-gemot may have taken place, seventeen are from Midlent, Easter, or the spring of the year, fourteen from Christmas or January, five from some time during the summer, five at Whitsuntide or May (two) or June (two), two from Lammas or August, three from sometime during the autumn of the year, five from September, two from October, two from November, and three from an unknown date. One might, therefore, conclude that the king took counsel with his witan most frequently at Christmas and Easter, and grant that greater numbers of witan were then in attendance on the king than at any other time of the year (except at a time of crisis when all the witan would be summoned). But it must be remembered that such festive meetings would much more readily find a place in the chronicles than the more prosaic courts of the king in his progress through-out the country at other times of the year.[2]

There is, moreover, little evidence in the lists for the view that the witan constituted a body that was summoned by the king on certain occasions or on the high festivals of the church year. On the contrary, the witena-gemots of Edward the Confessor were meetings of the king and the mag-nates who happened to be with him, held at various times and various places throughout the country. It is quite in accord with this view that the retinue of the king should be larger at certain places and on certain occasions. The number in attendance on the king at Christmas and Easter would no doubt be greater than at other times of the year, but the witness lists give us no warrant for assuming that the spiritual and the temporal magnates of the realm were ever explicitly summoned to attend a witena-gemot, except on very special occasions such as war or a political crisis.[3]

(April). . . ." Numerous references are given by Vigfusson. Whitsuntide was more exclu-sively a Christian feast.   [1] *ASChr*, C 1053.

   [2] In this connection it may be pointed out that during the reigns of the Norman kings, the *Chronicle* very frequently mentions where the king held his court on the three high festivals of the church (see *ASChr*, E 1085–7, 1091, 1094–1100, and the reign of Henry I *passim*). Yet no one would maintain that these sessions of the *curia regis* differed, except in numbers attending, from sessions of the *curia regis* held at other times of the year and more sparsely attended.

   [3] Note the number of attestations by certain classes of witan. On the twenty-six charters I have used from the reign of the Confessor, bishops attest as follows:

The myth of summoned witan, meeting once or twice or thrice a year, will not stand up to the evidence of the witness lists. The eleventh-century witenagemot, to judge from the evidence of the witness lists and the narrative sources, was essentially a court council. Had it been customary for an Anglo-Saxon king to summon his witan to his side once or twice a year, we might expect to find that the number of attestations on the royal charters would not vary greatly, but, as we have seen, they do.[1]

Before one may accept the view that witenagemots were held only when the king chose to especially summon the witan, it must be shown why the thegns, other than those who were royal officials of one sort or another, should be called to the king's side. The answer that they were summoned for feasting on the high festivals of the church year is hardly adequate.[2] There is every reason to suppose that men were then, as later, averse to undergoing the expense which attendance would involve.[3] In the case of the bishops and earls a summons would not be necessary except in

Charters	Bishops' signatures	Charters	Bishops' signatures
4	1	1	7
6	2	4	9
3	3	2	10
2	4	1	13
3	5		

Had the bishops been regularly summoned to gemots one would expect much less variation than these figures reveal. Even less variation would be expected in the figures of earls attending gemots, yet the earls attest our charters as follows:

Charters	Earls' signatures	Charters	Earls' signatures
1	0	9	4
1	1	4	5
8	2	1	6
2	3		

Our conclusion is strengthened when it is observed how many of the earls' signatures belong to the family of Godwin.

[1] The twenty-six charters I have used reveal the following:

Witnesses	Charters	Witnesses	Charters
10	2	21–25	5
11–15	5	31–35	8
16–20	5	52	1

[2] The fact that the Conqueror wore his crown three times a year in the presence of all the magnates of England (*ASChr*, E 1087) does not necessarily involve the assumption that he sent a special summons to them. In fact, I know of no evidence that he did. The language of the *Anglo-Saxon Chronicle*, too, bears out the fact that the witan were not usually summoned, except for some special crisis. Speaking of a specially summoned assembly, it says: "Her on þisum geare forðferde Siward eorl 7 þa *bead* man *ealre* witena gemot VII nihton ǽr Midlenctene 7 utlagode mann Ælfgar eorl" (E 1055, italics mine). Cf. also E 1047, 1048, 1052; *FlWig*, 1044).

[3] Liebermann speaks of the journey to the distant witenagemot as tiresome (*NA*, § 42). Cf. also Maitland, "Memoranda de Parliamento," *Maitland Selected Essays*, p. 69; McKisack, *Parliamentary Representation*, pp. 28–29.

emergencies, for these men were in such close touch with the king and so frequently in attendance at court that it would be superfluous to summon them. The very fact that the names of some of the outstanding thegns of the Confessor's reign never appear on the charters of the period shows that, with the exception of the thegns who held positions in the household of the king or were provincial administrators, thegns were not in the habit of attending on the king. The only occasions on which it may be assumed that thegns met with the king in large numbers are times of crises, such as 1051, when an armed force was necessary.

CHAPTER NINE

The Witan as Counsellors and Legislators

In his profound study of the mediaeval ideas of kingship and law Fritz Kern describes the relationship between the king, the law, and the community:

> We have seen that the mediaeval monarch is not absolute in theory. He is bound by the law. But in respect of form and practice, he seems to us to be absolute; for he is not obliged to attain that harmony with the law which is required of him, by any definite, formally prescribed method. The harmony between the ruler and the law is usually achieved without the observation of any fixed forms, though, in cases of doubt, the harmony of his actions with the law is demonstrated by the consent of the community or its representatives. But there is no binding rule as to what cases require this consent. In ordinary circumstances, it is presumed that all the monarch's acts are explicitly or implicitly in accord with the law and the community's sense of justice. . . .
>
> There are three degrees of popular participation in the government, i.e., participation of the representatives of the community, the *meliores et maiores*, and so on. The first is tacit consent; here the king acts formally alone, and so "absolutely" in form but not in substance. The second degree is advice and consent; the third is judicial verdict. It is typical of the Middle Ages that there are no hard and fast rules regulating the application of any of these three forms of participation, and that all three without any distinction, could result in equally valid acts of State.[1]

A cursory reading of the *Anglo-Saxon Chronicle* will bear out this view. At one time, for example, the king is said to "give a bishopric" to a certain individual.[2] At another, the king is said to hold a witenagemot and appoint a man to a bishopric.[3] It would seem that in the opinion of the

---

[1] *Kingship and Law*, pp. 188–9.

[2] For examples see *ASChr*, C 1045, E 1048, C 1049. Numerous other instances might be cited.

[3] *ASChr*, C 1050; *FlWig*, 1044. The former instance refers to the appointment of Robert to Canterbury. Another version of the *Chronicle* (E 1048) makes no reference to a witenagemot. It may be asked whether this means that all appointments were made in a witenagemot. But such a question is beside the point, which is simply that the chronicler makes no distinction, for he does not see one, between the act of the king alone and the act of the king in a witenagemot—an entirely logical view in eleventh-century England. I may remark here that I do not believe that Edward or any other Anglo-Saxon king ever appointed a prelate to a see without consulting at least some churchmen. But that he did appoint prelates without consulting many witan, is abundantly proven by the *Chronicle*, C 1044, in the case of the appointment of Siward. Nor, significantly, does the method of procedure in this instance seem, to the chronicler, a matter for condemnation.

chronicler the king is competent to act with or without the witan. In the same way the dismissal of the lithsmen in 1050 is recorded in one version of the *Chronicle* as an act of the king, in another, as the act of the king in a witenagemot.[1] In this instance there can be little doubt that the act was performed in a witenagemot, but it seems to be a matter of indifference to the chronicler. This may mean: (1) that the chronicler assumes that everyone will know that the dismissal would be the act of both king and witan; (2) that the participation of the witan is of no consequence in the opinion of the chronicler; or (3) that the question of what the king can do alone, and of what he can do only with the co-operation of the witan, is one that would never occur to the chronicler. Of these, the third appears the most reasonable answer, in view of the prevailing ideas on the relation of king and subject in eleventh-century England.[2] This, of course, is not the same as saying that every act of the king was good. It was that only if it was in accord with the law. It might be bad, just as an act of the king and his witan might be bad. Both the act of the monarch acting by himself, and the act of the monarch acting with the counsel of his witan, might on occasion be wrong, ill-advised, or contrary to the law. What was important was not the mode of action, but that the act, whosoever it be, be in accord with the law.[3]

From this indifference to the mode of action it follows that there can be no hard and fast definition of the functions of the witan. They might participate in all the acts of government or in none. There is, therefore,

[1] *ASChr*, C 1049, E 1047.

[2] Fritz Kern observes, p. 189: "Provided that he remained in accord with the law, it rested entirely at the monarch's discretion which of the three methods he adopted for the dispatch of business. Whether he settled the matter by personal decree, or after giving audience to, or even perhaps with the collaboration of counsellors, i.e., representatives of the community; or finally, by procuring the judgment of the high court or a court of princes, was decided entirely at his option." Cf. *ibid.*, pp. 78, 188. Attention may also be drawn to *CHMed*, p. 29: "It is the indivisible law which speaks through king and witan, and for them the divided and often antagonistic functions and rights of more advanced political theory have no meaning."

[3] Cf. Kern, *Kingship and Law*, pp. 189–90. Numerous instances could be cited from Anglo-Saxon history, showing that both the personal acts of a monarch and the acts of monarch and counsellors might be bad. Let the following suffice: "and king Eadward gave the bishopric to Ulf his priest, and ill bestowed it" (*ASChr*, C 1049); "And he [Hardecnut] was immediately received both by Angles and by Danes; though his counsellors afterwards cruelly requited it, when they counselled, that to sixty-two ships should be paid, for each rower, eight marks" (*ASChr*, E 1039); "And the aldorman Eadric then went to meet the king at Aylesford. Never was greater evil counsel counselled than that was" (*ASChr*, C 1016); one might also instance the outlawing and inlawing of Godwin once and Earl Ælfgar twice. For mediaeval man law was identical with that which was good, just, and right; an illegal act was an immoral act and *vice versa*. The sanctity of law and the necessity of acting in harmony with it are well brought out in the famous dictum of Njáll: "Með lögum skal land vort byggja, en með ólögum eyða" (*Sagan af Njáli Þorgeirssyni og sonum hans*, Viðeyar klaustur, 1844, chap. 70, p. 158).

little point in compiling a list of the functions of the witan, for they no doubt participated on occasion in every kind of act that the government performed. In other words, an act of a certain kind would on occasion be performed by the king alone, on occasion by the king and a few witan, and on occasion by the king and numerous, possibly all, the witan of the land. This is not to say that certain acts would not customarily be performed according to a certain mode. Actually that is all that one may hope to discover from a study of the sources for the Anglo-Saxon period of English history, i.e., how far it was customary for an Anglo-Saxon king to act alone in certain matters, with the counsel of a small number of witan, or with the counsel of "all the witan." What light do the sources for the reign of Edward the Confessor throw on this question?

The numerous references to the offering of counsel to the king by the witan in the pages of our primary source, the *Anglo-Saxon Chronicle*, prove conclusively that an Anglo-Saxon king did very frequently consult few or many witan. If, however, the arguments advanced in the preceding chapters have any validity, it would seem that Kemble went much too far in saying that the witan had a "right to consider every public act," if by these words he meant, as he seems to have, that the witan might demand to be consulted on all public business. It would rather seem that the actual position of the witan was that set out by Professor Stenton when he writes: "It was the duty of the council to advise the king on any problems which he *might choose to bring to its notice*."[1] The only objection that might be made to this statement is the use of the word "council," for it might imply that the witan were a much more self-conscious body than actually was the case.[2] What must be avoided is any suggestion that the witan of all England, or the great majority of them, possessed a *right* to be consulted on all acts of the king, or that, when the king is spoken of as having consulted his witan, the meaning is that he consulted a large number whom he had summoned and not just the few witan who happened to be at his side. It must be emphasized that the consultation of a few was equivalent to the consultation of all. The witan should not be thought of as forming a corporate body, nor should the word "witenagemot" be conceived of as meaning a council or assembly with a certain quorum necessary to validate its actions. Strictly there is no witenagemot, there are only witan.[3] The king consults the witan, and they, not a witenagemot or council, offer him counsel.

[1] *ASEng*, p. 544. Italics mine.
[2] I am not suggesting that Professor Stenton is not aware of this difference. We are all guilty of using the word on occasion when counsel or counsellors would be preferable.
[3] The fundamental objection to most accounts of the witenagemot is this assumption that numbers make a difference and that it was a corporate body. Cf. *NA*, § 50: "Another king was in 774 'deprived of counsel and consent of all his royal *comites* and of the

One might expect that in the sphere of foreign affairs the king would frequently consult his witan. However, the co-operation of king and witan in this field is hardly very evident in the reign of Edward the Confessor. The following examples may be instanced: In 1047 King Sveinn of Denmark asked for aid from England. His request was supported by Godwin, but opposed by Leofric and all the people.[1] The language of the sources is here, for our purposes, very unsatisfactory. There is little doubt that the request was discussed by the king and at least some of his witan. But it seems hardly warranted to envisage, as Freeman did,[2] a formal debate in a full witenagemot, on the basis of the sentence: "Ac hit þuhte unræd eallum folce." There is nothing in the account of the chroniclers, except the words "eallum folce," to suggest that other witan than those who happened to be with the king were summoned to discuss Sveinn's plea. It is, of course, not safe to draw conclusions from the silence of the sources in this matter, but all that may really be asserted is that Sveinn's request was discussed by the king and some of his witan, probably the great earls in particular. The same may be said of Sveinn's renewed request, if indeed the request was renewed, in the following year.[3] Nor does the account of the request of the Emperor Henry III to Edward for aid against Baldwin of Flanders give any details.[4]

We are told nothing in the *Anglo-Saxon Chronicle* as to who dispatched Bishop Ealdred to the emperor in 1054,[5] but Florence of Worcester says he was sent by the king.[6] One version of the *Chronicle* tells us that bishops Hereman and Ealdred went to Rome in 1050 "on the king's errand," another that the king sent them.[7]

companionship of his princes.' To deny (Chadwick 363) here to this plural its meaning of the corporate body of the witenagemot seems hypercritical indeed." Far from being hypercritical, it is eminently sound, and indeed the *ASChr*, E 774, says only that the Northumbrians drove out their king.

[1] *FlWig*, 1047. The *ASChr*, D 1048, says: "Ac hit þuhte unræd eallum folce."

[2] *NC*, II, 92.

[3] *ASChr*, D 1049, simply says: "Ac eall folc wiðcwæð." *FlWig*, 1049, again says that Godwin supported the request but Leofric opposed it.

[4] *ASChr*, C 1049, D 1050; *FlWig*, 1049. There is no mention of a discussion of the request. It is only said that the king acted upon it.

[5] *ASChr*, C 1054, D 1054. The latter says he went "on the king's errand." William of Malmesbury says he went on the king's business (*Vita Wulfstani*, bk. II, chap. IX).

[6] *FlWig*, 1054.

[7] *ASChr*, C 1049; E 1047. It is true that in later accounts of Edward's reign the share of the witan in the dispatch of the bishops is fully described, their mission being connected with the vow of pilgrimage to Rome made by the king. But little reliance is to be placed on these accounts, neither on that of Ailred of Rievaulx (B. Aelredus abbas Rievallensis, *Vita S. Edwardi regis et confessoris*, cols. 749–52) nor on the French metrical life based on this (*Lives*, ed. Luard, pp. 65–74, 219–28). Nor can I attach any significance for the Anglo-Saxon period to the statement in the French life, that Edward, because he had not obtained the consent of the barons and commons, could not undertake the pilgrimage. These are thirteenth-century ideas, although the principle of consent may apply to both

These events, with the exception of Welsh and Scottish affairs, are about all we know of the relations of England with foreign powers in the reign of the Confessor. There is also the alleged mission of Harold to William of Normandy, but it is shrouded in such mystery, and offers so little information on our subject that I have omitted it.[1] For the same reason I have not mentioned the alleged claim to the throne of England put forward by King Magnus of Norway and the reply of Edward.[2] One might add the reference to the pope of the question of the incorporation of the Devon and Cornish bishoprics into a single new diocese. However, it throws little light on the share of the witan in foreign affairs. King Edward simply says: "This, however, I make known to the Lord the Pope Leo, first of all, and confirm by his own attestation: then to all the English nobles."[3]

Relations between England and Wales were often troubled during the reign of Edward the Confessor, and no doubt discussed by the king and his witan. The latter seem to have had a hand in condemning Rhys to death, possibly at a Christmas gemot at Gloucester in 1052.[4] In 1055 when Earl Ælfgar secured the help of the Welsh, the witan seem to have counselled that he be reinstated in order to secure peace.[5] But nothing can be affirmed of the share of the witan in the Welsh war of 1056,[6] and only the king's action is mentioned in connection with the war of 1063. It is "at the king's order" that Harold marches against Wales, and after the death of Griffith "king Edward delivered [betæhte] the land over to . . . Blethgent and Rigwatla."[7] Nothing, for our purpose, is to be learned from the account of the war in 1065.[8] Even less is known of relations with Scotland. In 1054 Siward is said to have invaded that country "by order of the king."[9]

Thus little light is shed on the function of the witan as counsellors in matters of foreign policy from the accounts of the Confessor's reign. Only a few tentative conclusions may be made. Expediency would seem to have determined how extensively the king consulted his witan. In matters involving war and peace consultation may have been frequent and large

periods. Such constitutional ideas as are to be found in the poem are, however, those of the author's day and not necessarily those of the past. He refers, for example, to a *parlement commun* (p. 78).

[1] On it see *NC*, III, 144–70, 448–69.
[2] On this see Snorri Sturluson, *Heimskringla*, pp. 445–6.
[3] E. R. Pedler, *The Anglo-Saxon Episcopate of Cornwall*, p. 82. The information comes from *CD*, 791.
[4] *ASChr*, D 1053: "man rædde þ man sloh Ris."
[5] *ASChr*, D 1055: "man gerædde þone ræd."
[6] *ASChr*, C 1056; *FlWig*, 1056. Nor is it mentioned that the witan counselled the earlier expedition of Swegen against Wales in 1046 (*ASChr*, C 1046).
[7] *FlWig*, 1063; *ASChr*, D 1063.
[8] *ASChr*, D 1065; *FlWig*, 1065.　　　　　　　　　　　　　　[9] *FlWig*, 1054.

numbers of witan asked to give their counsel. Our sources usually speak
as if the king directed foreign affairs. It seems likely that this means that
normally the king consulted the witan who happened to be with him, and
that the chroniclers here speak only of his action, but that when questions
of war and peace arose larger numbers of witan were asked their advice,[1]
and that the chroniclers on such occasions associate the witan with the
king in their accounts.[2] Possibly F. M. Stenton sums up the situation in
the Confessor's reign as well as anyone when he says: "Throughout the
reign of Edward the Confessor it is the earls of Wessex, Mercia, East
Anglia, and Northumbria who direct the foreign policy of the kingdom."[3]

Of so-called legislation in the Confessor's reign there is little record.
There is, however, little doubt that the witan normally had some share
in the framing of "new" laws or the amending or restoration of old laws.
But their precise function in these matters is uncertain. It is probably
impossible to determine whether the witan played a very active part, or
whether the king proposed what seemed good to him and the witan consented. Possibly their share might vary from reign to reign. It is not
unlikely, however, that initiative lay with the king. S. B. Chrimes implies
this when he writes: "He [the king] might, and on occasion did, find it
necessary to declare, with the express or tacit assent of the 'wise men' of
his realm (the *witan*), what the law was on certain points, and even to
commit such declarations to writing."[4] A few of the thegns identified in
Appendix B (e.g., Thurgod, Siferth, Owine, Godric, Siric) are said to

---

[1] This is supported by the fact that all the examples of the witan deliberating and
deciding foreign policy which are cited by Liebermann (*NA*, § 54) are those of occasions
on which matters of extreme gravity were treated, with the sole exception of Sveinn's
request for aid in 1047. It is not strange that in the very troubled reign of Ethelred the
witan would often be consulted.

[2] Not, however, because they discerned any constitutionally significant difference
between the smaller and larger gathering, but because the business at the latter was of
greater importance and the occasion more impressive.

[3] *William the Conqueror and the Rule of the Normans*, p. 16.

[4] *English Constitutional History* (London, 1947), p. 73. Cf. the prologues of the laws,
Liebermann, *Gesetze, passim*. Snorri Sturluson's account of the legislative activity of the
Norwegian kings permits one to infer that the initiating power was the king, acting with
the counsel of a few "witan" (see *Heimskringla*, pp. 76, 215). No doubt the laws would
then be consented to by the people at a *þing*, or by such *proceres* as were deemed to represent the people. It is probable that in England the king and a few witan would draw up
the laws, which were then accepted by a larger number of witan, or were consented to
in the folkmoots. Some light is thrown on Anglo-Saxon "legislation" by D. Whitelock,
"Wulfstan and the Laws of Cnut," pp. 433–52. Cf. *NA*, § 60. It may be noticed here
that Liebermann's statement, "The doctrine that a king by himself could give ordinances
for his lifetime only, but required the consent of nobles for permanent legislation does
not emerge indeed before the twelfth century" (*Gesetze*, II, 477), is misleading, as Kern
points out: "The notion that the decrees of mediaeval monarchs were valid only during
their own reign is completely false. . . . Acts admittedly lawful . . . have the force of law
quite independently of any change of ruler; indeed, the older they are, the more sacred."
(*Kingship and Law*, p. 184.)

have been lawmen. Their function as witan may have been primarily that of helping the king declare law.[1] But it must be emphasized that there was comparatively little legislative activity. The written dooms represent only an infinitesimal fraction of the law.

On two occasions during the reign of Edward the Confessor old laws were renewed or confirmed. The first was at the time of the inlawing of Godwin in 1052: "And they [Godwin and his family, the king *et al.*] confirmed between them full friendship, and to all the people they promised good law."[2] The other was in 1065 when Harold, acting for the king, renewed (*nywade*) for the Northumbrians Cnut's laws.[3] Neither passage tells much beyond making it clear that it is the king's duty to maintain the "good, old" law.

[1] Steenstrup thinks that their duty was to proclaim the law (*Danelag*, pp. 195–218). On the function of lawmen in various Germanic societies see Dúason, *Rjettarstaða Grænlands*, pp. 40–41, and the authorities there cited. Cf. also Helen M. Cam, "Suitors and *Scabini*," pp. 191–2. Admittedly our information on them in England is very limited. I cannot agree with H. C. Coote that they were the remnants of the old Roman senate of the municipality (*The Romans of Britain*, p. 371; cf. Ellis, *Introd. to Domesday*, p. 205).

[2] *ASChr*, C 1052. In the *Quadripartitus* (*Gesetze*, I, 533) Edward is said to have confirmed Cnut's laws.

[3] *ASChr*, D 1065.

CHAPTER TEN

The Witan and the Election and Deposition of Kings

KEMBLE and Liebermann believed that the witan possessed great powers in the matter of the election and deposition of kings. The majority of historians seem to have agreed with them, although, in some cases, with qualified assent. The importance of this function of the witan has, however, been questioned by some, notably Chadwick and Purlitz.[1] In this matter there is possibly no hope of agreement, both because of the paucity of information and because of differences as to what is to be understood by election and deposition.

There can, however, be little question that in determining the succession to the throne, in the Middle Ages, both the "throne-worthiness" of a candidate and the consent of the community were important factors.[2] A royal family possessed a "kin-right" to the throne, but which member of it actually occupied the throne varied from generation to generation in many cases. Competence to carry out the kingly duties was, no doubt, an important consideration in determining the fitness of a candidate. The oldest son of the previous king would, if qualified, possess the strongest claim to the succession, but if he were a minor the king's brother might be preferred. How, when there were several suitable candidates in the royal family, the succession was determined is not clearly established. Normally, however, it would probably have been settled before the death of the king by him and his closest advisers, or after his death by the members of the royal family and a few of the leading men in the kingdom. There is little reason to believe that under normal circumstances the succession was settled in a national assembly or by all the witan. The *Anglo-Saxon Chronicle*, of course, frequently speaks of a king's having been elected (*gecoren*), but the expression means little as long as one does not know what exactly is involved in being elected. This may never be established. Judging from their language, the majority of modern historians would seem to think that the witan met in a formal meeting and, so to speak, cast their votes for this or that candidate. Chadwick held, however, that

---

[1] Chadwick, *Studies*, pp. 355–66; Purlitz, *König und Witenagemot*, pp. 12–50.

[2] A convenient and excellent summary of mediaeval ideas on "kin-right" and the election of kings is to be found in Kern, *Kingship and Law*, pp. 12–27.

election very likely meant simply recognition by the witan, i.e., the counsellors in attendance on the candidate, through some such act as the
swearing of an oath of allegiance. This seems most reasonable to me.[1]
When, on the other hand, several contenders strove for the throne, it is
difficult to believe that the question of the succession was settled by the
witan formally meeting and selecting this or that candidate. A more
normal procedure at that time would be for each candidate to attempt
to secure in one way or another the support of as many magnates as
possible and with their help seek to capture the Crown.[2] Examples may
also be cited of a man being acclaimed king by the witan who happened
to be with him when the death of the king occurred.[3]

It is probable, then, that election was basically, as Chadwick suggests,
"a recognition of lordship." Election in so far as it was an expression of
the principle of consent was an invariable accompaniment of an accession
to the throne. Each individual wita gave his allegiance to the king, and
he gave this as an individual and not as a member of a corporate body
or even as the representative of the nation.[4] It would also seem that an
individual might even feel justified in withholding his acceptance from
a king who was the choice of a majority of the magnates.[5] What is

---

[1] To say, as Liebermann does, that "the form of election need never have been disregarded, even when a king got his son recognised as future monarch" (*NA*, § 49) is
meaningless unless one is able to explain what is meant by the words "form of election."
The value of such an expression as "election" or "choice" of a king is very well shown
by the words of the *ASChr*, 924, "hine geces þa to fæder 7 to hlaforde," to describe the
acceptance by the Scots, Northumbrians, and Welshmen of King Edward as their over-
lord. Hardly a case of election in our sense of the word (Florence of Worcester, 924, uses
elegerunt). Needless to say, numerous instances may also be found, in the *Anglo-Saxon
Chronicle*, where there is no mention of election: see *s.a.* 860, 866, 871, 901, 940, 946, 955,
959, 975 (*CD*, 1312, speaks of this king as elected), 979. Three versions of the *Chronicle*
(B, C, D, 924) state that Athelstan was elected (*gecoren*) king by the Mercians; three
(A, F 925, E 924) say only that he succeeded to the kingdom.
[2] This seems to have been the method adopted by king Hákon *góði* of Norway when
he aspired to the throne of that country. He gained the support of Earl Sigurðr of Hlaðir
and then at a summoned *þing* was acknowledged king. Men in other parts of the country
then came or sent word that they wished to be his men (*Heimskringla*, pp. 70–71). Harold
Harefoot in England seems to have secured "election" only after canvassing support
(*Encomium*, pp. xxiii and lxiv; cf. W. H. Stevenson, "An Alleged Son of King Harold
Harefoot," p. 116).
[3] Edmund Ironside in 1016 (*ASChr*, C, D, E 1016) and the Ætheling Edgar in 1066
(*ASChr*, D 1066). Cf. also *ASChr*, E 1036.
[4] Chadwick, *Studies*, pp. 365–6.
[5] I am thinking of Godwin's refusal to acknowledge Harold as king in 1035 (*ASChr*,
E 1036). Plummer (*TSCP*, II, 208–10) argues that Harold was not chosen king until
1037, and was only regent until that time. I think, however, that it is as reasonable to
understand the *Chronicle* to mean that the kingdom was divided between Harold and
Hardecnut. The significant thing is that the magnates, rather than surrender their rights,
were willing to divide the country between two men. In the two years after 1035 Harold
was able to gain over enough of the reluctant nobles to make further opposition to him
impossible. Their submission made him king of all England. Since writing the above

important in this question of the succession to the throne is not that the witan are supposed to have had the power of "electing" the king, but that no man could be king until he had secured the support of the witan. Until the witan had consented to become his men, it was vain for an individual to style himself king. That this consent was seldom refused is evident from the fact that in the majority of cases the *Anglo-Saxon Chronicle* records nothing but the bare fact of succession. In this connection it may also be noticed that after England came under the rule of one king, only members of the royal family were considered "throne-worthy." This feeling was very strong in Anglo-Saxon England. The *Chronicle* (867) emphasizes, for example, that Ælla was *ungecyndne*, and in version C (1042) the chronicler says that the people received Edward "swa him gecynde wæs." This feeling, of course, limited the choice of the electors to members of the royal family, and would, I think, tend to strengthen the practice of settling the succession before the death of a reigning king.[1]

"The succession appears to have been settled beforehand by the reigning king, though of course such arrangements were largely dependent on the goodwill of the chief territorial officials."[2] This would appear to be a plausible statement of the usual procedure in England, and consequently any election would be synonymous with the swearing of allegiance to the new king. In the Middle Ages it was very frequently the practice throughout Europe for the reigning monarch to secure, during his lifetime, the recognition of his successor by the leading magnates,[3] and there is no reason to believe that England was an exception in this matter. Indeed there are several instances of such a disposal of the realm by the reigning monarch during his lifetime or on his death-bed: Æthelwulf is said to have disposed of the kingdom in a will,[4] and Edward the Elder to have left the government to his son Æthelstan;[5] Cnut made some arrangement

I have had access to Alistair Campbell's edition of the *Encomium*. He thinks that Harold secured constitutional election only in 1037, and was up to that time warden of all England on behalf of himself and his brother. On the return of the latter a division of the kingdom was contemplated (*Encomium*, pp. lxiii–lxiv).

[1] P. Grierson ("Election and Inheritance in Early Germanic Kingship," pp. 1–22) has argued that among the Ostrogoths, Visigoths, and Lombards no divinity attached to a particular royal line, but he does not extend this conclusion to include the Anglo-Saxons.

[2] Chadwick, *Studies*, p. 366. Cf. G. Barraclough, *Mediaeval Germany*, I, 52: ". . . 'election' in the sense of choice or designation of his successor normally falls to the reigning king himself."

[3] Numerous examples could be cited from the history of the Empire (cf. G. Barraclough, *The Origins of Modern Germany*, *passim* and especially pp. 25–26, 73–76) and of the Scandinavian kingdoms (cf. *Heimskringla*, *passim*). The recognition of William by the Norman magnates at the time of his father's departure on a pilgrimage is a well-known example.

[4] See *TSCP*, II, 82, where the authorities are cited, and *ASChr*, 855.

[5] *FlWig*, 924.

for the partition of his empire among his sons.[1] Even more important, in showing that normally kings would make provision for the succession, is the tremendous weight attached to the wishes of the dying monarch in regard to his successor. The most significant example of this in the Anglo-Saxon period is the alleged bequest of the throne made by Edward to Harold.[2] Even Freeman, who insisted that the disposal of the throne lay with the witan irrespective of the wishes of the late king, took great pains to show that Edward had actually designated Harold as his successor.[3] No one who reads his discussion will fail to be impressed by the importance that the chroniclers of the eleventh and subsequent centuries placed on a death-bed bequest. There are thus some grounds for holding that arrangements made during the lifetime of a monarch were the most important factors in determining to whom the throne would go. Such an arrangement in no way rules out the principle of consent, but this is so elementary and the necessity for any ruler to secure the adhesion of the principal lay and ecclesiastical magnates so great, that it should not require emphasis. What should be emphasized, I think, is not the positive right of the witan to elect a king, but rather the negative right of any subject to refuse, if he felt powerful enough, to accept a certain individual as king.[4]

[1] *Ibid.*, 1035; *ÍF*, XXVII, 306; *NC*, I, 318–19; L. M. Larson, *Canute the Great*, pp. 331–3. Further examples will be found in *NA*, § 49. Liebermann here cites *Beowulf* as showing that the ideal of Gautic kingship was an elective monarchy. Chadwick cites *Beowulf*, also, but as showing that the throne was regarded as any ordinary family property (*Heroic Age*, p. 372).

[2] It makes no difference whether Edward actually named Harold his successor or not. In fact, if the bequest is fictitious it is all the more important, as it would show that the wish of a dying king was considered of such great value that Harold invented the bequest in order to strengthen his case. Of the versions of the *Anglo-Saxon Chronicle* only E 1066 directly asserts that Edward designated Harold as his successor. Versions C and D 1065 do, however, say that Edward committed (*befæste*) the realm to Harold, and the *Vita Æduuardi* has the king say: "Hanc [the queen] cum omni regno tutandam commendo" (p. 433). The Icelandic versions of the bequest are interesting. The *Heimskringla* says that as the king lay dying Harold leaned over him and then said: "Því skírskota ek undir alla yðr, at konungr gaf mér nú konungdóm ok alt ríki í Englandi" (p. 498). After the king's death there was a witenagemot (*höfðingjastefna*) at which Harold repeated his assertion and was then elected king. According to the *Saga ens heilaga Eduardar* (*Flateyjarbok*, III, 468), the king, some years before his death, designates William as his heir and repeats this on his death-bed, but as his illness worsens, Harold leans over him and then makes the assertion quoted above.

[3] *NC*, III, 8–10, 385–400. Any attempt to prove definitely that Edward on his death-bed left the throne to Harold is likely to be fruitless. It is true that the statements of the *Anglo-Saxon Chronicle* to this effect carry considerable weight, as does that of Florence of Worcester, but the inherent probability of a death-bed bequest, in view of the Confessor's character and his previous unquestionable (in my opinion) designation of William as his successor, is, I think, very slight.

[4] This is abundantly illustrated in the history of the Empire before 1250 (see Barraclough, *Origins*, *passim*). Election may almost be said to mean, not a free gathering of magnates to elect whomsoever they wish, but a wooing of them by the aspirant to the

The history of the reign of Edward the Confessor sheds some light on the function of the witan in the election of kings. The succession of Edward was already settled in the lifetime of Hardecnut. It does not seem possible to understand in another sense the words of the *Anglo-Saxon Chronicle*: "7 þæs geres sona com Eadward his broðor on meddren fram geondan sæ Æðelredes sunu cynges þe wæs ær for fela gearan of þisan gearde adryfen 7 þeah wæs to cynge gesworon 7 he wunode þa swa on his broðor hirede þa hwile þe he leofode."[1] This, of course, does not rule out the participation of the witan in these arrangements. In fact, it almost goes without saying that they had a share in this matter, although a part of them seem to have been reluctant to recognize Edward, preferring, it would seem, a Scandinavian king, and scheming to deprive Edward of the Crown after his brother's death.[2] Any election, then, is out of the question, except in so far as it is implicit in the acceptance of Edward by the magnates and possibly in attempts to obtain recognition of him from recalcitrant magnates.[3] If this interpretation be right, the words, "7 eall folc geceas þa Eadward 7 underfengon hine to kyninge," can only mean that allegiance was sworn to Edward and he was acknowledged king.[4] This would then be one further example of the vagueness of the terminology of the *Anglo-Saxon Chronicle*.

Another matter in the reign of Edward the Confessor throws further light on the problem. This is the question of who was to succeed Edward. The very fact that this question loomed so large in the minds of con-

---

throne, in very many instances. It may be pointed out here that in the Scandinavian kingdoms the will of the reigning monarch would seem to have often been the decisive factor in determining the succession. An example of the importance of his wishes in this matter is the great weight attached to the wish of Magnus *góði* with regard to his successor (*Flateyjarbok*, III, 329–31; cf. also pp. 285–7).

[1] *ASChr*, D 1041. Version C uses almost the same words. I am well aware that Freeman vigorously opposed any such interpretation as that set out above. Actually, however, the very fact that Edward was invited to England by Hardecnut disposes of any argument that Edward was not marked out as the next king of the Anglo-Saxons. Alistair Campbell thinks that Edward was "The acknowledged heir to an ailing monarch, who knew his days were numbered" (*Encomium*, p. lxviii). *CD*, 762 (possibly spurious), a charter of Hardecnut, is witnessed by Edward (*praedicti regis frater verus*).

[2] Edward's mother would seem to have been one of these (see below, chap. XII). William of Malmesbury says that Eadsige and Godwin helped Edward to secure the throne to the irritation of the Danes (*GP*, p. 34).

[3] Only in this sense can I understand the statement of Florence of Worcester, 1042, that Edward was proclaimed king chiefly through the exertions of Earl Godwin and Bishop Lyfing.

[4] *ASChr*, D 1042. The *ASChr*, C 1042, omits all reference to an election and simply says: "7 eall folc underfeng ða Eadward to cinge." Versions C and D both add in almost the same words: "swa him gecynde wæs" (C 1042). Professor Stenton is of the opinion that Edward returned to England in 1041 on the invitation of Hardecnut who, "almost certainly, put him forward as his heir." He also rejects the view that Godwin was the chief agent in Edward's restoration (*ASEng*, p. 417).

temporaries of the Confessor suggests that such matters were not normally left to be settled at the death of a king but were already arranged during his lifetime.[1] Even if one could not rely on the evidence for a bequest to William by the king and witan, the fact that the Ætheling Edward was sent for all the way to Hungary would still destroy such an argument as the one that maintains that "an act of the King and his Witan in William's favour is impossible in itself and is confirmed by no kind of evidence."[2] I have elsewhere discussed the problem of both the promise to William and the return of the Ætheling Edward,[3] and it is unnecessary to say more here than that I believe that Edward and his witan did in 1051 promise the throne to William,[4] but that later, with the ascendancy of Earl Harold, an attempt was made to get the king to abrogate this by designating his kinsman Edward as his successor. To deny the witan competence in the former instance and allow it in the latter, as Freeman does,[5] is hardly possible. The witan had a share in both, but the will of the reigning monarch was probably the great, if not decisive, influence.[6]

It remains to say a few words about the events of the year 1066, as far as these relate to the disposal of the Crown. In the series of elections which Liebermann cites as sufficient to raise the practice of election beyond any doubt, he includes three examples from this year.[7] These are the elections of Harold, Edgar, and William. In the first case we have an instance of what can hardly be called an election, but is probably very typical of what the Anglo-Saxons understood by an election. The witan, who had gathered for the consecration of the abbey, were, after the death of Edward, confronted with a claim to the throne, on the part of Harold, which was based on some such arguments as his fitness for the position,

[1] I am not suggesting that such matters were arranged without consultation of the witan, whom I regard as having a share in all important business, but I am arguing against the view that the witan functioned as a sort of electoral college on the death of a king, and that they in this respect "towered above the crown" (*NA*, § 49).

[2] *NC*, III, 460. At the same time it strengthens the case for the designation of Edward as his heir by Hardecnut, for the two cases are very similar.

[3] In a forthcoming article.

[4] Cf. *ASEng*, p. 558: "It is in every way probable that the duke came in order to receive a recognition of his standing as successor designate to the crown." In a recent article ("Edward the Confessor, Duke William of Normandy, and the English Succession," pp. 526–45) Professor David Douglas has suggested that the statement of *Chronicle* D (1051), that William visited England, is an interpolation. He does, however, believe that Edward promised the throne to William.

[5] Cf. *NC*, III, 460, and II, 246. The weakness of Freeman's argument lies in his differentiation between what he calls the counsellors of Edward and the witan of England (*NC*, II, 197–200). They are one and the same.

[6] Even in the case of the Ætheling Edward, in which, I think, Harold may have imposed his will on the king, the Confessor does not seem to have yielded completely, if I am right in thinking that he refused to grant, or postponed granting, an audience to Edward.

[7] *NA*, § 49.

the lack of any other suitable candidates, and a real or alleged death-bed bequest to Harold by Edward. The witan were thus faced with a situation which left them hardly another alternative than that of acknowledging Harold as king. Nor is there much reason to believe that they did not all submit to him.[1] Consent was thus given, but an election, in any real sense of that word, was hardly made, and indeed parts of the country seem to have refused to submit to Harold, for he had to make a special visit to Northumbria to secure the allegiance of its magnates with the possible exception of Morcar, who may have become his man in London. This consent he finally, although with difficulty, obtained largely through the able assistance of Wulfstan.[2] The incident should serve as a warning against placing too much reliance in such conventional expressions as "a totius Angliæ primatibus ad regale culmen electus."[3] Of course, if the designation *subregulus*, which Florence of Worcester employs to describe Harold, be taken to mean that the earl was the formally recognized successor designate of Edward, the election becomes that much more unreal. It is, however, probable that no technical meaning is to be attached to the term, and that Florence used it simply because Harold's power and prestige in the last year or two of the reign were such that he was practically a viceregent.

After the death of Harold the witan were faced with the choice of finding another native or of submitting to William. They chose to make the Ætheling Edgar king. Their action here approximates much more to a genuine election than in the case of Harold, for Edgar was not in a position to push his claims if he were not voluntarily elected. However, there seems to be little doubt that the election was the work of a few witan,[4]

---

[1] An entirely erroneous impression of unanimity and of what the choice really meant is given by such a statement as the following: "The assembled people of England, in the exercise of their ancient and undoubted right, chose with one voice Harold the son of Godwine" (*NC*, III, 14). In another passage Freeman states that the Northumbrians had not been well represented at the gemot which elected Harold. At the same time he reveals very well his conception of what a witenagemot was, when he says that if the votes had been taken, not by heads, but by tribes, cities, or cantons, the Northumbrians, although present only in few numbers, would have had an equal voice in the national councils, "though the West-Saxons present might have been counted by hundreds or thousands" (*NC*, III, 37–38). Cf. J. H. Round, *Geoffrey de Mandeville*, pp. 437–8.

[2] *Vita Wulfstani*, pp. 22–23.

[3] *FlWig*, 1066. Similarly the *ASChr*, C, D 1042, E, F 1041, is employing conventional language when it says that *eall folc* chose Edward.

[4] The best account of Edgar's election is in *ASChr*, D 1066, where it is stated that it was the work of Ealdred, archbishop of York, and the garrison (*burhwaru*) of London. Edwin and Morcar are said to have promised to fight with Edgar, but whether they were present at the election is uncertain, although asserted by Florence of Worcester (1066). There is nothing to suggest that the election was the work of a fairly representative gemot, as Freeman thinks (*NC*, III, 351–4). Cf. Wilkinson, "Northumbrian Separatism," pp. 521–3.

acting at a time of crisis and under extraordinary circumstances. It is, thus, although an example of genuine election and of the right of the people to choose its rulers, hardly typical of normal procedure.

The third so-called election of 1066 can only by courtesy be given that name. William can by no stretch of the imagination be said to have been chosen or elected king, unless by those terms be meant the act of submitting to the overlordship of an individual. The chronicler recognizes this when he writes: "And then came to meet him archbishop Ealdred, and Eadgar child, and earl Eadwine, and earl Morkere, and all the best men of London, and then from necessity submitted [*bugon*] when the greatest harm had been done."[1]

The reign of the Confessor thus hardly supplies evidence that the witan formed a genuine electoral college, that they "towered above the king," or that the Anglo-Saxon monarchy was an elective one. On the other hand, as might be expected, it testifies that the title of king rested not solely on hereditary right, or the right to kingship which membership in the royal family implied,[2] but also on acceptance by the community (represented in England by the magnates or witan surrounding the king) of the claimant to the throne. He was, however, it seems, very often already marked out for the succession to the throne in the lifetime of his predecessor and only rarely elected by the witan, whose share in the election or creation of kings has probably been greatly exaggerated.

On the function of the witan in the deposition of kings the reign of the Confessor reveals little. Edgar can hardly be said to have been deposed, but rather to have voluntarily abdicated, if he was ever considered full king. An act analogous to the deposition of a king might be discerned in the expulsion of Earl Tostig by the Northumbrians. However, in a society where there exists no machinery to compel the peaceful abdication of a ruler whom the people wish to be rid of, it is almost impossible to establish a distinction between a legal deposition and a violent one. It is a fundamental principle of the Middle Ages that a king who breaks the law is no longer entitled to obedience or fealty. Any subject who feels himself unlawfully treated by the king is quite within his rights, not only in refusing obedience, but in resorting to force to gain his rights. For him the king is no king but a tyrant. Similarly, of course, a people is justified in expelling a ruler who does not observe the law. But in the final analysis a legal deposition is a rebellion against a ruler which is crowned with success. Thus the act of deposition does not consist in a formal vote of the witan

---

[1] *ASChr*, D 1066.

[2] That this was very strongly felt is shown by examples cited above, to which may be added the reference to the Ætheling Edgar, whom men wished to have as their king "eallswa him wel gecynde wæs" (*ASChr*, D 1066).

expelling the ruler, but in the successful execution of an act of renunciation, made by individuals acting as individuals banded together for the moment, but in no sense forming, or acting as, a corporate body. There is thus little point in saying that the witan possessed the right to depose the king, for this was a right which every individual possessed, i.e., the right of renouncing an unjust ruler. Nay, it was more than a right; it was the duty of every individual.[1]

It is a different matter, that in practice the witan would take the lead in renouncing a king. That was a matter of expediency, for only if a magnate felt himself powerful enough to oppose the king would it be practicable to renounce his allegiance. The Northumbrian crisis is a good example of what in practice deposition meant, and it illustrates well how impossible it is to distinguish, as Liebermann attempted to do, between "a legal act by the constitutional organ of the commonwealth" and "a sum of treacherous deeds of violence committed by individual nobles."[2] Such a distinction is meaningless in a society which recognizes both the right of resistance and the right of "self-help." As Kern points out, "success alone in the end determined whether a revolt was wicked or glorious."[3]

[1] Cf. Kern, *Kingship and Law*, p. 87: "The fundamental idea is rather that ruler and ruled alike are bound to the law; the fealty of both parties is in reality fealty to the law; the law is the point where the duties of both of them intersect." Essentially I agree with Kern's ideas on deposition (pp. 85–97).

[2] *NA*, § 50. It might be asked what steps the Northumbrians should have taken, had they wished to use, not violence as they did, but the recognized constitutional machinery of the day.

[3] *Kingship and Law*, pp. 90–91. The lenient treatment of defeated rebels, of which so many examples are found in the Middle Ages, is explained by the universal recognition of the right of resistance on the part of an individual who believed his rights to have been flouted. He was entitled to resort to "self-help."

CHAPTER ELEVEN

The Witan and Various Ecclesiastical and Civil Business

THERE seems to have been no fixed method of appointing prelates to vacant sees in the reign of Edward the Confessor. No doubt Edward consulted at least his most trusted advisers among the ecclesiastical witan before appointing a prelate, but his wishes were probably the determining factor in most cases. It is unlikely that the lay witan, with the possible exception of the earl within whose earldom the see or monastery lay,[1] were generally consulted. The statements made by the chroniclers are often vague as to the method of appointment. In the vast majority of cases they content themselves with saying either that so and so "succeeded" to a bishopric, or that the king gave the bishopric or monastery to an individual. In either case one is probably safe in assuming that the king bestowed the office after consulting a few witan. Exceptionally an appointment seems to have been made in a large witenagemot, but there does not appear to have been any rule as to when or why this was done.[2]

Whenever we are given any details as to an ecclesiastical appointment, it is invariably the will of the king that is the decisive factor. Thus in 1044 when Siward was made coadjutor archbishop of Canterbury, the matter was arranged between Archbishop Eadsige, Earl Godwin, and the king.[3] When the monks at Canterbury elected Ælfric to succeed Archbishop Eadsige, the king set aside their candidate and caused Robert to be appointed in a witenagemot at London.[4] When Manni wished to make Æthelwig his successor at Evesham, he asked the king to appoint him.[5] In the case of Wulfstan, even if we accept the story of a canonical election by the clergy and people of Worcester, it is still the king who grants them the right to hold a canonical election.[6] When Bury St. Edmunds became

---

[1] Such an inference may be drawn from Symeon of Durham when he writes: "Auxilio et favore comitis Tostii, qui Siwardo successerat, Egilwinus in episcopatum sublimatur" (*Opera omnia*, I, 92).

[2] Examples are the appointment of Manni in 1044 (*FlWig*, 1044); of Robert and Spearhafoc in 1051 (*ASChr*, C 1050); and possibly the appointments of Stigand in 1052 (*ASChr*, E 1052) and Wulfstan in 1062 (*Vita Wulfstani*, pp. 17–18).

[3] *ASChr*, C 1044, E 1043.

[4] *Vita Æduuardi*, pp. 399–400; *ASChr*, C 1050.   [5] *Chron. Evesham*, p. 88.

[6] *FlWig*, 1062. I find it somewhat difficult to reconcile Florence's account of a canonical election with the emphasis the *Vita Wulfstani* places on the election or approval by the king

vacant in 1065, "cogitat . . . rex . . . quem . . . in locum subroget," and having decided on Baldwin summoned the prior and community to Windsor, where they then elected Baldwin.[1] Another proof of the importance of the king is seen in the number of royal chaplains who were elevated to high positions in the church under Edward the Confessor.[2] All this points to the conclusion that on the whole the witan did not have a great part in the appointment of prelates. The king himself and possibly the high spiritual witan with an earl or two seem to have normally attended to this business.[3]

Deposition of bishops and abbots was also within the power of the king. It may be that the witan here played a more important role than in appointments. Thus the deposition of Stigand in 1043[4] was probably counselled by the earls and whatever other witan advised the despoiling of the king's mother. Nothing is known of the share of the witan in the refusal of the authorities to ordain Spearhafoc, but Archbishop Robert and Bishop Ulf seem to have been outlawed in the great gemot of 1052.[5] All these instances, however, are more of a political than of an ecclesiastical nature, as none of these men, not even, it seems, Spearhafoc, was rejected on the grounds that he was unfit for spiritual office. The pope is said to have forbidden the ordination of Spearhafoc, but for what reason is not known. The others were presumably expelled because they "counselled evil counsel." There is, in the reign of Edward the Confessor, no example of an ecclesiastic being deprived of his office for spiritual reasons, by the king and witan, unless it be that of Spearhafoc, and in his case the removal was probably the work of Robert acting with the permission of the king. It should be noticed that the expulsion of Archbishop Robert was deemed illegal by the papal curia and Stigand's appointment pronounced null and void. But it is significant that Stigand's partisans were so strong that he kept his office until the reform of the English church by Lanfranc and

and witan: "Ad curiam reversi, dum Wigornensis episcopi ventilaretur electio, nomen ejus tulerunt in medium" (*Vita Wulfstani*, p. 18). In either case, however, the will of the king is of primary importance.

[1] *Ungedruckte Anglo-Normannische Geschichtsquellen*, p. 245.

[2] On these see Knowles, *The Monastic Order*, p. 71; Larson, *King's Household*, pp. 140–2; *Regesta*, pp. xii–xv.

[3] Attention may be called here to the provisions of the *Regularis Concordia* on the election of abbots: "Abbatum . . . electio cum Regis consensu et consilio, sanctae regulae ageretur documento" (quoted in Knowles, *The Monastic Order*, p. 396). Even here the role of the king is very important, and the interference of the witan would seem to be largely excluded. I may add here that I do not regard writs announcing the bestowal of a bishopric as necessarily excluding action on the part of the witan, but I do think that the language is another indication of the primary importance of the king in this matter, e.g., "ich kyðe eow ðat ich habbe geunnen Gisan minan preste ðes biscopriche" (*CD*, 835).

[4] *ASChr*, C 1043.

[5] *ASChr*, E 1048, 1052.

William.[1] However, his retention of office is hardly to be ascribed to the witan but to Godwin and Harold.

The share of the witan in the regulation of other aspects of the life of the church does not stand out clearly in the sources for the reign of the Confessor. Yet there can be little doubt that at least the ecclesiastical witan played a major role in such matters.[2] The witan may have had some part in the fixing of the episcopal see at Exeter, although in the charter effecting this, the king makes the transfer known to "all the magnates of the Angles."[3] Possibly their share in such business has, however, been exaggerated. From the account of the attempt of Hereman of Ramsbury to obtain Malmesbury, it appears that such a decision might be made by the king after consulting no more than a few advisers. We are indirectly told that the first that Harold heard of the matter was when the monks of Malmesbury approached him and requested his aid in preventing Hereman from securing their monastery. Through his influence with the king, Harold was able successfully to oppose Hereman's design.[4]

Of the action of the witan in the union of the sees of Ramsbury and Sherborne in 1058, we are told nothing, nor do we know what hand they had in the dispatch of representatives to the synod at Rheims in 1049 or to that at Rome in 1050.[5] It is thus likely that the inner life of the church was largely regulated by the king and his closest ecclesiastical advisers. The lay witan may have, for the most part, interfered in church questions only when these particularly concerned them, and then only as individuals. They may also have played a considerable part in the framing of ecclesiastical laws, such as, for example, those of Cnut.

In civil matters the share of the witan, both spiritual and lay, may have been considerably more than in ecclesiastical business. It is not unreasonable to assume that king and witan co-operated in the appointment of earls. However, the reign of Edward the Confessor does not afford many clear examples of such co-operation.[6] Action by the king and witan in

---

[1] Papal influence in England, nevertheless, grew steadily throughout the reign of the Confessor. It is not correct to say, as F. E. Warren does, that "in the eleventh century we hear for the first time of bishops going to Rome for consecration or confirmation, and of the Roman court claiming at least a veto on the nomination of the English king" (*The Leofric Missal*, p. xxiv), but certainly the number of instances of papal intervention would seem to have been far greater in the reign of the Confessor than in any other reign in the preceding two centuries. More prelates travelled to Rome and there were more channels for papal influence. See Darlington, "Ecclesiastical Reform," pp. 385–428.

[2] See *NA*, § 56; Böhmer, *Kirche und Staat*, p. 50.

[3] *CD*, 791. Cf. Pedler, *Episcopate of Cornwall*, pp. 81–85.

[4] *GP*, p. 182. Freeman, who held that such an important piece of business could only be settled by the national assembly, has difficulty in explaining how this could have been done. He never explains why Harold was ignorant of the matter, if it was discussed in a full witenagemot (*NC*, II, 270).   [5] *GP*, pp. 180–1; *ASChr*, D 1051; E 1046.

[6] Yet all Liebermann's examples are drawn from this reign (*NA*, § 57).

the appointment of Odda and Ælfgar to earldoms in 1051 is implied in the words of the *Chronicle*: "7 man sette þa Oddan to eorle ofer Defenà-scire 7 ofer Sumersæton 7 ofer Dorseton 7 ofer Weales 7 mann sette Ælfgar Leofrices sunu eorles ðane eorldom on handa þe Harold ær ahte."[1] All other references in the *Anglo-Saxon Chronicle* to appointments of earls during the reign either mention the bare fact of succession or state that the king made the appointment.[2] Thus when Godwin died, Harold is simply said to have succeeded to his earldom and Ælfgar to the one Harold had held.[3] One version of the *Chronicle* reports Tostig's appointment non-committally: "Tosti feng to þan eorldome," but another version records: "se cyng geaf þone eorldom Tostige."[4] The bare fact of Ælfgar's succession to his father's earldom is all that the sources mention.[5] In 1065, when the Northumbrians deposed Tostig, they prayed that they might have Morcar for their earl, "7 se cyning þæs geuðæ."[6]

Not much is to be inferred from these references, but it seems clear that the king's action is of paramount importance, although there is little reason to believe that he did not consult some of his witan in most, or all, instances.[7] It might be concluded from the mention of the bare fact of succession in cases where son succeeds father, that the earldoms had become to some extent hereditary. Too much, however, should not be made of this. In fact, one may say that the language of the chroniclers, when describing the handling of these matters, is exactly what one might expect from members of a society whose modes of procedure were extremely fluid.

[1] *ASChr*, E 1048.

[2] Florence of Worcester adds nothing of importance.

[3] *ASChr*, C, D, E 1053.

[4] *ASChr*, D 1055, E 1055. It is to be noted that it is version E of the *Chronicle* which, according to Freeman, always emphasizes the popular nature of the government.

[5] *ASChr*, D, E 1057.

[6] *ASChr*, D, E 1065. Version C says only that the Northumbrians chose Morcar for their earl.

[7] An instance of the co-operation of the witan in large numbers is the restoration of the earldoms to Godwin and Harold when they were in-lawed in 1052, but this is hardly an example of normal procedure (*ASChr*, C 1052). Purlitz (*König und Witenagemot*, pp. 51–57) held that the king had the greatest share in the nomination of prelates and earls. He cites as examples of the king acting alone in these matters, in the reign of Edward the Confessor, the appointment of Siward to Canterbury, Hereman to Sherborne, Leofric to Crediton, Heca to Selsey, Ulf to Dorchester, Robert to Canterbury, and Spearhafoc to London (p. 53). He adds that he does not doubt that in the election of prelates "eine Mitwirkung der Witan bei derselben stattgefunden hat," but thinks it was only formal. The same procedure, he says, was followed in the appointment of ealdormen (p. 54), and he cites as examples of the king alone granting earldoms the appointment of Odda, and that of Blegent and Riwallo to Wales (p. 55). It is strange that Liebermann paid no attention to Purlitz, referring to him only once (*NA*, § 3), where he says that he generally followed Kemble, treating independently only the election and deposition of kings. This is hardly true.

In practice, the power of the king and witan to levy taxes for the public services cannot be doubted, but there are reasons to doubt that this was regarded as quite just or legal. It must, too, be emphasized that the only tax which is known to have been levied with some regularity by the king and witan was the *heregeld*.[1] There are also several references, in the *Anglo-Saxon Chronicle*, to the levying of taxes by the king and witan for the purpose of buying off the Danes.[2] Sometimes, however, the sources speak as if the king alone decreed the paying of tribute.[3]

To mediaeval man taxation was simply a form of confiscation of property. Kern asserts: "The State therefore can accomplish this attack on private rights [i.e., taxation] only with the free consent of all concerned (or at least of their representatives)."[4] In a certain sense, of course, the witan were regarded as representatives of the community, but it is doubtful whether they were regarded as competent to speak for all in such an important matter as taxation. In time of war the people would possibly acquiesce in the levying of taxes for the sake of securing peace, but in time of peace the levying of such taxes, it would appear, was felt to be an injustice. Indeed there is some reason to suspect that, even when they were levied with the sanction of the witan, they were still not regarded as having been levied by representatives competent to consent for the community.[5] There can, for example, be no doubt that the *strange gyld* imposed in 1041 was regarded as illegal by the inhabitants of Worcester. Yet apparently Hardecnut's witan agreed to it, for the king sent all his earls to punish the people for the slaying of his two huscarles who had been attempting to collect the tax.[6]

In the reign of Edward the Confessor there is no mention of the witan

---

[1] The *heregeld* seems to date from 1012–13 (*ASChr*, D 1052; cf. *Writs*, pp. 439–40).

[2] For example, *ASChr*, 991, 994, 1002, 1006, 1011, 1012. In 1004 it is the king and the East Anglian witan who decree the paying of tribute.

[3] *ASChr*, 1014. It is not stated in the *Chronicle* who imposed the tribute in 1018, the pay for the standing army in 1040, nor again the tax of 1041 (*ASChr*, *s.a.*), but in the latter two cases Florence of Worcester (*s.a.*) says they were imposed by the king. Purlitz (*König und Witenagemot*, pp. 59–61) doubts that the witan had much share in levying taxes. He says that the king himself lifted the *heregeld*. But he admits that the king and witan acted together on occasion. [4] *Kingship and Law*, p. 186.

[5] This may even be saying too much. Kern correctly writes: "We have here learnt two things: (1) that the monarch could, for example, exact taxation only after he reached an understanding with the community, and (2) that this understanding, at least in theory, took the form of negotiation with every individual, as to whether he was willing to pay" (*Ibid.*, p. 194). But it may be doubted whether this principle had become clearly established in eleventh-century England, where, except for the *heregeld* in the last two generations of the Anglo-Saxon state, new taxation was such an unheard of thing, that it is hardly to be expected that any principle whereby new taxation could legally be imposed would have evolved. This explains why, as Miss M. V. Clarke noticed, the idea of consent does not appear to have been in any way associated with royal revenue in the Anglo-Saxon period (*Mediaeval Representation and Consent*, p. 250).

[6] *ASChr*, C 1041; *FlWig*, 1041.

assenting to any taxes, although there is no doubt that Edward continued to collect the *heregeld*, or it would not have been necessary to abolish it in 1051. This abolition is said to have been performed by the king, and there is no mention of the witan acting in the matter.[1] The language used by the chroniclers, on this occasion, suggests that the tax was regarded as an unjust, and therefore illegal, one.[2] On the whole, I think, it may be said that it is doubtful if the Anglo-Saxons ever felt that the witan and the king—much less the witan alone—were competent to levy taxes on the nation. To employ modern terminology, it is questionable whether the witan and king ever had the constitutional right to impose new taxation. In a time of emergency, such as occurred during the reign of Ethelred, the community acquiesced in the levying of the *heregeld*. Since the war lasted such a long time, the tax, no doubt, acquired some status through age. No doubt, too, it continued to be unpopular. The very existence of this tax throughout almost forty years argues that Anglo-Saxon England had a government far less popular and far less representative than is often assumed, for, had it reflected the views of the majority of the community, there can be little doubt that a tax as unpopular as the *heregeld* would have been abolished long before it was. Again, had the witenagemot been a national assembly, whose members were regarded as representatives of the community rather than representatives of the king, the tax would either have been less unpopular or sooner abolished. Its very existence suggests that the Anglo-Saxon monarch was, in practice, though not in theory, more powerful than is commonly assumed.

Indeed, it may well be that the Anglo-Saxon monarchy and society bore a much closer resemblance to early Merovingian monarchy and society than to those of either eleventh-century France or Scandinavia, both of which it no doubt resembled in many ways. The peculiarly personal relationship between king and magnate in England, under even a weak king, worked in favour of the monarchy, much more than did the contractual and more strictly defined relationship between king and vassal in France. Only the most powerful personalities could turn feudalism into a source of strength to the Crown. Again, in Scandinavia the existence of *alsherjarþing* severely limited the exercise of power on the part of the king. In practice, an English king, if he took care not to offend the moral sense

---

[1] *ASChr*, D 1052; *FlWig*, 1051. On what evidence Liebermann bases his statement that the abolition was "enacted with the consent of the witan," I do not know (*NA*, § 59).

[2] *ASChr*, D 1052: "That tax distressed all the English nation during so long a space as is here above written. That was always paid before other taxes, which were variously paid, and with which the people were variously distressed." Later works emphasize even more strongly the unjust nature of the tax, but may reflect the views of their authors' contemporaries and not those of the Anglo-Saxons (see *Lives*, ed. Luard, pp. 51–52, 205–6). The other taxes mentioned in the above quotation from the *Chronicle* I believe to have been customary dues of various kinds.

of the community in too outrageous a fashion, and if he kept on good terms with the most powerful magnates, need hardly fear that his acts would be challenged. Much more, too, than the royal houses in most other countries, does the English royal house of Cerdic seem to have been regarded as pre-eminently "throne-worthy." I suspect that to a great extent the following statement of Chadwick may be as applicable to eleventh-century Anglo-Saxon society as to that of the Heroic Age: "Much has been written about the various powers possessed by the kings, but it is still by no means clear what they could not do, so long as they had a powerful and contented body of personal followers."[1]

It is recorded that on several occasions the witan co-operated with the king in planning the defence of the realm against the Danes and others.[2] The reign of Edward the Confessor offers some examples of this, although at times the king alone is mentioned in connection with the calling out of military forces. The decision to dismiss the lithsmen in 1050 and 1051 would seem to have been taken after consultation with large numbers of witan.[3] Again, the dispatch of ships to Sandwich in 1052, and the appointment of earls Ralph and Odda to command them, were decreed by king and witan.[4] It is possible that minor decisions of a military nature were made by the king and a small number of witan,[5] and that all major decisions were made by the king and all the leading magnates.[6] This is indeed what one would expect in a society where military forces are raised for the occasion and are commanded by the great magnates whom the king has appointed over the various localities. Co-operation of king and magnate is indispensable under such an arrangement, and very likely to be closer in this matter than in any other. That the Danish conquest made any appreciable difference here cannot be shown, although the existence of a standing army and a permanent navy would make it unnecessary to call out the *fyrd* except when grave danger threatened.[7] But the importance of the earls and of the thegns who were witan would still be great, since they, no doubt, became closely connected with the standing army. Its command would likely fall to some of the household officers of the king.[8] In any case harmony between king and magnates

---

[1] *Heroic Age*, p. 366. [2] See *NA*, § 58.

[3] *ASChr*, E 1047, C 1049, 1050. Larson has shown conclusively, I think, that only the naval forces, and not the standing army, were dismissed (*King's Household*, pp. 168–9).

[4] *ASChr*, E 1052.

[5] The king alone is mentioned as acting in *ASChr*, C 1045, 1049, and 1052. In the latter part of the Confessor's reign Harold is spoken of as the most important agent *ASChr*, C 1056, C, E 1063).

[6] Almost all the examples that Liebermann gives are of this nature (*NA*, § 58).

[7] See Appendix S.

[8] Kemble thought this might well have been the function of the stallers (*Saxons*, II, 122). The local levies seem often to have been led by the sheriffs (Morris, *Sheriff*, p. 27).

was absolutely necessary if the Crown were to possess any real military strength. The crisis of 1051 is a good illustration of this. Godwin was out-lawed in 1051 because the magnates were prepared to support the king. In 1052 Godwin had large forces and the magnates were unwilling to fight for the king, who, much against his will, had to yield. At all stages of the conflict king and magnates were in consultation. This, of course, is not to deny that the standing army may have considerably strengthened the royal power.

The question of what share the witan had in the booking of land is a complicated one. It is not at all certain what is meant by the terms "bookland" and "folkland". There is fairly general agreement that land held by book is land which has been freed from certain public burdens.[1] There is hardly as general agreement that folkland is land held under folk-right, land subject to rents and services for the maintenance of the king, and comprising all land from which these burdens have not been removed by action of the king and witan.[2] There would seem to be some reasons for thinking that this definition is too broad, and that folkland represents the ancient demesne of the Anglo-Saxon kings.[3] The subject, however, lies beyond the scope of this work, although the resolution of the problem would make it easier to assess the share of the witan in the booking of land. It may be said, however, that in what follows I assume that to book land means to remove from it certain burdens, to give the grantee the right to dispose of it at will, and to give it "immunity from challenge in the common moots and a procedure of defence which must have been a most enviable privilege in the conditions of law which then prevailed."[4]

There is no doubt that king and witan co-operated in the making of landbooks. It is another matter how important the share of each was. The conventional phrases used to describe the action of the witan may mean all or nothing,[5] but it would probably not be far wrong to view the king as the most important agent and the witan as witnesses rather than active parties, at least in the reign of Edward the Confessor.[6] This seems to be

---

[1] See *ASEng*, pp. 302–7; J. E. A. Jolliffe, "English Book-right," pp. 1–21; Turner, "Bookland and Folkland," pp. 357–86.   [2] Cf. *ASEng*, pp. 306–9.

[3] Turner, "Bookland and Folkland," advances what seem to be strong arguments for this view. I hope in the near future to discuss the whole question of what folkland was.

[4] Jolliffe, "English Book-right," p. 13.

[5] The formulae used in the Confessor charters are quoted note 2, p. 48, above. Jolliffe warns us: "To try to define the purpose for which king and witan intervene in the granting of book-land, or assess their several shares in the transaction, would be an anachronism" ("English Book-right," p. 6). Again he writes: "King and witan, 'rex cum consilio sapientum,' are the enacting power: to say more would be to force an unreal definition upon a practical age" (*ibid.*).

[6] Cf. Jolliffe, "English Book-right," p. 6: "Public enactment in its fullest sense, both as to the authority and the occasion, is what is sought, and the king may almost, though

confirmed by the fact that, whenever private charters are witnessed by king and witan, they are said to have been made with the "cynges fullra leafe and on his gewitnesse."[1] Even where the witan do not seem to witness, many private charters are said to have been made with the permission and consent of the king.[2]

The number of landbooks which are extant from the Confessor's reign testifies that it was customary to book land in the presence of the witan. That is almost all that the present state of our knowledge of this matter allows us to say. It would be futile, and possibly meaningless, to ask whether the consent of the witan was necessary when the king wished to book land. Such a question has meaning only if by "witan" are meant a large number of magnates gathered in a formal assembly, in which, to be valid, the transaction must be confirmed. If on the other hand the term describes merely the few magnates who happen to be with the king and whom he consults more or less formally, the question of validation does not arise. The king, no doubt, alienated land in the presence of both formal and informal assemblies, and it is doubtful whether he ever made an important grant without consulting at least a few witan, although I would hesitate to say that he did not feel competent to do so.[3] All that can really be said is that there was a customary, but not a fixed and

---

never quite, fulfil this requirement alone." Liebermann (*NA*, § 28) says that in the eleventh century the king and a court council disposed arbitrarily of Crown lands by means of the writ. This, as I have argued, establishes an unwarranted distinction between witan and court council, although it may be admitted that the announcement, by means of a writ, of a grant of land might be taken to mean that those to whom the writ is addressed had no share in the transaction announced in the instrument. But it is by no means certain that such an interpretation is correct. The writ tells us nothing as to how the action it announces was arrived at. Or is it to be seriously maintained that, because a writ states, "ich kyðe eow ðat ich habbe geunnen Gisan minan preste ðes biscopriche" (*CD*, 835), the king alone, without consulting any of his witan, made the appointment? Cf. V. H. Galbraith, "An Episcopal Land Grant of 1085," p. 556: 'For the sealed writ was in origin perhaps merely supplementary to the unaddressed diploma, whose provisions it notified in the form of a letter to the persons concerned. It . . . referred 'to an act of which it formed no part,' and we may doubt if it was even meant to be preserved." I may say here that I do not know of a genuine writ announcing a grant of land whose bestowal has been made in an extant genuine charter. It may, however, be mentioned that there is a writ (*CD*, 828) announcing that Atsere has given Lessness (K) to Westminster, and that this gift by Atsere is recorded in the forged *CD*, 824. But Dr. Harmer has shown that the writ itself is almost certainly a fabrication (*Writs*, pp. 299–301).

[1] *CD*, 956.

[2] Examples of both types are by no means confined to the reign of Edward the Confessor, but characterize the whole Anglo-Saxon period. See *CD*, 923 (1051–2); *ASC*, XCIV (1042); *CD*, 745 (1032), 898 (*ca.* 1023), 683 (*ca.* 985, Earl Ælfric also consents), 680, 681, 682 (all three *ca.* 977, and all with the permission of Earl Ælfhere in addition to that of the king), 1347 (975–9). Numerous other examples might be given.

[3] I think it likely that the advice and consent of the witan were felt to be desirable, not because the king was not competent to act without them, but to safeguard against a reversal of the grant by another monarch in the future.

invariable,[1] procedure in these matters. It may also be added that unquestionably the king and witan heard suits involving bookland, but I know of nothing from the reign of Edward the Confessor to add to what J. E. A. Jolliffe has written on that subject.[2]

[1] Had it been fixed and invariable the number of witan attesting land charters might be expected to vary much less than it actually does.

[2] "English Book-right," pp. 1–21.

CHAPTER TWELVE

The Witan and Judicial Matters

No discussion of the functions of the witan would be complete without an examination of its role in judicial matters. Suits concerning bookland were dealt with by the king assisted by the witan[1] and no doubt formed the bulk of civil suits heard. There are none of these from the reign of the Confessor to claim our attention. In criminal matters, cases of treason seem to have been the most frequent.[2] Of the latter several examples occur in which sentence of outlawry was pronounced and in some of which, at least, the witan had a share.

The reign of Edward the Confessor began, as is well known, with some dissatisfaction over his accession. It would seem that at least a part of the Danes in England would have preferred a Scandinavian king. Somewhat surprisingly Edward's mother seems to have been of this party. Her preference was, apparently, Magnus *góði* of Norway[3] and her activities must have brought her under suspicion. No formal trial, i.e. a trial at which she was present and permitted to make her defence before king and witan,[4] seems to have taken place, but the language of the chroniclers implies that the king and witan came to the decision to take action against her.[5] Earls Godwin, Leofric, and Siward took part in the despoiling of Emma, and were no doubt the most prominent in counselling the action. Both the date of the action and the language of the chroniclers argue against the assumption that the proceedings took place in a specially summoned meeting of all the witan. Emma's lands and treasures were seized by the

[1] See Jolliffe, "English Book-right," pp. 1–21. Cf. *NA*, § 61.

[2] Most of the examples Liebermann cites of the witan's exercise of jurisdiction in criminal matters are cases of treason (*NA*, § 61). I am unable to follow him when he distinguishes between the witenagemot and what he calls the "king's judicial court." He himself admits that both employed witan for doomsmen. I do not know in what the distinction between the two consisted, unless it be the number of witan employed. But for the eleventh century the number would be of no consequence.

[3] On this see *ASEng*, pp. 420–2; *NC*, II, 38–41; *TSCP*, II, 222–3.

[4] As will be seen from the account of the cases discussed below, the accused seems hardly ever to have been present, but to have been condemned *in absentia*.

[5] Especially *ASChr*, D 1043: "man gerædde þan cynge. . . ." The *ASChr*, C 1043, and E, F 1042, simply say that the king despoiled his mother. Florence of Worcester (1043) says that the king moved suddenly, and names the earls who acted with him. The reason for the despoiling of Emma, given by the above authorities, is unsatisfactory. We learn the true reason from an entry in the *Translation of St. Mildred* (Hardy, ed., *Descriptive Catalogue of Materials Relating to the History of Great Britain and Ireland*, I, 380), where Emma is said to have urged King Magnus to seize England. Cf. however *Encomium*, p. xlix.

king, and the witan probably had some share in the seizure, although it would be going too far to say that they adjudged her property forfeit to the king after a formal trial.

No details are known concerning the banishment in 1044 of Gunnhild, the niece of King Cnut, and her sons.[1] The same is true of Osgod Clapa's expulsion in 1046.[2] Both cases, however, were probably bound up with preference for the succession of a Scandinavian when Hardecnut died in 1042.

On the outlawry of Swegen in 1049 we possess more details,[3] but it is difficult to know exactly what happened. In 1046 Swegen made an expedition to Wales and on his return "ordered the abbess of Leominster to be fetched to him, and had her while it listed him, and then let her go home." Florence of Worcester says he wished to marry her.[4] In 1047 Swegen departed from England,[5] but whether voluntarily or as an outlaw is not known.[6] His affair with the nun was hardly cause for outlawry, and it is the only offence he is known to have committed.[7] The emphasis laid on his promise at the time of his return to England to be faithful to Edward might suggest that his departure was occasioned by a too favourable attitude toward Sveinn Úlfsson of Denmark, although this is belied by the friendly relations between Sveinn and Edward. Or can it be that when the king and witan refused Sveinn's request for aid, Godwin sent Swegen with ships, thus incurring the displeasure of Edward? It may of course be, that it was disappointment at not being allowed to marry the abbess that caused him to leave England.[8] In any case he did leave, and this made it necessary to grant his earldom to someone. It was, accordingly, divided between earls Harold and Beorn.[9]

Swegen remained abroad until 1049, when he returned at the time the king lay with his fleet at Sandwich. Whether outlawed or not, it was now necessary for Swegen to be reconciled with the king if he wished to regain his earldom. What steps he took to effect this cannot be known with certainty since the accounts in the sources vary. It seems certain, however, that Swegen obtained Beorn's aid in effecting a reconciliation with the

---

[1] *ASChr*, D 1045; *FlWig*, 1044.

[2] *ASChr*, C 1046, D 1047, E 1044; *FlWig*, 1046.

[3] The various accounts are conveniently arranged in *TSCP*, II, 229–31.

[4] *ASChr*, C 1046; *FlWig*, 1049.   [5] *ASChr*, E, F 1045.

[6] A judicious examination of Swegen's case is to be found in Wilkinson, "Northumbrian Separatism," pp. 513–14. Professor Wilkinson doubts that Swegen was formally outlawed, but thinks that he was in 1049 seeking "a personal reconciliation with the king."

[7] Cf. *TSCP*, II, 115.

[8] Freeman (*NC*, II, 57) held that Swegen, in his disappointment at not being allowed to marry the abbess, "threw up his earldom, left his country. . . ." Professor Stenton (*ASEng*, p. 423) thinks that Swegen had by his act "offended all responsible opinion," and that he then "abandoned his earldom, apparently because he was not allowed to marry her [the abbess]."   [9] *ASChr*, C 1049.

king. The story of Beorn's attempt to assist in this matter is immaterial to our purpose, which is to determine the share of the witan in the whole episode.

On one thing, no matter how they differ in detail, all the accounts agree. This is, that Swegen's plea for restoration was not dealt with in any formal assembly, but by the king and a few magnates. The will of the king seems to have been the deciding factor.[1] In one version of the *Chronicle* Swegen is said to have approached the king and secured restoration.[2] Harold and Beorn opposed this and evidently were able to persuade the king to reverse his decision and to order Swegen to leave the realm within five days. However, within two days Swegen won Beorn over to his side and persuaded him to intercede with the king. Another version states that Swegen made his request for reconciliation to the king.[3] Again Harold and Beorn opposed this, but the latter, it seems, was won over by Swegen. The king, however, refused to pardon the suppliant, who then persuaded Beorn to make another attempt to obtain a favourable decision from the king. But while Beorn was on his way to the court, Swegen slew him. According to both versions it was the king and the interested parties who played the leading roles. Clearly it was the king who could grant or withhold whatever Swegen was asking for.[4]

After Swegen slew Beorn "se cing þa 7 eall here cwædon Swegen for niðing."[5] Who was acting here with the king? What was the *here*? Liebermann distinguished between the *here* and the witenagemot when he wrote:

---

[1] Anyone familiar with the Icelandic sagas and those of the Norwegian kings cannot fail to be struck by the similarity between the attempt of Swegen to be reconciled with Edward and attempts of various individuals to obtain pardon at the hands of the Scandinavian kings for some act committed against the latter (Cf. *ÍF*, II, 179–95, 214–16; VIII, 159–61; *Heimskringla*, pp. 288, 292–7, 356, 478–9; *Fjörutíu Íslendinga-þættir*, ed. Þorleifr Jónsson, Reykjavík, 1904, pp. 140–3, 159–61, 517–23). It is to be remarked that, in spite of the great importance of national and provincial *þing* in the Scandinavian countries, especially Sweden, it is always the king who acts and decides, who punishes and pardons. Only on special occasions are matters of the gravest importance, such as war and peace, or the succession to the throne, dealt with at the *þing*. In other words, the government is the king's, although he sometimes relies heavily on the counsel of one or more of his courtiers. How much the more would this be the case in a society such as the Anglo-Saxon which knew no national assemblies? Indeed the *Anglo-Saxon Chronicle* everywhere speaks as if the government were the king's (including, of course, the witan or courtiers who happened to be with him). Only on occasion does it mention the summoning of all the witan, i.e., numerous magnates who do not habitually attend on the king, for the purpose of treating some very grave matter. Cf. in this connection a discussion of what to do with an individual who attempted to assassinate King Olaf (*Heimskringla*, p. 247). Note the informality of the proceedings.

[2] *ASChr*, E 1046.

[3] *ASChr*, C 1049.

[4] Professor Wilkinson takes essentially the same view ("Northumbrian Separatism," pp. 513–14).

[5] *ASChr*, C 1049.

"The *here* banishes Swen, but the witan confirm this outlawry."[1] He did not, however, exactly define the former. Freeman thought that the assembly which outlawed Swegen was a military gemot, although only of the standing army, and he had doubts as to the constitutionality of the act.[2] Larson regarded the *here* as the standing army of huscarles, the army which was founded or at least given definite organization by Sveinn or Cnut in England, and known as the *þingmannalið*. This explanation seems very reasonable.[3] Larson's view is strongly supported by Scandinavian sources which state that Beorn was slain in the *þingmannalið* in England.[4] Larson advanced strong arguments that the force was an organized guild with a code of laws, the same as, or similar to, the *Leges Castrenses* or *Viðrlög*.[5] In these it was provided that a member of the force who slew another member should stand trial before the *húskarlastefna*,[6] and if found guilty be driven off the king's estates with the name of *niðingr*, and be exiled from every land under Cnut's rule.[7] There seems little doubt that Larson is correct in his contention that it was this body, the *húskarlastefna* of the *þingmannalið*, that, together with the king, declared Swegen *niðingr* after the slaying of Beorn. It is not the witan but the standing army that decrees the exile of Swegen.[8] Nor is this strange, if indeed the *þingmannalið* was an organized body having its own code of laws. Beorn and Swegen had, very likely, been two of its commanders, and its competence to deal with Swegen was probably absolute, since he was no longer an earl, and was possibly even an outlaw.

[1] *NA*, § 39. What his authority for the latter part of this statement is, I do not know. He cites only the *ASChr*, where I can find no support for his view. On the *here* see Appendix S.

[2] *NC*, II, 67–68. Freeman assumed that the same assembly had previously rejected Swegen's application for restoration. Liebermann says (*NA*, § 61): ". . . the king by himself could revoke outlawry"; and Steenstrup writes (*Danelag*, p. 256): '. . . kongen alene kunde tilbagekalde den, som var landflygtig efter Dom."

[3] *King's Household*, pp. 152–69.

[4] "En þessi voru vpphauf vm mal þeirra Asmundar og Sueins konungs at Sueirn Gudnason hafde veget Biorn faudr hans j þingamanna lidi vestr aa Einglandi" (*Flateyjarbok*, III, 370). Larson erroneously translates *mal* as "conversation," but in this context it can only mean "relations," "matters," "affairs," or "business."

[5] See *Scriptores rerum Danicarum*, III, 139–64.

[6] A gathering probably similar to the Norwegian *hirðstefna* (see *Heimskringla*, p. 246; *ÍF*, XXVI, 344; XXVII, 304).   [7] *Scriptores rerum Danicarum*, III, 162.

[8] Professor Wilkinson ("Northumbrian Separatism," p. 514) believes that the *here* acted and declared Swegen *niðingr*, but feels that it might have hesitated to pass a formal sentence of outlawry on him. He adds: "Swegen was already, in fact, an outlaw. . . ." Whether this was so or not, the deeming of a man a *niðingr* seems equivalent to a legal sentence of outlawry. (Cf. Steenstrup, *Danelag*, p. 258: ". . . det at erklæres for niding indeholder ikke blot en moralsk, men en juridisk Dom, saa at der herved er udtalt en Fredløskjendelse over Svend." Steenstrup cites examples of similar cases.) Professor Wilkinson is, very likely, correct in saying that the differences between a witenagemot and the *here* were perhaps "more clearly recognised than Freeman would allow," and in rejecting an identification of witan and army.

After being thus severely dealt with, Swegen left the country. In the following year, however, he was back in England, reconciled to the king and fully restored to his honours. Any attempt to explain this strange event must be pure speculation, since the sources give very little information beyond the bare statement, "man geinlagode Swegen eorl,"[1] which might be held to imply action by the witan. About all that can be said is that the in-lawing is evidence of the very unstable political situation in England around 1050. No doubt the various forces were manœuvring for position although the crisis did not come until 1051.[2]

The crisis of 1051 ended with the outlawing of Godwin and his sons. The accounts of this episode pose a problem similar to that of the earlier outlawing of Swegen in 1049. What was the share of the witan and what the share of the *here* in these events?[3]

Both the origin and the detailed story of the crisis are largely irrelevant to the elucidation of this question. Godwin and the king came into conflict, and the former summoned his followers to Beverstone while the king was at Gloucester with a comparatively small retinue. In the face of Godwin's threat he summoned earls Leofric and Siward, who came with a small company, no doubt some of their huscarles.[4] When the seriousness of the situation became apparent, the earls, and almost certainly the king as well, sent for greater forces. This brought to the side of the king possibly some prominent witan, large numbers of the standing army or *þingmannalið*, and, it may be, some extraordinary levies also.[5] The *þingmannalið* or *here* was probably eager to fight, remembering its recent encounter with Swegen, but the witan may have counselled caution, possibly pointing out that time was on the side of the king. Negotiations apparently were carried on, since a rendezvous at London was ultimately agreed on. At that place Godwin and his sons were to appear and make their defence against the charges which had been levelled against them.

[1] *ASChr*, C 1050 and E 1047, only mention his return. Henry of Huntingdon (*Historia Anglorum*, p. 193) says he was in-lawed "cautela Godwini patris sui."

[2] See Appendix S.

[3] The best treatment of the crisis is Wilkinson, "Freeman and the Crisis," pp. 368–87, and in the main I follow the reconstruction of events therein set out. Professor Wilkinson's remarks on the various versions of the *Anglo-Saxon Chronicle* I regard as eminently sound. As to the origin of the crisis Professor David Douglas has recently argued ("Edward the Confessor, Duke William of Normandy, and the English Succession," pp. 526–45) that King Edward made a promise of the throne to Duke William and sent Archbishop Robert of Canterbury to the duke in 1051 "to ratify the grant in the presence of the duke." This brought on the crisis, Professor Douglas thinks.

[4] In the following account I have drawn upon *ASChr*, D 1052, which Professor Wilkinson has shown to be most reliable. Earl Ralph was probably with the king at Gloucester.

[5] The later statement, that after a rendezvous at London had been agreed upon "the people were ordered out over all this north end, in Siward's earldom, and in Leofric's, and also elsewhere," suggests, however, that only the *hireds* of the earls and the *here* of the king appeared at this time.

The language used by version D of the *Anglo-Saxon Chronicle* in reporting these events is not without significance. It is not a witenagemot that is decreed for London but a *stefna*, and "sceolde Godwine eorl 7 his suna þær cuman to wiþermale." This suggests that the *here* rather than the witan made the decision, although it would be rash to rely too heavily on the *Chronicle's* language alone, for this, as has been pointed out, is extremely loose and inexact. Yet it would seem equally rash to deny the *here* a large share in the proceedings at Gloucester. It may even be possible that at that meeting the *here* took the leading part, at London the witan. At Gloucester the spiritual witan, with the exception of two or three prelates, may well have been absent. Certainly they would be present at London. At Gloucester, under the threat of civil war, the decisions may well have been made in assemblies of the armed retainers of the king and earls. This, too, is what one might expect. Faced with the threat of armed conflict, kings often made their decisions after asking the opinion of their armies.[1] All the more would this be the case where the army was a professional force, having a definite organization and a code of laws governing the behaviour of its members, one of whom, we have seen reason to believe, was Swegen.[2] It seems not unreasonable to conclude that the assembly at Gloucester was primarily one of the *here*, and that the decisions made there were made by the king and *here*, rather than by the king and witan.[3] The two are, of course, not entirely distinct, for many witan would be members of the *here*, and their functions as witan and warriors might and would overlap. But the *here* was more limited in its functions than the witan, for it could deal with only such matters as affected its members or were of a military nature. In addition the spiritual witan were not members of the *here*. Therefore, when the crisis was not resolved by armed conflict, the absent witan would naturally, if only for practical reasons, be summoned to support the king.

[1] Numerous examples could be cited from the sagas of the Norwegian kings (*Heimskringla, passim*) of decisions made in the presence of, and with the acquiescence of, the whole army just prior to battle, or when the arrival of an enemy force was feared.

[2] Presumably Godwin and his other sons were also members.

[3] The distinction between the *here* and the witenagemot has been, as noticed above, suggested by Professor Wilkinson ("Northumbrian Separatism," p. 514). He has also in his "Freeman and the Crisis" (pp. 378, 379) suggested that the gathering at Gloucester was not a witenagemot, but one of partisans in arms. With this I would largely agree, but would call the gathering one of the *here*, rather than one of partisans in arms. I would also add that it was not a witenagemot, not because Edward and the witan present were not competent to deal with the matter, but because it was not expedient to deal with it so, and because the *here* was under the circumstances (the absence of many witan and the military nature of the gathering) the logical body to settle whether the matter was to be put to the issue of arms or settled by more peaceful means. However, it must always be remembered that we are probably making distinctions which would never have occurred to an Anglo-Saxon.

Thus, when the assembly at Gloucester ended without recourse to armed conflict and it was decided to settle the dispute in a council, it would inevitably follow that both the witan and the *here* would act with the king at London, even though the latter had acted alone, or at least played the most prominent part, at Gloucester.[1] In such an important matter the king would, for practical reasons, wish for the support of every influential man in the community. Either witan or *here* would be quite competent to outlaw Godwin and his sons, but the action of both would have greater weight.

That both bodies acted at London is borne out by the language of the *Chronicle*, but the *here* appears to have anticipated the action of the witan, for Swegen was outlawed ("man utlagode þa Swægn eorl") and then on the morrow the king held a witenagemot. This seems the most logical explanation, although it cannot be asserted that *man* does not mean the witan rather than the *here*. Yet it would seem strange that the witan would outlaw Swegen before they outlawed his father and brothers. It is quite understandable that the *here* would do this because the slaying of Beorn in 1049 still rankled.

It would seem that Godwin was summoned to appear before both the king (and presumably his witan) and the *here*. At least it is difficult to understand otherwise the language of the *Chronicle*: "Þa ne onhagode him to cumenne to wiðermale ongean þone cyng 7 agean þone here þe him mid wæs for þa on niht awæg 7 se cyng hæfde þæs on morgen witenagemot 7 cwæð hine utlage 7 eall here hine 7 ealle his suna."[2] It is emphasized that Godwin was unwilling to come *before* the king and *before* the *here*, and the sentence is said to have been pronounced both by the king and by the *here*.[3] It would thus seem safe to conclude that sentence of outlawry was pronounced on Godwin and his sons by the king and his witan, and in addition by the *here* acting in the *húskarlastefna*. This is in harmony with

[1] I believe that, in view of what has been said above, one is justified in placing considerable emphasis on the language of the *Chronicle*, and that it greatly strengthens the view that it is the *here* that acts at Gloucester. It decides on a *stefna* at London, using a word that designates meetings of the standing army, i.e., the *húskarlastefna*. Again, Godwin is summoned to come to *wiðermale*. This word is no doubt the same as the OIcel *viðrmæli*, which, besides its ordinary sense of "conversation" or "a talking together," seems to have had a more technical sense, that of "defence," rebuttal," or "counter-plea" (indeed this sense may be detected in the Icelandic proverb, "Viðurmælis er hver maður verður"), and this, in our case, is the only sense it can have (see Vigfusson, *Icelandic-English Dictionary*, s.v. *viðrmæli*, and especially Marius Hægstad og Alf Torp, *Gamalnorsk Ordbog med Nynorsk Tyding*, s.v. *viðrmæli*). It seems then not unreasonable to suppose that *wiðermale* is used in a technical sense meaning a defence offered to a charge laid under the *Viðrlög*.

[2] *ASChr*, D 1052. Italics mine.

[3] Larson's account (*King's Household*, pp. 166–7) agrees with mine in emphasizing the part played by the *here* in the crisis, but he seems inclined to identify *here* and witenagemot to a far greater extent than I think is warranted.

the concept of the witan advanced in this work. A witenagemot never performs an act, the individual witan do; the *here* performs many acts in its corporate capacity, its individual members never.[1]

In the in-lawing of Godwin the *here* appears to have had a minor role, if any. Of course, Godwin was able to regain his position because of the armed forces he was able to muster. The witan, however, played an important part in preventing bloodshed and arranging a pacific settlement. King Edward seems to have vigorously opposed any reconciliation with Godwin, but to have been overruled by the witan led by Bishop Stigand who, it appears, was the principal mediator.[2] This is a singular instance in which the witan seem to have imposed their will on the king.[3] They play, thus, the major role in the restoration of Godwin, and have, no doubt, to bear the responsibility for the outlawing of the Frenchmen,[4] for this must have been as distasteful to the king as the restoration of Godwin.

During the remainder of the reign only two individuals are known to have been outlawed. On the twice repeated outlawry of Earl Ælfgar the sources give little information which would enable one to assess the share of the witan in the proceedings. According to one version of the *Chronicle*,[5] Ælfgar was outlawed in 1055 in a witenagemot at London. This version also gives one to understand that it was Earl Harold who arranged the terms of reconciliation. From this one might suspect that Harold was the man responsible for Ælfgar's outlawry in the first place. Nor is it unreasonable to see in this episode a part of Harold's manœuvring for position.[6] Even less is known of the details of the second outlawing of Ælfgar in 1058 and his subsequent restoration.[7]

---

[1] Cf. *ASChr*, C 1049, D 1052.

[2] *ASChr*, E 1052. His role is comparable to that of Leofric at Gloucester (*FlWig*, 1051).

[3] How else is one to understand the words of *ASChr*, E 1052: "Then the king however refused for some while; so long until the people who were with the earl were much excited against the king and against his folk; so that the earl himself with difficulty stilled his people. Then went Bishop Stigand to them, with God's support, and the wise men, both within the town and without, and they resolved that hostages should be fixed on each side and it was so done"? Had the king proceeded to extremes, it is impossible to say what would have happened.   [4] *ASChr*, C 1052.

[5] *ASChr*, C 1055. The other versions, D and E 1055, mention only his outlawry, the former saying he was almost without guilt, the latter that he was charged with being a traitor and confessed this, although involuntarily. Version E is silent as to how he was restored, but D says that after the greatest evil had been done, then "man gerædde þone ræd þ man Ælfgar eorl geinnlagode 7 ageaf him his eorldom 7 eall þ him ofgenumen wæs." Florence of Worcester (1055) says he was "sine culpa" and that Harold arranged the terms of his reinstatement.

[6] Freeman was uneasy as to Harold's share in the matter: ". . . he [Harold] may possibly have felt that he was himself in some sort the cause of all that had happened, if he had promoted any ill-considered charges against his rival" (*NC*, II, 264). Professor Stenton (*ASEng*, p. 566) speaks of Ælfgar as having been outlawed twice "by a court under Harold's influence."

[7] Only *ASChr*, D 1058 (echoed by *FlWig*, 1058) mentions it, giving no details. Professor

The witan of England can hardly have played an important part in the outlawing of Earl Tostig in 1065. This was really the work of the Northumbrians, and the role of the witan must have been limited to persuading Edward to accept the inevitable. There is no reason to suppose that Edward and the witan banished Tostig, but they did give way to the demands of the Northumbrians that he depart from England.[1]

In none of the above cases can the witan really be said to have performed the function of a high court of justice, for it is not known that any of the individuals outlawed (unless it be Tostig) appeared before them as before a tribunal to make his defence. On the contrary, the sentences, if they may be called such, were pronounced on the culprit in his absence and, it seems, in accord with the wishes of the monarch rather than on the basis of evidence of guilt.[2] This is, of course, not surprising, for the issues are political rather than judicial, and are decided by the armed strength of the protagonists. The witan, no doubt, offer counsel, but they can hardly be said to hand down a verdict, much less a judgment arrived at after a judicious examination of the facts of the case.[3] The witenagemot as a high court of justice is, therefore, little in evidence during the reign of Edward the Confessor. The activities of the witan in the above cases belong rather to the political than the judicial sphere.

Stenton (*ASEng*, p. 566) suggests that the allocation of the earldoms in 1057 may have driven Ælfgar to rebellion.

[1] See *ASChr*, C, D 1065, E 1064; *Vita Eduuardi*, pp. 421-3. The best recent treatment of the revolt is Wilkinson, "Northumbrian Separatism," pp. 504-26.

[2] By and large it may be said that in dealing with a king, an individual who had offended the former could expect justice at the king's hands in proportion to his own ability to oppose the king or to rally friends to his support. This is strikingly apparent in the Scandinavian cases cited above, and there is little reason to think that conditions were much different in England.

[3] Or, if this is too modern terminology, after offering the defendant every opportunity to clear himself. Godwin, it is true, was offered this to some extent in 1051, and he did clear himself in 1052 before his reconciliation with the king, but both instances smack of formality, and have little real meaning as far as a judicial trial is concerned.

CHAPTER THIRTEEN

Conclusion

THE foregoing examination of the witan in the reign of Edward the Confessor seems to substantiate the view that the witenagemot was little more than a court council. Its essential members were the great prelates and the great earls. In addition there attended such thegns as filled the household offices and provincial posts and, rarely, the clergy of the royal chapel and writing office. The word "witenagemot" had no technical meaning beyond the literal meaning of a meeting of the witan, that is a meeting of such royal counsellors as happened to be with the king or such as he summoned *ad hoc*. In no case should it be understood as meaning a corporate body, which, in its corporate capacity, had either well-defined functions or clearly accepted jurisdictions. A witenagemot was the occasion on which the king and his counsellors transacted business of one kind or another. Even the word "witan" can hardly be said to have meant anything except as it was used to describe the men whom the king consulted, his counsellors, who are in the main only the members of his court. These courtiers are the equivalent of the Scandinavian "hirðmenn," "ráðgjafar," or "handgengnir menn," the men who in Cnut's reign are called "cynges rædesmen," or men like Stigand who is called King Edward's "rædgifa 7 his handprest." The witan are men of substance who hold important ecclesiastical or civil offices. They are individuals on whom the king relies for the government of the country. There is nothing to show that they were a numerous body, and there is nothing to show that any of them had any constitutional right to be counsellors of the king.

The witenagemot is a national assembly only to the extent that the king's court is the centre of the government of the country. In fact it is difficult to discuss the witenagemot without implying to it much more modern characteristics than it actually possessed. As is well known, representative government, which appeared in the later Middle Ages, was an institution of very slow growth, and it is necessary, in discussing government in the early Middle Ages, to avoid reading into words the implications of later ages. Royal officials in the Middle Ages had a dual function. They were representatives of the Crown and they were also representatives of the folk. But they were not representatives of the latter in the sense that the folk had different interests than the king. There is no antithesis between the two parties. Both exist to maintain the law; in fact, that is almost the sole function of both parties. Both co-operate to ensure that to every individual justice be done. The greatest safeguard of the rights of both king and folk lies in the deep-felt and almost implicit idea of the supremacy of law. Certain methods of procedure are right, not because they are constitutional, but because they are old and satisfactory. To an Anglo-Saxon, what was important was not machinery but principles, not methods but results. The state exists, not to tell one what is right, but to preserve a way of life which is right. Modern society is legislative society. Mediaeval society is preservative society.

Nineteenth-century historians, with their veneration for constitutional government, focused their eyes on the machinery through which, and to which, the nineteenth-century system of government had evolved, and not on basic ideas. To them constitutional government existed only where institutions similar to those of their ideal government could be found. It was almost inconceivable to the nineteenth-century historians that without these institutions the rights and liberties of the subject could be maintained. For them the conflicting interests of the state and the individual were real. They saw in the primitive society of the Anglo-Saxons a conflict between government and subject, which only a much later and more complex society could feel and consciously envisage. Without machinery to protect him the Anglo-Saxon was, in their eyes, helpless before the tyranny which characterizes all governments.

In actual fact, this is very far from the truth. The Anglo-Saxon was protected, not by machinery, but by the current and deeply affirmed principle of the supremacy of law, to which all alike owed obedience and for the maintenance of which all alike were duty bound to strive. In a society as primitive and unselfconscious as that of the eleventh-century Anglo-Saxons, no machinery could be devised which would serve to curb the desire for power on the part of individuals or the king, if the fundamental ideas of right and wrong were not genuinely felt and sincerely accepted by the majority of the people. With the development of more absolutist ideas after the Conquest, it required three or four centuries for the baronage to devise machinery which was at all capable of curbing the ambitions of powerful kings.

With identical machinery at all times, the Icelandic republic experienced in the period 930–1264 vastly different circumstances. It knew in the tenth century a period of aristocratic rule, during which the idea of the supremacy of law was strong. This idea limited to a great extent any abuse of power, the opportunity for which was afforded by the unequal distribution of wealth among a relatively small number of chieftains. In the eleventh century, Iceland, with the same machinery, and with the old pagan ideas of the supremacy of law still vital and possibly reinforced by new Christian conceptions, experienced a golden age, in which the rule of law was facilitated by the break-up of the great estates of the previous century and by a more equitable distribution of wealth. The twelfth century witnessed the decay of old heathen principles, and the new Christianity was unable to fill the void quickly enough. At the same time the introduction of the tithe was making possible the resumption of wealth and power into the hands of a few families. As a result, Iceland, still with the same machinery of government, experienced a period of lawlessness and anarchy which ended only with the exhaustion of the state and the passing of the republic.

The witan of England were not a corporate body; they were not a body with definite rights and fixed functions; they did not constitute a national assembly in any real sense of that term; they were not representatives of the nation in the nineteenth-century meaning of that word. In short, any attempt to discuss them from the standpoint of representative and parliamentary government must end in misunderstanding.

The witan were creatures of the king, but they were not creatures in the same sense as the officials of the royal household in the later Middle Ages. These latter, as the bureaucracy developed and the central government extended its jurisdiction, became conscious of a dichotomy of Crown and subject. Inevitably as royal government grew, the need of the Crown for revenue increased and the interests of the monarch grew greater than the interests of even the greatest subject. What seemed of vital importance to the royal bureaucrats of the later Middle Ages was often an unnecessary or foolish venture from the standpoint of the subject. Much of the business of the Crown was of no interest to the individual subject and he saw no personal benefit accruing from it. It was the resultant cleavage which forced the later Middle Ages to attempt the reconciliation between strong government and individual liberty.

Anglo-Saxon England, on the other hand, hardly knew these problems which accompany centralization and the growth of wealth and culture. The witan certainly felt no cleavage between the interest of folk and Crown. They were servants of both; in fact both king and witan were but representatives of the sole existing reality, the race, whose welfare was assured in the maintenance of the good, old law. Both king and witan are toiling toward the same goal. To say that either has certain exclusive functions, or that the one is superior to the other, is to introduce distinctions which have no meaning.

The importance of the witan does not lie in their existence as a curb upon royal power. It lies rather in their representation, unconscious though it may have been, of the principle that all elements of society—Crown or witan or folk—exist for the purpose of guaranteeing the fundamental principles on which the well-being of society depends. In this there can be no distinction between king and witan. Co-operation to this end is the only real duty of both. It is in this embodiment of the co-operative principle of government that the witan are important. It was this that they unconsciously handed down to William the Conqueror and his successors. Parliament and our present institutions of central government are, as far as machinery is concerned, basically of feudal origin. But much of the spirit of these institutions—and that is the all-important factor[1]—is of Anglo-Saxon origin, and this spirit, which also permeated the institutions of local government, is our most important legacy from the Anglo-Saxons. In many ways the Conquest was a calamity; it may well be, however, that the need of William the Conqueror to pose as the successor of the Anglo-Saxon king helped to preserve the fundamental Anglo-Saxon idea of king and witan, king and folk, as partners, not rivals, in the work of government. It has leavened the whole of our history.

[1] Cf. Davis, *EHR*, XXVIII, 427, where, writing on Liebermann, he says: "Like them [Stubbs and the Germanists] he prefers to think of this system [the Anglo-Saxon] as an ideal, as a set of traditions and general principles, which did not change very much from one generation to another."

Opinions of Some Historians on the Functions of the Witan

HERE I have quoted Kemble's canons and then cited the pages whereon they are discussed, or alluded to, by some outstanding scholars.

CANON I

Kemble: First and in general, they possessed a consultative voice, and the right to consider every public act, which could be authorized by the king (*Saxons*, II, 204).

    Liebermann, *NA*, § 53.
    Stubbs,   *CH*, I, 140, cf. 141, 148.
    Stenton,   *ASEng*, p. 544.
    Morris,   *CH1216*, p. 59.
    Jolliffe,   *CHMed*, p. 25.

CANON II

Kemble: The witan deliberated upon the making of new laws which were to be added to the existing folcriht, and which were then promulgated by their own and the king's authority (*Saxons*, II, 205–6).

Is it not manifest that he [Ethelred], like Ælfred, really felt the legislative power to reside in the witan, rather than in the king? (*ibid.*, p. 213).

[It is hardly necessary to say that the expression, "legislative power," must be greatly qualified, whatever Kemble may have meant by it. As Jolliffe says: "Of legislation, as we understand it, there was, of course, almost nothing" (*CHMed*, p. 29).]

    Liebermann, *NA*, § 60.
    Stubbs,   *CH*, I, 157; cf. 141–3.
    Stenton,   *ASEng*, p. 544.
    Morris,   *CH1216*, pp. 60, 61.
    Jolliffe,   *CHMed*, pp. 24, 25; cf. p. 177.

CANON III

Kemble: The witan had the power of making alliances and treaties of peace, and of settling their terms (*Saxons*, II, 213).

    Liebermann, *NA*, § 54.
    Stubbs,   *CH*, I, 148.
    Stenton,   *ASEng*, p. 544.
    Morris,   *CH1216*, p. 61.
    Jolliffe,   *CHMed*, p. 103.

CANON IV

Kemble: The witan had the power of electing the king (*Saxons*, II, 214).

Liebermann, *NA*, §§ 49, 50. Cf. Chadwick, *Studies*, pp. 355–66.
Stubbs,   *CH*, I, 151.
Stenton,   *ASEng*, pp. 544, 543.
Morris,   *CH1216*, p. 60.
Jolliffe,   *CHMed*, pp. 31–32.

CANON V

Kemble: The witan had the power to depose the king if his government was not conducted for the benefit of the people (*Saxons*, II, 219).

Liebermann, *NA*, §§ 49, 50.
Stubbs,   *CH*, I, 153, 155.
Stenton,   *ASEng*, p. 203.
Morris,   *CH1216*, p. 35.
Jolliffe,   *CHMed*, pp. 31–32. Cf. Kern, *Kingship and Law*, p. 86.

CANON VI

Kemble: The king and the witan had power to appoint prelates to vacant sees (*Saxons*, II, 221).

Liebermann, *NA*, § 56. Cf. Böhmer, *Kirche und Staat*, p. 50.
Stubbs,   *CH*, I, 149–50.
Stenton,   *ASEng*, p. 544, 538–9. See also Knowles, *The Monastic Order*,
             p. 396.
Morris,   *CH1216*, pp. 61–62.
Jolliffe,   *CHMed*, p. 136.

CANON VII

Kemble: [The witan] had also the power to regulate ecclesiastical matters, appoint fasts and festivals, and decide upon the levy and expenditure of ecclesiastical revenue (*Saxons*, II, 222).

Liebermann, *NA*, § 56. See also Böhmer, *Kirche und Staat*, p. 50.
Stubbs,   *CH*, I, 143.
Stenton,   *ASEng*, p. 538. See also Knowles, *The Monastic Order*, p. 650.
Morris,   *CH1216*, p. 243. See also Rose Graham, *Ecclesiastical Studies*,
             p. 164.
Jolliffe,   *CHMed*, p. 29.

CANON VIII

Kemble: The king and the witan had the power to levy taxes for the public services (*Saxons*, II, 223).

Liebermann, *NA*, § 59.
Stubbs,   *CH*, I, 148.
Stenton,   *ASEng*, p. 544.
Morris,   *CH1216*, p. 63.
Jolliffe,   *CHMed*, pp. 127–31.

CANON IX

Kemble: The king and witan had power to raise land and sea forces when occasion demanded (*Saxons*, II, 224).

[Kemble admits that the king "always possessed of himself the right to call out the ban or armed militia of the freemen" but adds that in extraordinary circumstances "the authority of the witan was added to that of the king; and that much more extensive levies were made than by merely calling out the *hereban* or *landsturm*," e.g., naval forces (*ibid.*, pp. 224–5).]

> Liebermann, *NA*, § 58.
> Stubbs,   *CH*, I, 148.
> Stenton,   *ASEng*, p. 544.
> Morris,   *CH1216*, p. 61.
> Jolliffe,   *CHMed*, p. 29.

CANON X

Kemble: The witan possessed the power of recommending, assenting to, and guaranteeing grants of land, and of permitting the conversion of folcland into bocland, and vice versa (*Saxons*, II, 225).

> Liebermann, *NA*, §§ 28, 29, 62.
> Stubbs,   *CH*, I, 145, 157.
> Stenton,   *ASEng*, pp. 308, 544.
> Morris,   *CH1216*, p. 63.
> Jolliffe,   "English Book-right," p. 6; cf. *CHMed*, p. 74.

CANON XI

Kemble: The witan possessed the power of adjudging the lands of offenders and intestates to be forfeit to the king (*Saxons*, II, 228).

> Liebermann, *NA*, §§ 61, 62.
> Stubbs,   *CH*, I, 147.
> Stenton,   *ASEng*, p. 544.
> Morris,   *CH1216*, p. 62.
> Jolliffe,   *CHMed*, p. 28.

CANON XII

Kemble: Lastly the witan acted as a supreme court of justice, both in civil and criminal cases (*Saxons*, II, 229).

> Liebermann, *NA*, § 61.
> Stubbs,   *CH*, I, 147.
> Stenton,   *ASEng*, p. 544.
> Morris,   *CH1216*, p. 62.
> Jolliffe,   *CHMed*, pp. 28, 29, 108, 177.

List of Witnesses Signing Royal and Private Charters

In all cases I have listed the charters on which the name of a witness appears as follows: in ordinary type, the charters I believe genuine; in ordinary type but within brackets, the charters I regard as doubtful; in italics, the charters I deem spurious.

Ædridg, thegn. Signs CD, 771.

Ælfgar, earl of Mercia (*ob. ca.* 1062). He was earl of East Anglia during Harold's exile 1051–2 and succeeded to it again when Godwin died in 1053. In 1057 on the death of his father he became earl of Mercia and retained this until his death sometime after 1062. I am inclined to think that he lived until 1065 (why does DB, O, 154 report that Oxford paid dues to Earl Ælfgar TRE if another earl held it for four years before the Conquest, as Freeman thought (*NC*, II, 312)?). Ælfgar's signature before he became earl seems to occur very infrequently, or at least cannot be readily distinguished from other thegns of the same name. Signs CD, 788 (*þe Erles sunu*), 805, 811, 956; (810); *785, 813, 963, 964.*

Ælfgar, thegn, the brother of Ordgar and Esbern (CD, 1334). I am unable to identify this man beyond saying that I believe he came from the southwest of England (cf. *ASC*, pp. 434, 448, and 459). Signs CD, 768, 774, 775, 776, 780, 781, FASM, II, Exeter xii; CD (770, 778); *771*, It is also possible that the Ælfgar who signs CD, 811, as *consiliarius* and CD, 787, as *nobilis* (both genuine) is the same man. He has been identified as a Somerset thegn (*TCPB*, p. 80) in the case of CD, 811, and is possibly the witness on the doubtful CD, 816. It should be mentioned that Ælfgar of Minehead, So (CD, 1334), is a possibility for some of the above charters. The puzzling thing about the witness lists is that Earl Ælfgar does not seem to sign more than one or two charters before he became earl, for there seems to be little doubt that it is Ælfgar, the brother of Ordgar, who signs most of the above charters. It would be tempting to identify Earl Ælfgar as the brother of Ordgar, but this seems impossible (*NC*, II, 443–6). There are so many Ælfgars in the reign of the Confessor that we cannot in most cases be certain which one is meant (see *PNDB*, *s.* Algar and Ælfgar).

Ælfgar, thegn, the father of Beorhtric (CD, 804). He held lands in Gl and Wo. Signs CD; 805.

Ælfgeat, thegn. On CD, 767, the name occurs twice, but I think that its first appearance must be the result of a clerical error, since it precedes those of the bishops, and the witness list as a whole appears jumbled. I am unable to identify this man or men, except to say that one may be the sheriff of Mx (CD, 858). Another possibility is a So thegn (*PNDB*, *s.n.*). Signs CD, 811; FASM, II, Exeter xii; CD (767, 778, 816); *772*.

Ælfgeat, notarius. Who this purports to be I do not know. An Ælfgeat *presbyter* held lands in C and So (*PNDB*, *s.n.*). Signs CD, *825*.

Ælfgifu Emma, queen mother. She was the wife of (1) Ethelred and (2) Cnut. Her death occurred March 6, 1052. She was despoiled by the king in 1043, but whether she was still in disgrace when she died is not known (see Appendix M). Signs *CD*, 768, 773, 774, 775, 788, 1332; (767, 962); *771, 779, 916.*

Ælfnoð, thegn. This is probably the Ælfnoð who held lands of Peterborough (*DB*, L, 345b, 346; *LD*, index, *s.n.* Alnod). Signs *CD*, 806, 819; *813, 815, 824, 825, 912.*

Ælfric, archbishop of York 1023–51. Signs *CD*, 768, 774, 775, 776, 780, 781, 783, 784, 787, 791, 797, 1335; *FASM*, II, Exeter xii; *CD* (767, 769, 770, 778); *771, 772, 779, 785, 786, 794, 912, 916.*

Ælfric, bishop. This name occurs on *CD*, *813*, but no bishop of that name was living in 1062. There was a bishop with that name at Elmham (1038/9–1042/3), on whom see *Writs*, p. 549.

Ælfric, abbot of Pershore *ca.* 1033–*ca.* 1055 (*ASC*, p. 460). Signs *CD*, 797, 807; *771, 772, 912, 939.*

Ælfric, monk of Worcester. This is probably the brother of Earl Odda, and Miss Robertson is very likely right in thinking that the scribe misread *min* for *mon* when copying this charter on which alone this name with such a designation appears (see *ASC*, p. 457). Signs *CD*, 797.

Ælfric, thegn. This is a very common name and it is difficult to be certain in each case as to the identity of the man. Ælfric Withgar's son (*CD*, 978) certainly witnesses some of the charters on which the name Ælfric appears. He was Queen Emma's deputy in the eight-and-a-half Bury hundreds and a landowner in the eastern counties (*ASC*, p. 425, *ASW*, p. 188). Signs *CD*, 788, *HLC*, pp. 300–2; *CD* (769, 962).

Ælfric, thegn. Another Ælfric is probably a thegn in the southwest, perhaps a So thegn (*PNDB*, *s.n.*). This Ælfric might be the brother of Earl Odda (*CD*, 804; *NC*, II, 380). Signs *CD*, 781, 787; *FASM*, II, Exeter xii. It may be mentioned that an Ælfric was sheriff of Hu (*CD*, 903) and another sheriff of C (*DB*, C, 189), but I do not think they witness any of these charters.

Ælfsige, abbot. There is an abbot of this name at Peterborough but he died in 1042 (*ASChr*, E 1041) and was succeeded by Earnwig (*ibid.*) who resigned in 1052 (*ibid.*, E 1052). Miss Robertson says (*ASC*, p. 405) that Ælfsige was abbot of Peterborough from 1005 to 1055, but this is an error. The Ælfsige who signs these charters is therefore likely to be the Ælfsige abbot of St. Benedict at Hulme (1019–*ca.* 1046). Signs *CD*, 774, 775; (769).

Ælfstan, abbot of St. Augustine 1023/7–1046 (cf. *ASC*, p. 420). Signs *CD*, 774, 775, 776, 780; (769); *772, 779, 916.*

Ælfstan, thegn. The name occurs frequently. The most likely man seems to be the one who held lands in So, Do, Ha, Br, Gl, Ht, and Bd, as well as in W, where Boscombe, with which he is often identified, is located (*PNDB*, *s.n.*). *CD*, 767, grants him Sevenhampton, W (*DB*, W, 71b). He is very likely the sheriff of *CD*, 945, although of what shire is uncertain. Kemble (*Saxons*, II, 167) made it Ht. Signs *CD*, 773 (as staller), 774, 775, 776, 780, 781; *FASM*, II, Exeter xii; *CD* (767, 769, 770, 778, 793, 816); *772, 779, 800, 813, 912.*

Ælfstan, monk of Worcester. Miss Robertson thought that the *mon* after this name on *CD*, 797, might be an error for *min* (*ASC*, p. 457), but this does not seem likely for an Ælfstan *sacerdos* signs *HLC*, pp. 247–8. He became prior of Worcester in 1061 (Harmer, *Writs*, pp. 550–1). Signs *CD*, 797, *HLC*, pp. 247–8.

Ælfweald, bishop of Sherborne, 1045/6–1058 (*ASC*, p. 447; *GP*, p. 183. The terminal date is erroneously given as 1050 in *RAS*, p. 36, and in Knowles, *The Monastic Order*, p. 700). Signs *CD*, 784, 787, 956; *HLC*, pp. 300–2; *CD* (792, 793); *772, 813, 916.*

Ælfweald, thegn. This name is likely that of a landowner in Wo (*VCH*, Wo, i, 316a, 318a, 318b, 320a). Signs *CD* (823); *801, 813.*

Ælfweald, thegn. This is the brother of Leofwine (*q.v.*). Signs *CD* (962).

Ælfweard, bishop of London 1035–44. Signs *CD*, 768, 774, 775, 788; (769); *771, 772.*

Ælfweard, abbot. This name occurs only once, *CD*, 775, with the title of *dux* along with others who must be abbots but are also titled *duces*. There is little doubt that this is Ælfweard, bishop of London. He was previously abbot of Evesham (from 1014) and retained that office after he became bishop (*FlWig*, 1044).

Ælfweard, thegn. This name is very common and occurs frequently. In at least two instances it would seem to belong to a So thegn (*ASC*, 489). Signs *CD*, 787, 1332.

Ælfweard, thegn. On most of these charters the name is probably that of Ælf-weard of Longdon, Wo (*ASC*, p. 459 and also 449). Signs *CD* (769, 770, 778, 792, 793); *800, 939 (de Knifarton).*

Ælfwig, abbot of Bath *ca.* 1060–5 (*TCPB*, p. 19; *RB*, LII, 98), or Ælfwig, abbot of the New Minster, Winchester, and brother of Godwin. The latter was abbot of the New Minster *ca.* 1063–6 and was slain at Hastings. The name Ælfwig occurs on *CD* (778, 817); *772, 813, 817.* The signature of either of these two men on *CD*, 778, is almost certainly impossible. There is, however, great mystery about the brother of Godwin (see *NC*, II, 459–61), and he may have been an abbot earlier than 1063. It is also possible that -*wig* may have been written instead of -*wine* (cf. *PNDB*, p. 125). This would remove the difficulties, for Ælfwine of the New Minster would be acceptable.

Ælfwig, thegn. There was a sheriff of Gl with this name (Morris, *Sheriff*, p. 35). He may be our man. The name occurs twice with the title of *praefectus* on *CD* (767), but I suspect that it is repeated in error. It occurs only on doubtful or spurious charters. Signs *CD* (767, 792, 793); *800.*

Ælfwine, bishop of Winchester 1032–47. Signs *CD*, 773, 774, 775, 776, 780, 781, 783, 784, 788, 1332, 1335; *FASM*, II, Exeter xii; *CD* (767, 769, 770, 778); *771, 772, 779, 785, 813.*

Ælfwine, abbot. There are three abbots of this name:

(1) Ælfwine of Buckfast. His dates are not known but probably include the early years of the Confessor's reign. I conjecture that he may have attested *CD*, 1332; (767).

(2) Ælfwine of the New Minster *ca.* 1032–57 (on the dating see *ASC*, pp. 418, 437). I conjecture that he may have attested *CD*, 773 and 956; *FASM*, II, Exeter xii.

(3) Ælfwine of Ramsey 1043–79 (when Æthelsige of St. Augustine was appointed

to assist or succeed Ælfwine is not clear, for the latter lived long after the Conquest (*NC*, IV, 509–11)). Of the three this man is the most important, for he was an intimate of the Confessor. Signs *CD*, 774, 775, 776, 780, 781, 787, 791, 1332; *HLC*, pp. 300–2; *CD* (778, 796); *772, 779, 800, 809, 813, 824, 963, 964.*

Ælfwine, thegn (possibly known as the Red). This is probably the son of the Ælfwine Wulfræd who is well known from Cnut's reign. He lived in K (*CrawCol*, p. 50; *ASC*, p. 464). Signs *CD*, 773, 788; (*769, 962*).

Ælfwine, thegn. This is probably a tenant of the bishop of Winchester and/or of the Confessor (*ASC*, p. 464). Signs *FASM*, II, Exeter xii; *CD* (770).

Æstan, thegn. This is a Bk thegn, the father of Leofwine (*q.v.*). Signs *HLC*, pp. 247–8.

Æthelfrid, thegn. He held lands in Do and So (*PNDB, s.n.* In this work Æthel-is spelled Æðel, but I have disregarded this and in all cases referred to such names as *s.n.*). Signs *CD*, 811; (*816*).

Æthelmær, bishop of Elmham 1047–70, brother of Stigand (*ASC*, p. 431). Professor Knowles, for some reason, gives the terminal date as 1055 (*The Monastic Order*, p. 698). Signs *CD*, 956; (*816*); *785, 801, 813.*

Æthelmær, thegn. This is likely the son of Kola *þæs cyninges heahgerefa* (*ASChr*, A 1001), who met the Vikings who came up the Exe at Pinhoe, D. Signs *CD*, 787; *FASM*, II, Exeter xii; *CD* (767, 796, 816).

Æthelmund, thegn. Signs *CD*, *813*.

Æthelnoð, abbot of Glastonbury 1053–78. Signs *CD*, 811, 822; *HLC*, pp. 300–2; *CD* (816, 817); *801, 813, 815, 964.*

Æthelnoð, thegn. This is probably intended to be the Æthelnoð *cild*, who held lands in K, Sr, So, D, Co, E, Sx, and Ha, and who is called by Florence of Worcester (1067) *satrapam Agelnothum Cantwariensem* (*PNDB, s.n.*). He was probably sheriff of K, although this is only conjecture. Signs *CD*, *800, 824.*

Æthelric, bishop of Durham 1042–56. His signature is found only on the spurious *CD*, 779.

Æthelric, bishop of Selsey 1057–70 (*ASChr*, E 1058). Signs *CD* (810, 816).

Æthelric, thegn. There are so many thegns by this name in southwest England that identification is impossible (see *PNDB, s.n.*). Signs *CD*, 1332; *FASM*, II, Exeter xii; *CD* (767, 793); *770, 800.*

Æthelric, thegn. This is Bishop Beorhtheah's brother in Wo. Signs *HLC*, pp. 247–8; *CD* (767).

Æthelric Rufus, thegn. I am unable to identify this man. Signs *CD* (962).

Æthelsige, abbot of St. Augustine, Canterbury (May 26, 1061–?). He was sent on an embassy to Scandinavia in 1068 and outlawed in 1070. Later he returned to Ramsey and died there in 1087. On him see *TCPB*, p. 78; *NC*, IV, 509–11. Signs *CD*, 822; (*817*); *771, 809, 813, 824, 825, 963, 964.*

Æthelsige, thegn. This is a So thegn who was the steward of Queen Eadgyð (*PNDB, s.n.*). Signs *CD*, 811; *916.*

Æthelstan, bishop of Hereford 1012–56. Signs *CD*, 768, 774, 775, 776, 780, 781, 784, 797; (*767, 769, 778*); *771, 779, 912, 916.*

Æthelstan, abbot of Abingdon 1044–8. Signs *CD*, 776, 780, 781; *FASM*, II, Exeter xii; *CD* (778).

Æthelstan, thegn. This is likely a landowner in L (*LD*, index *s.n.* Adestan). Signs *CD*, 819.

Æthelweard, abbot of Glastonbury (*ob.* 1053). Signs *CD*, 774, 776, 780, 781, 787, 791; *FASM*, II, Exeter xii; *CD* (767, 769, 792, 793, 796); *772, 779, 785*.

Æthelweard, thegn. Probably this is the Æthelweard *Tochesone* of D (*PNDB*, *s.n.*) at least in the latter case. Signs *HLC*, pp. 300–2; *FASM*, II, Exeter xii.

Æthelwig, abbot of Evesham 1059–77. Signs *CD*, 811, 822; *HLC*, pp. 247–8; *CD* (778, 823); *772, 809*.

Æthelwig, priest. I do not know who this is unless it be the above abbot before he was raised to that office. Signs *CD*, *796*.

Æthelwig, thegn. This may be the thegn surnamed *banesona*, who held in D and So and whose lands passed to Alured de Hispania (see *PNDB*, *s.n.*). One of the wealthiest thegns of Nf and Sf had this name and was connected with Thetford (*EHR*, XXXVII, 233; *PNDB*, *s.n.*), but I cannot connect him with these charters. Signs *CD*, 775; (767, 816); *771, 964* (Æthelwig of Thetford might be intended in these two forgeries).

Æthelwig, thegn. Who this is, I do not know. Signs *CD* (816).

Æthelwine, bishop of Durham 1056–71. As in the case of his predecessor, Æ. signs only once, and that on a spurious charter, *CD, 813*.

Æthelwine, dean of Worcester. He may have become prior (see *ASC*, p. 457). Signs *CD*, 797, 807; *912*.

Æthelwine, thegn. This is most likely Æthelwine the father of Turchil and sheriff of Wa (*PNDB*, *s.n.*). Signs *CD* (769).

Æthelwine, thegn. This is Æthelwine the Black (*Chron Rameseiensis*, p. 209) who was sheriff of Hu. Signs *CD* (962).

Æthelwine, thegn. This may be the Æthelwine who held in So and whose lands went to Alured de Hispania (*TCPB*, p. 80). Signs *CD*, 811; *FASM*, II, Exeter xii.

Agemund, thegn. He is possibly a thegn of L (*PNDB*, *s.n.*, and *LD*, index *s.* Agemund). Signs *CD*, 819.

Áskell, thegn. He was the son of Toki and an important landowner in L (*LD*, pp. xl–xli, xliv, and index *s.* Aschil, s. of Toke). Signs *CD*, 808.

Azur, thegn. This is a well-known thegn of Wo (*ASC*, p. 458; *NC*, II, 381). Signs *CD*, 805, 807; *HLC*, pp. 247–8; *CD* (823).

Azur, thegn. This is probably a thegn in Br, who in *DB* is called *dispensator regis E.* (*PNDB*, *s.n.*). Signs *FASM*, II, Exeter xii; *CD* (769); *813 (regis dapifer)*.

Azur, thegn. This man, called the Red, may be a thegn of K (*ASC*, p. 437). Signs *CD*, 773.

Baldwin, abbot of Bury St. Edmunds 1065–98. His signature never occurs except on spurious charters. Signs *CD, 809, 813 (regis capellanus), 824, 825*.

Beorhtmær, abbot of Croyland. His dates are usually given as 1018–48, but Miss Robertson thinks he may have been alive as late as 1053 (*ASC*, p. 458). I am of the same opinion. Signs *CD*, 956.

Beorhtric, abbot of Malmesbury 1062–70. Signs *CD* (817); *964*.

Beorhtric, priest. This is possibly the above abbot before he was elevated to that office. Signs *CD* (792, 793); *800*.

Beorhtric, thegn. The name occurs often on the witness lists. In some cases it probably belongs to a Wiltshire thegn and companion of Eadric of Laxfield (see *Feudal Documents*, p. xciii). Signs *CD*, 774, 775, 776, 780, 781; *FASM*, II, Exeter xii; *CD* (767, 769, 778, 796); *772*, *800*.

Beorhtric, thegn. This man would seem to be the son of Ælfgar, lord of Gloucester. On him see *NC*, IV, 109–10, 517–19; *TCPB*, p. 80. Signs *CD*, 805 (*Ælfgares sunu*), 807, 811 (*consiliarius*); *HLC*, pp. 247–8, 300–2; *CD* (810, 816, 823); *813, 815, 964*. This Beorhtric may well have signed some of the charters I have attributed to the other one.

Beorhtweald, bishop of Ramsbury 1005–45. Signs *CD*, 768, 774, 775, 1332; *FASM*, II, Exeter xii; *CD* (767, 769, 778); *771, 772, 779, 916*.

Beorhtwine, bishop of Sherborne 1023–45. Signs *CD*, 774, 775, 776, 780, 781; (767); *771, 772, 916*.

Beorhtwine, thegn. This is probably the B. *predives* who gave land to the church of Worcester (*ASC*, p. 461). Signs *HLC*, pp. 247–8; *CD* (823); *813*.

Beorhtwine, thegn. This may have been a thegn of Edward in Do (*PNDB*, *s.n.*). Signs *FASM*, II, Exeter xii.

Beorn, earl of the Middle Angles *ca.* 1045. He was slain by Swegen in 1049. King Sveinn Úlfsson of Denmark was his brother. Signs *CD*, 781, 784, 787; (778); *912*. He never signs as *minister*.

Bondi, thegn. This is the well-known staller of Edward. He held lands in Dr, Bk, Bd, Gl, O, Nth, and E. Round thinks he was sheriff of Bd (*EHR*, XIX, 91). Signs *CD*, 811, 822 (*steallere*); (810, 816); *813* (*regis palatinus*), *824, 825*.

Brand, abbot of Peterborough, November 1, 1066–9. Signs *CD*, *963*.

Burgræd (*Burhtredus*), thegn. Feilitzen identifies him as a thegn holding lands in Bd, Bk, and Nth (*PNDB*, *s.n.*). He was a very important landowner (see *VCH*, Bk, I, 240b, 241a; *VCH*, Nth, I, 287). Signs *CD* (962).

Carl, thegn. This may be the Carl who held lands in Sx, Sr, Ha, W, and So (*PNDB*, *s.n.* Karl). There is a Carl, father of Godric and Godwine, in K (*VCH*, K, III, 223, 231). I think, however, that the former is the witness on these charters. Signs *CD*, 774, 775, 776, 780, 781; *FASM*, II, Exeter xii; *CD* (767, 769, 778); *771*.

Ceolmaer, thegn. One man with this name is mentioned in *DB* (Wo, 176b). He held Doddenham, Wo. Signs *HLC*, pp. 247–8.

Ceolric, thegn. This was probably a thegn in So (*PNDB*, *s.n.*). Signs *CD*, 791.

Ceolweald (*Celfpendus*), thegn. A man of this name is mentioned in *DB*, holding lands in Sf (*PNDB*, *s.n.*). Signs *CD*, 791.

Cola, thegn. Signs *CD*, *825*.

Cynesige, archbishop of York 1051–60. Signs *CD*, 806, 807, 956; *HLC*, pp. 300–2; (796 (*presbyter*)); *800* (*presbyter*).

Cynesige, thegn. The only entries under this name in *DB* are in So and Co. Signs *CD* (793).

Cyneweard, thegn. This may be the C. to whom, along with Godwin and Bishop Hereman, *CD*, 948, is addressed, although it is strange that *DB* shows no lands under that name in Br, and it may well be that Kemble (*Saxons*, II, 167) is wrong in making him sheriff of Br. The man we have here may have been a royal reeve or local magnate in Wo. Lands by men of this name are found in *DB* in Wo, E, Gl, and Wa (*PNDB*, *s.n.*; Morris, *Sheriff*, p. 43). Signs *CD*, 807; (767 (*praefectus*)), (792 (*praepositus*), 796 (*praepositus*)); *800* (*praepositus*).

Dodda, thegn. It is difficult to identify this man and the signatures may belong to more than one individual. The most likely man is a Co thegn (*PNDB*, *s.n.*; but cf. *ASC*, pp. 448, 490). Signs *CD*, 787, 791, 1332; *FASM*, II, Exeter xii; *HLC*, pp. 300–2; *CD* (767, 770); *771, 813*.

Duduc, bishop of Wells 1033–60. Signs *CD*, 768, 774, 775, 776, 780, 781, 784, 787, 791, 807, 956, 1332; *FASM*, II, Exeter xii; *HLC*, pp. 300–2; *CD* (767, 770, 778, 793), *771, 772, 779, 800, 912, 916*.

Eabpisus, thegn. This may be an error for Ealwine or some such name, but identification is impossible. Signs *CD*, 791.

Eadgyð, queen. Edward married Eadgyð, the daughter of Godwin, in January 1045. She died December 18, 1075. Signs *CD*, 776, 780, 781, 783, 805, 807, 808, 819, 822, 956, 1335; (778, 810, 816, 817, 823); *779, 785, 794, 809, 813, 815, 824, 825, 916, 963, 964*.

Eadmær, thegn. This seems to be Eadmær *at Burham*, who signs also under Cnut (*ASC*, p. 411; *CrawCol*, p. 151). He held in K. Signs *CD*, 773; *HLC*, pp. 300–2; *CD* (769).

Eadmær, thegn. This is probably Eadmær *atre* who had lands in D, So, and E, and likely the man known as E. *attile* (*atule*) of Ht, Mx, and Bk (*PNDB*, *s.n.*). Signs *CD*, 811.

Eadmund, abbot of Pershore *ca.* 1060–85. Signs *HLC*, pp. 247–8; *CD, 813, 825, 964*.

Eadnoð, bishop of Dorchester 1034–49. Signs *CD*, 768, 774, 775, 776, 780, 781, 784; (767, 769, 778, 962); *771, 779, 912, 916*.

Eadnoð, thegn. This is intended to be King Edward's staller, killed in 1067 or 1068. His lands lay in Br, W, Ha, So, and possibly elsewhere (*ASC*, p. 489; *PNDB*, *s.n.*; Morris, *Sheriff*, p. 37; *NC*, IV, 514; *VCH*, Br, I, 295, 337a, 346a). Signs *CD*, *824, 825*.

Eadric, thegn. This is possibly the Eadric of Laxfield who was a wealthy thegn of Nf and Sf (*Feudal Documents*, pp. xc–xcii; *ASC*, p. 426). He might also be a wealthy Kentish thegn (*ASC*, p. 451). Signs *HLC*, pp. 247–8; *CD, 813*.

Eadsige, archbishop of Canterbury 1038–50. Previously he was bishop at St. Martin's (1035–8). Signs *CD*, 768, 774, 775, 784, 787, 788, 791, 1332; *FASM*, II, Exeter xii; *CD* (767, 769, 770, 778, 792, 793, 796); *771, 772, 779, 785, 786, 794, 800, 912, 916, 939*.

Eadweald, priest. The only priest with this name of whom I know was probably attached to Christ Church. He signs under Cnut *CD*, 745, 746, 751. Signs *CD*, 788; (767).

Eadweard, king 1042–66. Signs *CD*, 768, 773, 774, 775, 776, 780, 781, 783, 784, 787, 788, 791, 797, 805, 806, 807, 808, 811, 819, 822, 956, 1332, 1335; *FASM* II, Exeter xii; *HLC*, pp. 247–8, 300–2; *CD* (767, 769, 770, 778, 792, 793, 796, 798,

810, 816, 817, 823, 962); *771, 772, 779, 785, 786, 800, 801, 809, 813, 815, 818, 824, 825, 912, 916, 939, 963, 964.*

Eadwig, thegn. This may be intended to be Eadwig *cilt* of He. Signs *CD, 813.*

Eadwine, abbot of Westminster 1049–*ca.* 1070. Signs *CD* (810); *771, 809, 824, 825.*

Eadwine, earl of Mercia *ca.* 1065–71 (on the date see above *s.n.* Ælfgar, earl). He was the son of Earl Ælfgar and a brother of Morcar. His lands were chiefly in Wa, St, Sa, Y, and Wo. Signs *CD* (816); *801, 809, 824, 825, 964.*

Eadwine, thegn. It is difficult definitely to identify this man. He may have been the above Eadwine before he became earl, or a wealthy EA thegn (Nf, Sf). In the latter case, however, the date of the first charter would seem somewhat early (*Feudal Documents*, pp. cxiii–cxiv; *ASW*, pp. 119–200). There is a sheriff of an unknown county with this name and with possessions in O and Wa (Morris, *Sheriff*, p. 43), but this is probably the son of Burgræd (*q.v.*) and too young to sign these charters. Signs *CD* (769, 796).

Eadwulf, thegn. I cannot identify this man, but men with this name held lands in Y, Nf, D, and Sf. He signs *CD*, 791, and may have been a Devon thegn. *CD*, 787, is a grant to an Eadwulf in Co (see also *Iadulf*).

Ealdred, archbishop of York 1060–9. He was previously bishop of Worcester (*ca.* 1046–62), administered Ramsbury from *ca.* 1055–8 after the resignation of Hereman, and also held the see of Hereford 1056–60 *donec antistes constitueretur.* Only on *CD*, 808, 819, 822; (810, 816, 817, 823) does he sign as archbishop. Signs *CD*, 784, 791, 805, 806, 807, 808, 819, 822, 956; *FASM*, II, Exeter xii; *HLC*, pp. 247–8; *CD* (770, 792, 793, 798, 810, 816, 817, 823); *772, 800, 801, 809, 813, 824, 825, 912, 916, 939, 963, 964.*

Earngeat, thegn. This is a Wo thegn (*PNDB*, s.n.). Signs *HLC*, pp. 247–8; *CD* (823).

Earnwig, abbot of Peterborough 1042–52 (*ASChr*, E 1041, 1052). Signs *CD*, 797.

Ecglaf, thegn. Unknown. He can hardly be the huscarl of this name, whom Freeman mentions, from the neighbourhood of Durham (*NC*, IV, 203). Signs *FASM*, II, Exeter xii; *CD* (770); *772.*

Ecgwulf, thegn. There is an Ecgwulf in L (*LD*, p. 64, no. 29) who seems to be the only man with this name in *DB*. I doubt that he is the witness on these charters. Signs *CD*, 787, 791; *FASM*, II, Exeter xii; *CD* (770).

Esbern, thegn. This is probably the brother of Ordgar and Ælfgar (*CD*, 1334). Signs *CD* (767), *813.*

Esgar, thegn. This is King Edward's staller. He has been called sheriff of Mx (Morris, *Sheriff*, p. 37), but Dr. Harmer doubts that he was (*Writs*, p. 561). His lands lay in many counties (*PNDB*, s. Ásgeirr). Signs *CD*, 806, 808 (*regis dapifer*), 811 (Feilitzen (*PNDB*, s. Ásgeirr) says that this Esgar may be a So man and not the staller, but in *TCPB* (p. 80) he is identified with the staller), 822, 956; (810, 816, 823); *771, 801, 809, 813, 824, 825, 916.*

Everwacer, thegn. This man held lands in So and D (*PNDB*, s.n.; *TCPB*, p. 80). Signs *CD*, 811; (816).

Freowine, thegn. Signs *CD*, 916.

Giso, bishop of Wells 1061–88. Signs *CD*, 811, 822; *809, 813, 824, 825.*

Godmann, priest. This is the chaplain of King Edward and the father of Godric, abbot of Winchcombe (Symeon of Durham, II, 171). He is probably the Godman *presbyter* who held lands in D (*PNDB, s.n.*). Signs *CD*, 791; (*767*).

Godric, abbot of Winchcombe 1054–*ca.* 1069. Signs *HLC*, pp. 247–8; *CD* (*823*); *785, 801.*

Godric, prior of Christchurch, Canterbury. Signs *CD*, 773.

Godric, priest. This is likely a monk of Worcester. Signs *HLC*, pp. 247–8.

Godric, deacon. This is likely a monk of Worcester. Signs *HLC*, pp. 247–8.

Godric, thegn. This is probably Godric of Burham (K), a privileged landholder (*PNDB, s.n.*; *ASC*, p. 439). Signs *CD*, 773; (*769*).

Godric, thegn. This is Godric, the son of Carl, another landholder in K (*ASC*, p. 398). Signs *CD* (*769*).

Godric, thegn. This is Godric, the sheriff of Br (*CD*, 840, 945; *VCH*, Br, I, 293–4, 331–4, 348–50; *NC*, IV, 22–24, 494–6). Signs *CD*, 781; *FASM*, II, Exeter xii.

Godric, thegn. This is a lawman of L (*LD*, pp. xxix, xxxii, and 3, no. 1). Signs *CD*, 808 (*filius Eadgyfu*), 956.

Godric, thegn. This is probably Godric *finc* who held 7 hides at Charlton, Wo (*ASC*, p. 461). Signs *HLC*, pp. 247–8.

Godsunu, thegn. This name must be corrupt. Signs *CD* (*767*).

Godwine, bishop at St. Martin's, Canterbury, *ca.* 1049–61. The date of his appointment is uncertain but he was probably made bishop when Siward resigned (*ASChr*, C 1048, D 1049; *FlWig*, 1049). His signature does not occur on the charters unless he is the Godwine meant on *CD, 825.*

Godwine, bishop of Rochester 995–1046. There may possibly have been two incumbents of this see with this name in this period, but Knowles lists only one (*The Monastic Order*, p. 698). Signs *CD*, 773, 784; (*769*); *771.*

Godwine, abbot of Winchcombe *ca.* 1042–53. Signs *CD*, 797; *FASM*, II, Exeter xii; *CD*, *771, 785, 912, 916, 939.*

Godwine, earl of Wessex *ca.* 1018–53. Signs *CD*, 768, 773, 774, 775, 776, 780, 781, 783, 784, 787, 788, 791, 797, 807, 1332, 1335; *FASM*, II, Exeter xii; *CD* (*767, 769, 770, 778, 792, 793, 796*); *771, 772, 779, 786, 794, 801, 912, 916, 939.*

Godwine, priest. It is difficult to identify this man unless he be the above bishop at St. Martin's, whose appointment is sometimes dated 1050 or 1051 (*BKN*). This would permit his signing the genuine charter. Signs *CD*, 791; (*792, 793*); *800.*

Godwine, deacon. This is likely a monk of Worcester. Signs *HLC*, pp. 247–8.

Godwine, thegn. There was a sheriff of So by this name (*CD*, 834–6, 838) and he almost certainly is the witness on these charters. Signs *CD*, 787, 1332; *FASM*, II, Exeter xii; *CD*, *813, 916.*

Godwine, thegn. The Godwine *praepositus civitatis Oxnafordi* of *CD*, 950, is likely the man who attests *CD* (*793*) as *praepositus civitatis.*

Godwine, thegn. A Kentish thegn who probably witnessed *CD* (*770*) (*CrawCol*, p. 151).

Grimcytel, bishop of Selsey 1039–47. Signs *CD*, 768, 774, 775, 776, 780, 781, 784; (*767, 778*); *771, 779.*

Gyrth, earl of East Anglia 1057–66. Signs *CD*, 811; *HLC*, pp. 300–2; *CD* (810, 816, 817); *771, 801, 813, 815, 824, 825.*

Hakon, thegn. This will be a L thegn (*LD*, index *s*. Hacon). Signs *CD*, 819.

Harold, earl of Wessex and later king. It is not definitely known when Harold became an earl, but judging from the charters, he signs as an earl for the first time in 1045. However, he is mentioned as earl in a will whose date is probably 1044 (*ASW*, XXXI and p. 192). Dr. Harmer has suggested that the conflicting dates for Harold's earldom are probably to be explained by differing dates for the beginning of the year. She dates his appointment 1044/5 (*Writs*, p. 563). He signs *CD*, 776 and 780, as *minister*, but 781 as *dux*. Signs *CD*, 776, 780, 781, 787, 791, 806, 808, 811, 819, 822, 956; *FASM*, II, Exeter xii; *HLC*, pp. 300–2; *CD* (792, 793, 796, 810, 816, 817, 823); *785, 786, 800, 801, 809, 813, 815, 824, 825, 916, 939, 963, 964.*

Heca, bishop of Selsey 1047–57. He was a royal chaplain before his appointment (*FlWig*, 1047). Signs *CD*, 956; (792, 793).

Herdingus, thegn. He was the son of Eadnoð staller (*NC*, IV, 515, *ASC*, p. 489) and held in So and Br. He signs only twice, once as *pincerna* on the doubtful *CD* (816), and again as *reginae pincerna* on the spurious *CD*, *813.*

Hereman, bishop of Ramsbury 1045–55. He resigned in the latter year but later became bishop of Ramsbury-Sherborne 1058–78, and transferred that see to Old Sarum in 1075 (*Writs*, p. 563–4). He was a royal chaplain (*FlWig*, 1045). Signs *CD*, 776, 780, 781, 783, 784, 787, 791, 811, 822, 956, 1335; (767, 792, 793, 796, 798, 810, 816); *786, 800, 801, 813, 824, 825.*

Hugo (Hugelinus), thegn. He seems to have been King Edward's chamberlain, His lands lay in Hu, Br, O, and Wa (*VCH*, Hu, I, 354a). Signs *CD* (810 (*camerarius*), 823); *771, 809* (*cubicularius*).

Iadulf, thegn. There is an Iadulf (or Eadwulf) in Y (*DB*, Y, 329) but I doubt that it is the present witness. It may be that the Iadulf who witnesses these documents is the Eadwulf who was prominent in the rising against Walcher of Durham in 1080 (*NC*, IV, 456–7). He may also have been some L thegn. Signs *CD*, 806, 808, 819.

Ingold, thegn. Signs *CD*, *801.*

Leofcild, thegn. This may have been a sheriff of Essex (*CD*, 869, 870; *Writs*, pp. 564–5; *ASW*, p. 191). Signs *CD*, 788; (769).

Leofnoð. It is difficult to identify this man. Feilitzen suggests a Co thegn (*PNDB*, *s.n.*). Signs *HLC*, 300–2; *CD* (770).

Leofric, bishop of the united sees of Cornwall and Devon 1046–72. His episcopal seat was at Crediton until 1050, when for greater security he removed it to Exeter (*Writs*, p. 565). He was a royal chaplain (*FlWig*, 1046) and probably attests *CD* (767) as priest. *FASM*, II, Exeter xii, records the grant of Dawlish, D, made by the Confessor to him (cf. *DB*, D, 101b). He also signs *CD*, 784, 787, 811, 956; *HLC*, pp. 300–2; *CD* (792, 793, 796, 798, 810, 816, 817); *786, 800, 801, 813, 824, 825, 963.*

Leofric, abbot of Peterborough 1052–66. He was a nephew of Earl Leofric. He also held the abbeys of Burton, Coventry, Croyland, and Thorney. On his pluralism see Darlington, "Ecclesiastical Reform," p. 403. Signs *CD*, 956; *785, 813, 824, 825.*

Leofric, earl of Mercia 1023/32–57. On the date of his appointment see *Writs*, p. 565. Signs *CD*, 768, 773, 775, 776, 780, 781, 783, 784, 787, 788, 791, 797, 805, 807, 1332, 1335; *FASM*, II, Exeter xii; *CD* (769, 770, 778, 792, 793, 796, 823); *771, 772, 779, 785, 786, 794, 800, 818, 912, 916.*

Leofric, priest. Two priests of this name sign *CD* (767). One is probably the Leofric who became bishop of Exeter, but who the other is I do not know and the name may have been repeated in error.

Leofric, thegn. There is a Leofric who is referred to as *praepositus* holding in Wo (*PNDB, s.n.*) who may be the same man as the one Kemble makes sheriff of that county (*Saxons*, II, 168). There is also a Leofric, brother of Leofnoð and son of Osmund (*CD*, 950), who held in Bd, but the name is such a common one that identification is difficult (*PNDB, s.n.*). Signs *CD* (767), *916.*

Leofsige, abbot of Ely. His dates are usually given as 1029–45, but Miss Robertson argues that this may be wrong and that he did not die until 1054 or 1055 (*ASC*, p. 467). Dr. Harmer, while rejecting Miss Robertson's actual arguments, agrees on other grounds in dating Leofsige's death in 1055 (*Writs*, p. 566). Signs *CD*, 774, 775, 956; (769, 778); *800, 801.* There is a second abbot Leofsige signing with him on *CD*, 956, but I have no idea who this could be (cf. *ASC*, p. 467).

Leofsige, thegn. It is difficult to say who this is. It might be *homo Tosti comitis* in Bd. Signs *CD* (778).

Leofstan, abbot of Bury St. Edmunds 1044–65. Signs *CD* (810), *813.* Another abbot of this name signs the latter and spurious charter, but no other is known.

Leofweard, abbot of Muchelney, before and after the Conquest (*ASC*, p. 488; *DB*, So 91). Signs *CD* (816).

Leofwine, bishop of Lichfield 1053–70 (Tait, "An Alleged Charter of William the Conqueror," pp. 155–8). He was previously abbot of Coventry. Signs *CD*, 956; (816, 823), *813, 964.*

Leofwine, earl. The date of his appointment and the territories embraced by his earldom are uncertain. Freeman argued that he was appointed *ca.* 1057 (*NC*, II, 382–3, 583–5). The earliest instance in which his signature as *dux* occurs, with the exception of the spurious *CD*, *771*, is *HLC*, pp. 300–2 (1059). It cannot be asserted that wherever the signature *Leofwine minister* occurs it is that of the future earl, although it is possible that he was old enough to sign at the beginning of the reign of the Confessor. He held lands chiefly in K, Sx, So, D, Mx, Ha, and Bk. He was killed at Hastings 1066. Signs as *minister* or *nobilis CD*, 787; *FASM*, II, Exeter xii; *CD* (767, 769, 792, 793); *800*; as *dux HLC*, pp. 300–2; *CD* (810, 816, 817); *771, 809, 813, 815, 824, 825, 963.*

Leofwine, thegn. The one who signs *CD* (962) is called *filius* Æstan, and is mentioned in *DB* as holding lands in Bk and Nt (*PNDB, s.n.*). This may be the man who signs *HLC*, pp. 300–2. If it is not, identification is difficult (see *PNDB, s.n.*; *VCH*, Bk, I, 275).

Locre (*Locar*), thegn. There is only one man of this name in *DB* and he held lands in Nt (*DB*, Nt, 285). Signs *CD*, 819.

Lyfing, bishop of Crediton and Cornwall 1027–46, of Worcester 1038–46. Signs

CD, 768, 774, 775, 776, 780, 781, 1332; *FASM*, II, Exeter xii; *CD* (767, 769, 770, 778); *771, 772, 779, 912, 916*.

Lyfing, priest. This is possibly the *presbyter homo Eddeue* of Ht (*DB*, Ht, 137). Signs *CD* (792, 793).

Lyfing, thegn. He was the king's staller. Signs *CD*, 956; *FASM*, II, Exeter xii; *CD* (767); *801, 813* (*regis dapifer*). It is possible that the second genuine charter is not attested by the staller but by some thegn of the same name in Ha, W, or So (cf. *ASC*, p. 463, and *PNDB*, s.n.).

Mærgeat, thegn. Probably intended to be the same individual as the only one with this name in *DB*. He held lands in Lei, Wa, and L. He was the father of Æthelric (*PNDB*, s.n.). Signs *CD*, *912*.

Mærleswegen, thegn. This is the well-known sheriff of L, who had lands there and in Gl, So, Y, and D (*VCH*, Y, II, 172). Signs *CD*, 806, 808.

Manni (Wulfmær), abbot of Evesham 1044–59. Signs *CD*, 797, 807, 956; *771, 912, 916, 939*.

Manni, thegn. There is a Manni, father of Wulfsige, holding lands in Mx, and a Manni the Swarthy in Sf (*PNDB*, s.n.). Signs *FASM*, II, Exeter xii.

Morcar, earl of Northumbria 1065–71. His signature appears only twice (*CD*, *916* (min) and *825* (comes)), in both cases on spurious charters.

Nefetofi, thegn. I am unable to identify this man. Probably the name is corrupt. Signs *CD* (792, 793); *800*.

Norðmann, thegn. There is a Norðmann, sheriff of Nth (*CD*, 863, 904; *PNDB*, s.n.; Morris, *Sheriff*, p. 35), but the name is common and it is difficult to say who signs the genuine charter. Signs *HLC*, pp. 247–8; *CD* (816).

Odda, earl of Devon, Somerset, Dorset, and Cornwall 1051, and he may have been earl of Worcester and Gloucester after Godwin's return (*ASC*, pp. 456–8. *VCH*, Wo, I, 260, says he belonged to the foreign party). He was a kinsman of King Edward (*NC*, II, 380). He died 1056. Signs most of these charters as *minister, nobilis*, or *miles*. He signs *CD*, 797, as monk, but as Miss Robertson has argued this may be the result of a scribal error, *mon* for *min* (*ASC*, p. 457). As *dux* he signs *CD*, 805; he also appears as such in *CD*, 804, and *FAC*, IV, 32. Signs *CD*, 768, 774, 775, 776, 780, 781, 787, 791, 805, 1332; *FASM*, II, Exeter xii; *CD* (767, 769, 770, 778); *771, 779*.

Ordgar. On most of these charters the witness would seem to be the *Ordgar Deuonensis* of the spurious *CD*, *939*: he was the brother of Ælfgar (*q.v.*) and held in southwest England. He must have been an important royal thegn. *CD*, 1332, grants a D estate to Ordgar. There is an Ordgar, sheriff of C (Morris, *Sheriff*, p. 35), but I cannot connect him with these charters. Signs *CD*, 768, 774, 775, 776, 780, 781, 783, 787, 1332; *FASM*, II, Exeter xii; *CD* (767, 769, 770, 778); *771, 779, 939*.

Ordlaf, thegn. I am unable to find another example of this name in the reign of the Confessor, although it occurs in earlier times, e.g., Ordlaf the earl in 901 (*GP*, p. 395): *CD*, 901, must be addressed to this earl by Edward the Elder and not by the Confessor. Signs *CD*, 787.

Ordric, abbot of Abingdon ca. 1052–66 (*Chron Abingdon*, I, 464, 482). Signs *CD*, 822; (792, 796, 810, 817); *800, 813*.

Ordwig, thegn. Miss Robertson identifies him as the man who held Acton Beauchamp of the church of Worcester (*ASC*, p. 459). Signs *CD*, 807, *823*.

Ordwulf, thegn. The name occurs frequently in the D and So entries of *DB* (*PNDB*, *s.n.*). Signs *CD*, 774, 775, 787, 791; *HLC*, pp. 300–2; *FASM*, II, Exeter xii; *CD*, *771*, *779*.

Osbeorn, chaplain. The man meant is very likely the one who later became bishop of Exeter (1074–1103), and was an intimate of King Edward (*GP*, p. 201; *VCH*, Sr, I, 281). Signs *CD*, *815*, *825*.

Osbeorn, thegn. This is probably the son of Richard Fitz Scrob. He held lands in He, Wo, and Sa (*Writs*, p. 569). Signs *CD* (778).

Osbert, canon of St. Mary, Rouen. I have no information on this man, but he must have been the agent of his church in connection with the subject matter of the charter he signs, *CD* (810).

Osgar, thegn. He may be Osgar *de Bedeford* (*DB*, Bd, 218) or the reference may possibly be to Esgar staller (*q.v.*). Signs *CD*, 1335.

Osgod, thegn. This is probably the Osgod Clapa who was the king's staller and held land in the eastern counties. He was outlawed in 1046 (*ASW*, p. 196). Signs *CD*, 768, 774, 775, 776, 780, 781, 783, 1335; *FASM*, II, Exeter xii; *CD* (767, 769, 770, 778); *771*, *772*, *779*.

Osgod, thegn. This is Osgod *apud Heailea* (Hagley, Wo; *PNDB*, *s.* Ásgautr). Signs *CD*, 805, 807; (823).

Osmær, thegn. This is probably a D thegn (*ASC*, pp. 448–9). Signs *CD*, 787, 1332; *FASM*, II, Exeter xii; *CD* (770).

Oswulf, thegn. This is probably Oswulf *filius Frane tegnus regis E.*, who had lands in Ht and Bk (*PNDB*, *s.n.*). Signs *CD*, 787; (778).

Oswulf, thegn. This is Oswulf *fila*, a thegn of E (*ASW*, p. 191). Signs *CD*, 787, 788.

Owine, thegn. This must be a thegn of Wo, but I have no information on him. Signs *CD*, 805; *912*.

Owine, thegn. This individual may be, as Miss Robertson thinks (*ASC*, p. 468), a lawman of Lincoln. If that is so it is likely the Owine referred to in *LD*, p. 64, no. 29. Signs *CD*, 956.

Peter, priest. This is probably the chaplain of the Confessor, and later of the Conqueror, who became bishop of Lichfield (1072–85). On him see *VCH*, Br, I, 300; *VCH*, So, I, 406, 471b, 522. Signs *CD*, 791; *813*, *815*, *825*.

Ralph, earl of Hereford *ca.* 1050–7. He was a nephew of the Confessor and is said to have accompanied him to England. Signs *CD*, 791, 956; (792, 793, 796); *785*, *800*.

Ralph, thegn. He was the king's staller under Edward and possibly an earl under William, dying *ca.* 1070. His lands lay in Nf, Sf, Co, and L (*ASC*, pp. 463–4; White, *Complete Peerage*, IX, 568–71). Signs *CD*, 791 (*minister*), 808 (*regis dapifer*), 811 (*minister*), 822, 956 (both as staller); (810, 816, both as *minister*); *801*, *813*, *824*, *825*, *916*.

Regenbald, priest. He seems to have been the most important of the king's chaplains in the latter part of Edward's reign, and is often, after the Conquest, called chancellor. Whether he had this title under the Confessor is a much debated question, for most of the documents in which he appears as such are either of doubtful authenticity (e.g., *CD*, 809, 813, 824, 825, 891; *ASC*, CXVIII) or post-Conquest (*DB*, He, 180b). He held lands in He, Bk, Do, So, Br, and Wo. Signs *CD*, 791 (*presbyter*), (792, 793, 796 (all as *presbyter*), 810 (*regis sigillarius*)); *800* (*presbyter*), *815* (no title), *809, 813, 824, 825* (all as *cancellarius*).

Robert, archbishop of Canterbury 1051–2. He was bishop of London 1044–51, and all the signatures below are from that period. He never signs as archbishop. Signs *CD*, 784, 791; (792, 793); *785, 800.*

Robert fitz Wymarc, thegn. This is the well-known staller of King Edward (*NC*, II, 230; *CD*, 859; *Feudal Documents*, p. xcii). It cannot be proved that he was sheriff of E, as Freeman thought (*NC*, II, 230), but cf. Morris, *Sheriff*, p. 37 and the authorities there cited. He is likely the *Rotbert* and *Rodbeard* of *CD*, 811 (*TCPB*, p. 80) and *810*. He held lands in E, Sf, W, So, He, Hu, Sa, Ht, and C. Signs *CD*, 811; (810, 816 (*procur.*)); *771, 809, 813* (*regis consanguineus*), *815* (staller), *824, 825, 916.*

Rodbeorht, priest. I do not know who this is, unless it be Bishop Robert of Hereford (1079–95). Signs *CD* (792, 793, 796); *800, 825.*

Rymhtricus, thegn. The name must be corrupt; should possibly be Brihtric. Signs *CD*, 791.

Sæweald, abbot of Bath *ca.* 1065–77 (*RB*, LII, 98). Signs *CD* (816).

Siferth, thegn. Abbot Brand had a kinsman of this name in Lincoln (*LD*, p. xliv, cf. p. xlii). Miss Robertson thinks he was a lawman of Lincoln (*ASC*, p. 468). Signs *CD*, 956.

Sihtric, abbot of Tavistock 1046–82. Signs *CD*, 787; *813.*

Siric, thegn. This is possibly the L man mentioned in *LD*, p. 200, no. 5, and p. 201, nos. 12, 13. Miss Robertson thinks he was a lawman of Lincoln (*ASC*, p. 468). Signs *CD*, 956.

Siweard, coadjutor bishop to Eadsige, archbishop of Canterbury, 1044–8. He was abbot of Abingdon and signs the first six charters as abbot, the next two as bishop, and the rest as archbishop. Signs *CD*, 773, 774, 775; (767, 769); *916*; 784; (778); 776, 780, 781, 783, 1335.

Siweard, bishop of Rochester, 1058–75. He was abbot of Chertsey (*ca.* 1042–58) before he became bishop (*RB*, LII, 97–98) and signs the first six charters as abbot. Signs *CD*, 776, 780, 1332; (769, 778); 779; (810); *824, 825, 963.*

Siweard, earl of Northumbria *ca.* 1033–55. Signs *CD*, 768, 774, 775, 776, 780, 781, 784, 787, 791, 797, 956, 1332; *FASM*, II, Exeter xii; *CD* (767, 770, 778, 792, 793, 796, 962); *772, 779, 785, 794, 800, 818, 912, 916, 939.*

Siweard, thegn. This is probably the Siweard who held in Wo and He and was a kinsman of King Edward (*VCH*, Wo, I, 321a). Signs *CD* (823).

Siweard, thegn. This may be the Siweard Bearn who held in Br, Db, and elsewhere (*PNDB*, s. Sigeweard). Signs *CD* (816); *813, 824, 825.*

Spearhafoc, abbot of Abingdon 1048–50, and bishop-elect of London 1051. Signs *CD* (793).

Stigand, archbishop of Canterbury 1052–70. He was previously bishop of Elmham (1044–7), and bishop of Winchester (1047–70). Signs *CD*, 773, 784, 787, 788 (as priest), 791, 797, 806, 808, 811, 819, 956; *HLC*, pp. 300–2; (792, 793, 796, 798, 810, 816, 817); *786, 800, 801, 813, 815, 824, 825, 912, 963, 964.*

Swegen, earl of Oxfordshire, Gloucestershire, Herefordshire, Somersetshire, and Berkshire. He was the oldest son of Godwin, and seems to have been made earl as early as 1043. He was outlawed in 1049, returned to England in 1050, and shared the outlawry of his father in 1051. He died 1052 on his way home from a pilgrimage. I think the signature *Swegen* of *CD* (962) is his, prior to his appointment as earl. Signs *CD*, 768, 774, 775, 776, 780, 781, 784; *FASM*, II, Exeter xii; *CD* (767, 769, 770, 778, 962); *771, 779, 912, 916.*

Swegen, thegn. Signs *CD, 815.*

Swithgar, notarius. His signature appears only on spurious charters. Signs *CD, 809, 813, 824.*

Thored, thegn. This man is difficult to identify. I cannot think that he is the same man (or one of two) who signs Kentish charters under Cnut (*ASC*, pp. 410–11). Feilitzen identifies him as the Thored to whom the doubtful *CD* (778) grants Ditchampton, W, and who is mentioned as a benefactor of St. Mary, Winchester, in *DB*, W, 68. But this does not tell us much about the thegn, if he is our man. Signs *CD*, 774, 775, 776, 780; (778); *771.*

Thurgisl. This is likely King Edward's thegn in Bd (*PNDB, s.n.*). Signs *CD* (962).

Thurgod, thegn. He is called *lagen* and seems to have been one of the lawmen of L (*LD*, p. 95, no. 1; p. 96, no. 7; p. 97, no. 13; p. 99, no. 29; p. 187, no. 6; Steenstrup, *Danelag*, p. 197; *ASC*, p. 468). He held lands in Y, Nt, O, and L. Signs *CD*, 956.

Thuri, earl. The only earl with this name is the *Ðuri comes* who held under Hardecnut (*NC*, I, 347, II, 375–6), and who may possibly have lived until *ca.* 1044 (*NC*, II, 375–6). If this is so, he could sign *CD, 962* and, if my dating is correct, 797. These are the only two charters from the reign of the Confessor on which his name occurs. On his earlier signatures see *Writs*, p. 574.

Thurkill, thegn. This is probably a thegn in Br (*VCH*, Br, I, 294, 351b). The name, however, is a common one, e.g., *Turchillus uuit* of He (*PNDB, s.* Þorkell; *ASC*, p. 400) and *Turchil the Dane,* "one of the leading thegns of the eastern Midlands" (*VCH*, Hu, I, 330). Signs *FASM*, II, Exeter xii; *CD* (767, 778).

Thurstan, thegn. I do not know who this is unless it be the EA thegn whose bequests are contained in *CD*, 788, and *ASW*, XXXI. Signs *FASM*, II, Exeter xii.

Tofi, thegn. This is, I think, the Tofi who was at one time (from *ca.* 1061 until sometime after the Conquest) the sheriff of So (*CD*, 821, 837, 839; *Writs*, p. 575; Morris, *Sheriff*, p. 35). He is sometimes confused with Tofi the Proud, who, it cannot be denied, could have signed the second and third charters. I think this unlikely because of their provenance. On the two men see *ASC*, p. 400; *ASW*, p. 186; *NC*, I, 521–2. Signs *CD*, 791, 1332; *FASM*, II, Exeter xii; *CD* (767, 778, 792, 816); *800.*

Toki, thegn. It is difficult to identify this man. There is a large landowner of this name, the son of Outi, who held lands in Nth, Lei, Db, Nt, Y, and L. Steenstrup thinks he was a lawman (*Danelag*, p. 197; cf. *LD*, p. xxx). Then there is the well-known Toki, the father of Aki. The latter had trouble with Bishop Ealdred of Worcester (*CD*, 805; cf. *CrawCol*, p. 144; *ASC*, pp. 447–8). King Edward had a huscarl of this name (*DB*, Mx, 129). It is not certain, however, that any of these men sign these charters (cf. *PNDB*, *s.n.*). Signs *CD*, 1332; (767).

Tostig, earl of Northumbria 1055–65. He was outlawed in 1065 and died at Stamford Bridge in 1066. Signs as *minister CD*, 787, 791; *FASM*, II, Exeter xii; *CD* (767, 792, 793, 796); *800*; as *dux CD*, 806, 808, 811, 822; *HLC*, pp. 300–2; *CD* (810, 816, 817); *771, 785, 801, 813, 815, 818, 916, 963*.

Toti, thegn. I am unable to identify this man, unless he be Toti, the father of Azur, who held in Bk (*PNDB*, *s.n.*). Signs *CD* (767).

Ufic, thegn. I am unable to identify this man, but he may have been from E (cf. *ASW*, pp. 191–2). Signs *CD*, 788.

Ulf, bishop of Dorchester *ca.* 1049–52. Signs *CD* (792, 793, 796); *794, 800*.

Ulf, thegn. He is called "son of Tofi" and occurs frequently in *LD* (see pp. xiv, xli–xliv, lxxxviii, and the index *s.* Ulf, Tope sune; cf. also *ASW*, pp. 207–8). An Ulf was sheriff of Mx (*CD*, 843), and a portreeve of London (*CD*, 872; Round, *Geoffrey de Mandeville*, pp. 353–4). As far as I know none of the portreeves of London attest charters, but writs are addressed to them (see Kemble, *Saxons*, II, 174). The first is certainly our man. Signs *CD*, 806, 819; *815*.

Ulf, thegn. He is called Ulf of Lincoln and is probably identical with *Ulf fenisc*, a very large landowner in the Danelaw. Steenstrup thinks he was a lawman (*Danelag*, p. 197), but this is not certain, although his importance cannot be denied (cf. *LD*, pp. xxxi, xxxvii, and the index *s.* Ulf, Fenisc of Fünen). Signs *CD*, 806, 808.

Ulfcytell, thegn. This is most likely the U. *cild* of C (*ASW*, XXXI, p. 194), or the U. who was sheriff of He (*CD*, 802), but there are many men with this name (*PNDB*, *s.* Úlfkell). Signs *FASM*, II, Exeter xii; *CD* (767); *916*.

Vikingr. This may be a landholder from Sf (*DB*, Sf, 375b, 376) or a *homo comitis Haroldi* of C (*ASW*, pp. 194–5). Again it may be neither of these men. Signs *CD* (816).

Wagen, thegn. This is probably the Wagen who held lands in Wo and was one of the men of Earl Leofric (*ASC*, p. 458; *CrawCol*, p. 144). He may be the same man as the Wagen who held Wooten Wawen (*VCH*, Wa, I, 284). Signs *CD*, 805; *939*.

Walter, bishop of Hereford 1061–79. He was a royal chaplain (*GP*, p. 300). Signs *CD* (816, 823); *809, 813, 824, 825*.

Walter, no title but probably thegn. Signs *CD*, *815*.

Waltheof, earl of Northumbria 1065–75. He only held part of this earldom under the Confessor. Signs *CD* (810, 816).

Wigot, thegn. This is a very wealthy landowner of Wallingford (Br) who had lands in Sx, Sr, Ha, Br, Ht, and Bk (*PNDB*, *s.* Vigot). He was a kinsman of King Edward (*CD*, 862; *EHR*, LI, 99). It is not at all certain that Wigot was sheriff of O, as Freeman (*NC*, IV, 497) would make him, for the bulk of his land seems to have lain elsewhere. (*PNDB*, *s.* Vigot; *NC*, IV, 497–9; cf. *EHR*, XLVIII, 14, where Darlington writes: "In some instances magnates addressed by name are not known to have held land in the region concerned, and it is reasonable to regard them as royal officials." Darlington is speaking of post-Conquest times, but the same would apply to pre-Conquest England.) However, it does not seem possible to arrive at a definite conclusion. In any case his signature occurs only on one doubtful charter and three spurious ones. Signs *CD* (816); *813, 824, 825*.

Wigot, thegn. He is called Wigot of Lincoln (see *LD*, p. 241, no. 16). Signs *CD*, 809, 819.

Wihtsige, thegn. I do not know who this man is unless he be Wynsige (*q.v.*). Signs *CD* (793); *800*.

William, bishop of London 1051–75. He was a royal chaplain (*FlWig*, 1051), and signs the first three charters as priest. Signs *CD* (792, 793); *800*; 811, 956; (816, 817); *813, 815, 824, 825, 912, 963.*

Wistan, abbot of Gloucester. His dates are given as 1058–72 (*Historia et cartularium monasterii Sancti Petri Gloucestriae*, I, 9), but I am not certain that they are right. A Wistan *sacerdos* signs a Wo charter (*HLC*, pp. 247–8, which I have dated 1060). This may not be the same man. A Wistan monk signs *CD*, 797, 807. Wistan signs as abbot only the doubtful *CD* (823) and the spurious *964*.

Wulfbeald, thegn. Men with this name held lands in Sf and Sx. Signs *CD* (769).

Wulfgar, thegn. This is probably *Wulger æt Hiwerc* of *CD*, 897, a So thegn (*PNDB*, *s.n.*). Signs *FASM*, II, Exeter xii.

Wulfmær, thegn. This may be intended to be a Nf thegn. Freeman says he was a sheriff (*NC*, V, 543). Signs *CD*, *912*.

Wulfnoð, abbot of Westminster 1032–49. Signs *CD*, 773; *779*.

Wulfnoð, thegn. It is difficult to identify this man. Edward had a huscarl of this name (*CD*, 845) who is probably the same man as the king's thegn who held lands in Ha (*DB*, Ha, 53b, 54). In *CD*, 843, a Thurstan huscarl is called *praefectus palatinus* in the Latin version of the writ. This may explain why Wulfnoð is called *praefectus* in *CD*, 767. Signs *HLC*, pp. 300–2; *CD* (767, 770); *772.*

Wulfric, abbot of Ely 1045–65. Miss Robertson thinks Wulfric's appointment may be dated ten years too early (*ASC*, p. 467). He is said to have been a kinsman of Edward (*NC*, III, 68). Signs *CD* (817); *813.*

Wulfric, abbot of St. Augustine, Canterbury, 1045–61. Signs *CD*, 773; (810).

Wulfric, thegn. This is probably intended to be Wulfric *æt Wernæforda* (Warnford, Ha) (*PNDB*, *s.n.*). Signs *CD*, *824, 825.*

Wulfsige, bishop of Lichfield 1039–53. Signs *CD*, 774, 775, 776, 780, 781, 797; (798); *771, 785, 912, 916, 939.*

Wulfsige, abbot of Chertsey. His dates are uncertain, but he signs between 1042 and 1045 (*ASC*, p. 418). Signs *CD* (767, 778).

Wulfsige, thegn. This might be the Wulfsige *þæs cynges gerefa* of *CD*, 789 (*ASC*, p. 440), but nothing more is known of him. I suspect that our man is a So thegn of King Edward (*PNDB*, *s.n.*). Signs *FASM*, II, Exeter xii.

Wulfstan, bishop of Worcester 1062–95. Signs *CD*, 797, 807 (both as monk); *HLC*, pp. 247–8 (as *sacerdos*); (816, 823); *771, 801, 809, 824, 825.*

Wulfstan, thegn. Signs *CD*, *800.*

Wulfweald, abbot of Chertsey 1058–84. He was also abbot of Bath, where his dates would seem to be 1061–84 (cf. *RB*, LII, 97–98). Signs *CD* (810); *771, 824, 825.*

Wulfweard. This unknown abbot appears in the genuine *FASM*, II, Exeter xii, on the doubtful *CD* (769, 778, 792, 793), and on the spurious *CD*, *800.*

Wulfweard, thegn. This is likely Wulfweard the White who held lands in K, Mx, Bk, O, Gl, W, Ha, So, Do, and possibly Br and L (*ASC*, pp. 462–3; *PNDB*, *s.n.*; *VCH*, Bk, I, 216–17). Signs *FASM*, II, Exeter xii; *CD*, *801*, *825*.

Wulfwig, bishop of Dorchester 1053–67. Some years after the Conquest the episcopal seat of Dorchester was moved to Lincoln (*NC*, IV, 285). Davis confuses Wulfwig with Ulf the Norman, who was promoted to Dorchester in 1049 (*Regesta*, pp. xiii–xiv). Signs *CD*, 806, 808, 819; (816); *779*, *801*, *813*, *818*, *824*, *825*, *963* (*cancellarius*).

Wulfwig, monk of Worcester. Signs *CD*, 797; *HLC*, pp. 247–8 (*sacerdos*).

Wynsige, thegn. He was the king's chamberlain (*camerarius*) (Larson, *King's Household*, p. 129; *PNDB*, *s.n.*). He held in Bd and Bk. He is usually called Wenesi. Signs *CD* (816 (*cubicularius*), 823). He may also sign *CD* (793); *800*.

Yfingus, regis dapifer. This seems an error for Lyfing (*q.v.*). Signs *CD*, *813*.

Number and Classification of Witnesses on the Charters

I. Number and Classification of Witnesses on Genuine Charters:

Title	Royal charters		Private charters	
King	18		8	
Queen	7		4	
Queen Mother	3		3	
	——	28	——	15
Archbishop	33		8	
Bishop	97		27	
Abbot	45		21	
Priest	4		7	
Dean	1		4	
Monk	4		2	
	——	184	——	69
Earl	66		17	
Thegn	163*		37**	
Reeve or sheriff	1		1	
Regis dapifer or staller	2		7	
Consiliarius	2		..	
	——	234	——	62
Total		446		146

* Or 168 if we count thegns designated by titles of royal officials.
** Or 45 if we count thegns designated by titles of royal officials.

II. Number and Classification of Witnesses on Doubtful Charters:

Title	Royal charters		Private charters	
King	11		2	
Queen	4		..	
Queen Mother	1		1	
	—	16	—	3
Archbishop	17		1	
Bishop	70		5	
Abbot	43		3	
Priest	23		1	
Chancellor	1		..	
Canon	1		..	
	—	155	—	10
Earl	46		4	
Thegn	106*		20	
Reeve or sheriff	11		..	
Camerarius	1		..	
Regis procurator aulae	4		..	
Pincerna	2		..	
Cubicularius	1		..	
	—	171	—	24
Total		342		37

* Or 125 if we count thegns designated by titles of royal officials.

III. Number and Classification of Witnesses on Spurious Charters:

Title	Royal charters		Private charters	
King	15		4	
Queen	9		2	
Queen Mother	3		..	
	—	27	—	6
Archbishop	28		6	
Bishop	98		8	
Abbot	67		12	
Priest	6		..	
Deacon	1		..	
Chancellor	5		..	
Notarius	3		..	
Chaplain	5		..	
	—	213	—	26
Earl	68		14	
Thegn	102*		5	
Reeve or sheriff	2		..	
Regis dapifer or staller	6		..	
Reginae dapifer	1		..	
Camerarius	1		..	
Cubicularius	4		..	
Procurator aulae regis	1		..	
Regis pincerna	1		..	
Regis aulicus	1		..	
Regis palatinus	1		..	
Regis consanguineus	2		..	
	—	190	—	19
Total		430		51

* Or 119 if we count thegns designated by titles of royal officials.

List of Archbishops Attesting Charters

Name and see	Number of attestations on charters	
	Genuine	Doubtful
Ælfric, York, 1023–51	13	4
Cynesige, York, 1051–60	4	..
Eadsige, Canterbury, 1038–50	9	7
Ealdred, York, 1060–9	3	4
(bishop of Worcester, 1046–62)	8	4
Robert, Canterbury, 1051–2	none	none
(bishop of London, 1044–51)	2	2
Siweard, coadjutor bishop at St. Martin's, Canterbury, 1044–8	5	..
(abbot of Abingdon)	3	2
(as bishop)	1	1
Stigand, Canterbury, 1052–70	6	4
(bishop of Elmham, 1044–7) (bishop of Winchester, 1047–70)	5	3
(as priest)	1	..

List of Bishops Attesting Charters

Name	Number of attestations on charters		
	Genuine	Doubtful	Spurious*
Ælfweald, Sherborne, 1045/6–58	4	2	..
Ælfweard, London, 1035–44	4	1	..
Ælfwine, Winchester, 1032–47	12	4	..
Æthelmær, Elmham, 1047–70	1	1	..
Æthelric, Durham, 1042–56	..	..	x
Æthelric, Selsey, 1057–70	..	2	..
Æthelstan, Hereford, 1012–56	8	3	..
Æthelwine, Durham, 1056–71	..	..	x
Beorhtweald, Ramsbury, 1005–45	5	3	..
Beorhtwine, Sherborne, 1023–45	5	1	..
Duduc, Wells, 1033–60	14	4	..
Eadnoð, Dorchester, 1034–49	7	4	..
Giso, Wells, 1061–88	2	..	..
Godwine, St. Martin's, Canterbury, 1049–61	..	..	x
Godwine, Rochester, 995–1046	2	1	..
Grimcytel, Selsey, 1039–47	7	2	..
Heca, Selsey, 1047–57	1	2	..
Hereman, { Ramsbury, 1045–55, 1058–78 / Sherborne. 1058–78 }	11	7	..
Leofric, { Crediton, 1046–50 / Cornwall, 1046–72 / Exeter, 1050–72 }	5	8	..
Leofwine, Lichfield, 1053–70	1	2	..
Lyfing, { Crediton and Cornwall, 1027–46 / Worcester, 1038–46 }	8	4	..
Siweard, Rochester, 1058–75	..	1	..
(as abbot of Chertsey, ca. 1042–58)	3	2	..
Ulf, Dorchester, 1049–52	..	3	..
Walter, Hereford, 1061–79	..	2	..
William, London, 1051–75	2	2	..
(as priest)	..	2	..
Wulfsige, Lichfield, 1039–53	6	1	..
Wulfstan, Worcester, 1062–95	..	2	..
(as monk or priest)	3	..	..
Wulfwig, Dorchester, 1053–67	3	1	..

* Where the individual attests some genuine or doubtful charters I have paid no attention to the number of his spurious attestations. Where the individual's name appears only on spurious charters I have indicated this by an "x."

List of Abbots Attesting Charters

Name	Number of attestations on charters		
	Genuine	Doubtful	Spurious*
Ælfric, Pershore, 1033–55	2	..	..
Ælfsige, St. Benet of Holme, 1019–46	2	1	..
Ælfstan, St. Augustine, Canterbury, 1023/7–46	4	1	..
Ælfweard, Evesham, 1014–44	1	..	..
Ælfwig, Bath, ca. 1060–5	..	2	..
Ælfwig, New Minster, Winchester, 1063–6	..	..	x
Ælfwine, Buckfast, ca. 1046	1	1	..
Ælfwine, New Minster, Winchester, ca. 1032–57	3	..	..
Ælfwine, Ramsey, 1043–79	9	2	..
Æthelnoð, Glastonbury, 1053–78	3	2	..
Æthelsige, St. Augustine, Canterbury, 1061– ca. 1070	1	1	..
Æthelstan, Abingdon, 1044–8	4	1	..
Æthelweard, Glastonbury, ob. 1053	7	5	..
Æthelwig, Evesham, 1059–77	3	2	..
Baldwin, Bury St. Edmunds, 1065–98	..	..	x
Beorhtmær, Croyland, 1018–48/53	1	..	..
Beorhtric, Malmesbury, ca. 1062–70	..	1	..
Brand, Peterborough, 1066–9	..	..	x
Eadmund, Pershore, ca. 1060–85	1	..	..
Eadwine, Westminster, 1049–70	..	1	..
Earnwig, Peterborough, 1042–52	1	..	..
Godric, Winchcombe, 1054–ca. 1069	1	1	..
Godwine, Winchcombe, 1042–53	2	..	..
Leofric, Peterborough, 1052–66	1	..	..
Leofsige, Ely, 1029–? 1055	3	2	..
Leofsige, unknown	1	..	..
Leofstan, Bury St. Edmunds, 1044–65	..	1	..
Leofweard, Muchelney, dates unknown but before and after the Conquest	..	1	..
Manni, Evesham, 1044–59	3	..	..
Ordric, Abingdon, ? 1052–66	1	4	..
Sæweald, Bath, ? 1065–77	..	1	..
Sihtric, Tavistock, 1046–82	1	..	..
Siweard, Chertsey, ca. 1042–58	3	2	..
Siweard, Abingdon, before 1044	3	1	..
Spearhafoc, Abingdon, 1048–50	..	1	..

* Where the individual attests some genuine or doubtful charters I have paid no attention to the number of his spurious attestations. Where the individual's name appears only on spurious charters I have indicated this by an "x."

Appendix F—*continued*

Name	Genuine	Attestations Doubtful	Spurious
Wistan, Gloucester, ? 1058–72	..	1	..
Wulfnoð, Westminster, 1032–49	1	..	..
Wulfric, Ely, ? 1055–65	..	1	..
Wulfric, St. Augustine, Canterbury, 1045–61	1	1	..
Wulfsige, Chertsey, *ca.* 1042–5	..	2	..
Wulfweald, { Bath, 1061–84 Chertsey, *ca.* 1058–84 }	..	1	..
Wulfweard, unknown	1	4	..

Abbeys Whose Abbots Attest Charters

Name	Value of holdings in DB* £	s.	d.
Abingdon (Br)	462	3	3
Bath (So)**	81	13	6
Buckfast (D)	17	8	4
Bury St. Edmunds (Sf)**	639	18	4
Chertsey (Sr)	198	14	0
Croyland (L)	52	6	0
Ely (C)	768	17	3
Evesham (Wo)	129	2	3
Glastonbury (So)	827	18	8
Gloucester (Gl)**	99	0	0
Malmesbury (W)**	178	10	0
Muchelney (So)**	54	16	0
Pershore (Wo)	81	15	0
Peterborough (Nth)	323	0	8
Ramsey (Hu)	358	5	0
St. Augustine, Canterbury (K)	635	0	0
St. Benet of Holme (Nf)	96	5	4
Tavistock (D)	78	10	0
Westminster (Mx)	583	11	2
Winchcombe (Gl)	82	0	0
New Minster, Winchester (Ha)	390	4	0

* The calculation is that of Professor Knowles (*The Monastic Order*, pp. 702–3).
** Occurs only on doubtful charters.

List of Earls Attesting Charters

Name	Number of attestations on charters		
	Genuine	*Doubtful*	*Spurious**
Ælfgar, 1051–? 1065	3	1	..
(as *minister*)	1	..	..
Beorn, 1045–9	3	1	..
Eadwine, ? 1065–71	..	1	..
Godwine, 1018–53	17	7	..
Gyrth, 1057–66	2	3	..
Harold, 1045–66	11	7	..
(as *minister*)	2	..	..
Leofric, 1023/32–57	17	7	..
Leofwine, 1057–66	1	3	..
(as *minister*)	2	4	..
Morcar, 1065–71	..	..	x
Odda, 1051–6	1	..	..
(as *minister*)	11	4	..
Ralph, 1050–7	2	3	..
Siweard, 1033–55	13	7	..
Swegen, 1043–7	7	4	..
(as *minister*)	..	1	..
Thuri, *ob. ca.* 1044	1	1	..
Tostig, 1055–65	5	3	..
(as *minister*)	3	4	..
Waltheof, 1065–75	..	2	..

* Where the individual attests some genuine or doubtful charters I have paid no attention to the number of his spurious attestations. Where the individual's name occurs only on spurious charters I have indicated this by an "x."

List of Lower Clergy Attesting Charters

Name	Number of attestations on charters	
	Genuine	Doubtful
Ælfstan, monk, priest, and prior (1061), Worcester	2	..
Æthelwine, dean of Worcester	2	..
Eadweald, priest, ? Christ Church	1	1
Godmann, royal chaplain	1	1
Godric, priest of Worcester	1	..
Godric, prior of Christ Church	1	..
Godric, deacon, Worcester	1	..
Godwine, priest	1	2
Godwine, deacon of Worcester	1	..
Peter, royal chaplain, later bishop of Lichfield	1	..
Regenbald, royal chaplain	1	3
Stigand, priest, later archbishop of Canterbury	1	..
Wistan, monk and priest, Worcester, later abbot of Gloucester	3	1
Wulfstan, monk and priest, later bishop of Worcester	3	..
Wulfwig, monk and priest, Worcester	2	..

List of Thegns Attesting Charters*

Name	Location of principal lands**	Number of attestations on charters	
		Genuine	Doubtful
Ælfgar	SW	9	3
Ælfgar	Gl, Wo	1	..
Ælfgeat	Mx or So	2	3
Ælfnoð	L	2	..
Ælfric	Sf	2	2
Ælfric	So	3	..
Ælfstan	So, Do, Ha, Br, Gl, Ht, Bd, W	7	6
Ælfweald	Wo	..	1
Ælfweald	Bk, Ht	..	1
Ælfweard	Wo	..	5
Ælfweard	So	2	..
Ælfwig	Gl	..	3
Ælfwine	K	2	3
Ælfwine	Ha	1	..
Æstan	Bk	1	..
Æthelfrið	Do, So	1	1
Æthelmær	D	2	3
Æthelric	K	3	2
Æthelric	Wo	1	1
Æthelric Rufus	?	..	1
Æthelsige	So	1	..
Æthelstan	L	1	..
Æthelweard	D	2	..
Æthelwig	Nf, Sf	1	2
Æthelwine	Wa	..	1
Æthelwine	Hu	..	1
Æthelwine	So	2	..
Agemund	L	1	..
Áskell	L	1	..
Azur	Wo	3	1
Azur	Br	1	1
Azur	K	1	..
Beorhtric	W	6	4
Beorhtric	Gl, D, Do, Wo	5	3
Beorhtwine	Wo	1	1
Beorhtwine	Do	1	..
Bondi	Br, Bk, Bd, Gl, O, Nth, E	2	2

* Thegns whose names appear only on spurious charters are not listed here.
** In some cases the location is conjectural (see Appendix B, s.n.).

Appendix J—*continued*

Name	Location of lands	Attestations Genuine	Doubtful
Burgræd	Bd, Bk, Nth	..	1
Carl	Sx, Sr, Ha, W, So	6	3
Ceolmær	Wo	1	..
Ceolric	So	1	..
Ceolweald	Sf	1	..
Cyneweard	Br, Wo, E, Gl, Wa	1	3
Cynesige	So, Co	..	1
Dodda	Co	5	2
Eabpisus	?	1	..
Eadmær	K	2	1
Eadmær	Ht, Mx, Bk, D, So, E	1	..
Eadric	Nf, Sf, or K	1	..
Eadwine	Nf, Sf	..	2
Eadwulf	Y, Nf, D, Sf, Co	1	..
Earngeat	Wo	1	1
Ecglaf	?	1	1
Ecgwulf	?	3	1
Esbern	SW	..	1
Esgar	Sr, Ht, Bk, Wa, Mx, C, Sf, Nf, Br, O, Nt, E	5	3
Everwacer	So, D	1	1
Godric	K	1	1
Godric	Br	1	..
Godric	L	2	..
Godric	Wo	1	..
Godric	K	..	1
Godsunu	?	..	1
Godwine	So	3	2
Godwine	O	..	1
Godwine	K	..	1
Hákon	L	1	..
Herdingus	So, Br	1	..
Hugo	Hu, Br, O, Wa	..	2
Iadulf	L or Y	3	..
Leofcild	E	1	1
Leofnoð	Co	1	1
Leofric	Wo or Bd	..	1
Leofsige	Bd	..	1
Leofwine	Bk, Ht	1	1
Locre	Nt	1	..
Lyfing	Ha, W, So, He, Db, Bk, Ht, Y, K, Nth, La, E	2	1
Mærleswegen	L, Gl, So, Y, D	2	..
Manni	Mx or Sf	1	..
Nefetofi	?	2	..
Norðmann	Nth	1	1

Name	Location of lands	Attestations Genuine	Doubtful
Ordgar	D, So, W	10	4
Ordlaf	SW	1	..
Ordwig	Wo	1	1
Ordwulf	So	6	..
Osbeorn	Y or He	..	1
Osgar	Bd	1	..
Osgod	EA	9	4
Osgod	Wo	2	1
Osmær	D	3	1
Osmund	?	..	1
Oswulf	Ht, Bk	1	1
Oswulf	E	2	..
Owine	Wo	1	..
Owine	L	1	..
Ralph	Nf, Sf	5	2
Robert fitz Wymarc	E, Sf, W, So, He, Hu, Sa, Ht, C	1	2
Rymhtricus	?	1	..
Siferth	L	1	..
Siric	L	1	..
Siweard	Wo, He	..	1
Siweard	Br, Db, Wa	..	1
Thored	W	4	1
Thurgisl	Bd	..	1
Thurgod	L	1	..
Thurkill	Br or He	1	2
Thurstan	?	1	..
Tofi	So	3	4
Toki	Nth, Lei, Db, Nt, Y, L, Wo	1	1
Toti	?	..	1
Ufic	?	1	..
Ulf	L	2	..
Ulf *fenisc*	L	2	..
Ulfcytell	C or He	1	1
Vikingr	Sf or C	..	1
Wagen	Wo, Wa	1	..
Wigot of Wallingford	Bk, Sx, Sr, Ha, Ht, Bk	..	1
Wigot of Lincoln	L	2	..
Wihtsige	?	..	1
Wulfbeald	Sf, Sx	..	1
Wulfgar	So	1	..
Wulfnoð	Ha	1	2
Wulfsige	So	1	..
Wulfweard	K, Mx, Bk, O, Gl, W, Ha, So, Do, Br, L	1	..
Wynsige	Bd, Bk	..	2

Thegns Who Were or May Have Been Sheriffs

Ælfgeat, Mx
Ælfstan, Ht
Ælfwig, Gl
Æthelnoð, K
Æthelwine, Wa
Æthelwine, Hu
Bondi, Bd

Godric, Br
Godwine, So
Leofcild, E
Leofric, Wo
Mærleswegen, L
Norðmann, Nth
Tofi, So

Scandinavian Names on the Charters

(26 thegns, 6 earls, 1 bishop, 1 abbot)

Agemund (Ögmundr), thegn
Áskell, thegn
Azur (Ösurr), thegn (three men)
Beorn (Björn), earl
Bondi (Bóndi), thegn
Carl (Karl), thegn
Esgar (Ásgeirr), thegn
Grimcytel (Grímkell), bishop
Gyrth (Gyrðr), earl
Hákon, thegn
Harold (Haraldr), earl and king
Locre (Lokkr?), thegn
Mærleswegen (Anglo-Scandinavian, Mærle-Sveinn), thegn
Manni, abbot
Manni, thegn

Norðmann (Norðmaðr, but possibly OE), thegn
Odda (Oddi), earl
Osgod (Ásgautr), thegn (two men)
Thored (Þórðr), thegn
Thurgod (Þorgautr), thegn
Thuri (Þórir), earl
Thurkil (Þorkell), thegn
Thurstan (Þorsteinn), thegn
Tofi (Tóvi), thegn
Toki (Tóki), thegn
Tostig (Tósti), earl
Ulf (Úlfr), thegn (two men)
Ulfcytel (Úlfkell), thegn
Wagen (Vagn), thegn
Wigot (Vigot), thegn

The Authenticity of the Charters

I. Royal Charters:

CD, 767, 1043.* Doubtful. The witnesses whose dates are known are compatible with the date given, but the witness list appears garbled. It begins with the king and queen followed by the two archbishops. Then come the signatures of two bishops, one earl, one priest, two thegns (*ministri*), one *praefectus*, six bishops, four abbots, one priest, two earls, three priests, five thegns (*milites*), one undesignated name, two thegns (*ministri*), two *praefecti*, four thegns (*ministri*), one *praefectus*, and seven thegns (*ministri*). Also some of the names occur twice (Alfgeat *minister*, Ælfwig *praefectus*, Leofric *presbyter*), and while it is impossible to say with certainty that they have been repeated in error, the garbled appearance of the list points to that conclusion. I would, however, hesitate to brand the charter and witness list as out and out forgeries, for *DB*, 71b, shows Sevenhampton, W, to have been held by Ælfstan.

CD, 769, 1042–4. Doubtful. The only name on the witness list which might cast doubt on its genuineness is that of an abbot Wulfweard. No abbot of this name is known from this period; there is an abbot Wulfweald of Chertsey but he does not seem to have become abbot until 1058 (*RB*, LII (1940), 97–98). Abbot Wulfweard occurs also on *CD*, 778, 792, 793, and 800, all of which are not above suspicion. There must, however, have been an unknown abbot of this name, for it appears on the genuine *FASM*, II, Exeter, xii. The land Cliff, K, which *CD* (769) gives to an Æðelred is shown as held by an Ælfric in *DB*, K, 9, but the latter may have been the son of the original grantee. The absence of any reference to the *trimoda necessitas* may be suspicious.

CD, 770, 1044. Doubtful. The charter bears this date, but this is not reconcilable with the signature of Ealdred who did not become bishop of Worcester until 1046. If the charter did not bear the date 1044 it might be assigned to 1046, as far as the witness list is concerned, but then the Indiction would be wrong.

CD, 771, 1044. Spurious. The witness list is irreconcilable with any date.

CD, 772, 1044. Spurious. Impossible are the names of bishops Ælfweald of Sherborne and Ealdred of Worcester and that of abbot Æthelwig of Evesham.

CD, 774, 1044. Genuine. Both this and *CD*, 775, refer to land given to Winchester and both estates are in *DB*, So, 87b, and O, 155, reported to have been held by Stigand, who had presumably kept them after he became archbishop in 1052. The Conqueror had then restored them to the church. The only name that occasions difficulty is that of Ælfgifu Emma who was despoiled by Edward in 1043. It is possible that a reconciliation took place between the king and his mother, for her name appears also on *CD*, 773, which seems to

* The date is either the actual date of a genuine document or the purported date of doubtful or spurious document.

be genuine and from about 1045. It is an argument against reconciliation that her name does not occur on a charter after 1045, but I think the reason for its absence is that she ceased to sign after Edward married Eadgyð. The case for reconciliation is further supported by the fact that a writ, addressed to Earl Ælfgar, who received his first earldom in 1051, grants Ælfgifu land (*CD*, 876), which after her death passed to Bury St. Edmunds with the approval of the king (*CD*, 878). Both these writs are deemed authentic by Dr. Harmer (*Writs*, pp. 148–9).

CD, 775, 1044. Genuine. A careless scribe has written *dux* for *abbas* after each of the six abbots whose names appear on this witness list. The occurrence of the name Ælfweard among those of the bishops and those of the abbots is not serious, for Ælfweard who was bishop of London (1035–44) had previously been abbot of Evesham (from 1014), and did not relinquish this office when he became bishop. This, however, is the only instance in which he attests in both capacities. I am inclined to believe that *CD*, 774, 775, 776, and 780 are all genuine Winchester charters, and that a careless scribe has made mistakes in copying the first two. If forgeries, they are most skilfully done.

CD, 776, 1045. Genuine.

CD, 778, 1045. Doubtful. The names of abbots Ælfwig and Æthelwig cause difficulty. It is, however, recorded in *DB*, W 68 that the land which this charter grants Þórðr was given to the church of Winchester by him. The two abbots may be unknown ones, who have not been traced elsewhere.

CD, 779, 1045. Spurious. This is a Westminster forgery (*ASC*, p. 433; *Encomium*, p. 60), but the witness list is so skilfully concocted that only the signature of Ælfgifu, who signs *Ælfgyfu imma*, points to a forgery.

CD, 780, 1045. Genuine. The witness list contains exactly the same names as *CD*, 776.

CD, 781, 1045. Genuine (cf. *ASC*, p. 463).

CD, 783, 1046. Genuine.

CD, 784, 1046. Genuine, unless the signatures of Eadsige as archbishop and Siward as bishop arouse suspicion. The two similarly sign *CD*, 778, and Siward was bishop at St. Martin's.

CD, 785, 1047. Spurious. The only date at which this could have been made is 1047, for bishops Ælfwine of Winchester (1032–47) and Æthelmær of Elmham (1047–70) both sign. However, other witnesses are irreconcilable with this date, e.g., earls Tostig, Ralph, and Ælfgar. The abbots Lyfing and Godric, designated as abbots of Coventry and Evesham respectively, are entirely mythical. The only abbots with these names from about this time are those of Peterborough (1052–66) and Winchcombe (1054–*ca.* 1069).

CD, 786, 1049. Spurious. The witness list as it stands is compatible with the date but it is very short and contains no abbots or thegns.

CD, 787, 1049. Genuine.

CD, 791, 1050. Genuine. Kemble marked this charter, which transfers the see of Crediton to Exeter, spurious, but there seem to be slight reasons to doubt its genuineness. The witnesses are entirely in accord with the date. I think the charter must at least be founded on genuine materials (cf. *EHR*, XI, 731).

CD, 792, 1050. Doubtful. The only difficulty lies in the name of Ordric, abbot of Abingdon, who seems to have become abbot in 1052, when Rotholf died. Is it possible that Ordric was abbot of Abingdon in 1050 and that Rotholf only enjoyed the fruits of the abbey or that Ordric is an error for Spearhafoc whose name appears on the almost identical witness list of *CD*, 793?

CD, 793, 1050. Doubtful. It must be said that these Abingdon charters, although having respectable witness lists, are somewhat suspicious. *CD*, 793, for example, purports to record the gift of Sandford, O, to Earl Godwin. Yet in *DB*, O, 156b, the earl is not mentioned in connection with the land. This may, however, not be serious. Its transference to the abbey is supposed to have taken place after the death of Godwin in 1054 when Harold gave it to the abbey (*Chron Abingdon*, I, 469). This transaction is recorded in *CD*, 800 (*q.v.*).

CD, 794, 1044–50. Spurious. The Croyland forgery with a truncated witness list.

CD, 796, 1052. Doubtful. This, another Abingdon charter, does not strengthen one's faith in that abbey's documents. It purports to be made in 1052, an impossible date for the witness list. Archbishop Eadsige, who signs, died in 1050. Cynesige and Robert, who sign as priests, became archbishops in 1051. The name of Abbot Ordric is, as noted above, difficult to reconcile with the date 1050 (supposing 1052 to be a scribal error). If an earlier witness list has been appended to this charter, as has been suggested (*Chron Abingdon*, II, 525), his name seems out of place. It may be noticed that *DB*, Br, 59 shows Chilton to have been held of Earl Harold TRE.

CD, 797, 1044. Genuine. The date assigned to this charter by Kemble, 1052–3, is unacceptable, for Archbishop Ælfric, who signs it, died in 1051. The date would seem to be fixed by the signatures of Earl Thuri, who may have lived as late as 1044 (*NC*, II, 375–6), and of Manni who was appointed to Evesham in that year. As Miss Robertson has argued (*ASC*, p. 457), the designation of Odda and Ælfric as monks is probably a scribal error.

CD, 798, 1053. Doubtful. This charter is witnessed by the king and five bishops, one of whom is Stigand who became archbishop in 1052. The charter grants Barkley, Ha, to "meo fideli ministro . . . Lutrise." Kemble thinks the name may be Leofric, but it might be anything. The land is shown in *DB*, Ha, 44 in the possession of Ælfsige *presbyter* both at the time of the survey and TRE. Lutrise may be an error for Ælfsige, but why is he then called *minister* and not *presbyter* or did he later become a priest? Or was Ælfsige the son of Lutrise? *DB* says he holds of the king and held of Edward and the charter grants the land freely. It is among the lands listed in *DB* as held by the Canons of Holy Trinity, Twineham. The date and the Indiction do not agree.

CD, 800, 1054. Spurious. This charter from Abingdon purports to record the gift of Sandford to the abbey, but the witness list is incompatible with the date given in the charter. Were the list genuine (and it may well be that a list from an earlier charter was appended to this one) its date would be fixed by the signature of Ulf, who became bishop of Dorchester in 1049, and that of Archbishop Eadsige who died in 1050. The only names not entirely reconcilable with this date are two. Leofsige, abbot of Ely, is usually said to have died in 1045, but Miss Robertson has convincingly argued that he lived another ten years (*ASC*, p. 467). The other name is that of Abbot Ordric.

CD, 801, 1055. Spurious. This is indicated by the attestations of such men as Archbishop Ealdred, Bishop Wulfstan, and the earls Gyrth and Eadwine. Yet it cannot be later than 1055, for Leofsige of Ely signs. The charter is an Evesham fabrication.

CD, 806, 1055–60. Genuine. Kemble dated this charter 1051–60 but it must have been made after the appointment of Tostig as earl and before the death of Archbishop Cynesige. *DB*, L, 345b, shows the land, Walcott, in the hands of the abbey of Peterborough (cf. also *Peter Chron*, p. 41).

CD, 808, 1060. Genuine (cf. *DB*, L, 345b; *Peter Chron*, p. 40).

CD, 809, 1060. Spurious. The date cannot be accepted nor are the witnesses reconcilable with any date, for they include the attestations of both Earl Leofric (*ob.* 1057) and Abbot Baldwin of Bury St. Edmunds who was not appointed until 1065.

CD, 810, 1061. Doubtful. If this charter is not genuine I am inclined to think that it is at least based on genuine materials. *DB*, D, 104 shows the land, Ottery, in the possession of St. Mary, Rouen, and declares that it also held this land TRE. The only name on the witness list not compatible with the date is that of Earl Waltheof. It is not impossible that this charter was made some time after the bequest. It is written in the past tense and ends: "Hic sunt designata nomina testium qui fuerunt in praesentia quando exhibui praefatae donationis cartulam." It could thus have been made in 1065, about which time Waltheof is thought to have received an earldom, if it be granted that Earl Ælfgar may have lived until 1065. The year of his death is not known but often given as 1062.

CD, 811, 1061. Genuine. In spite of Giso's alleged statement before the witness list I believe this charter to be almost certainly genuine and in any case based on genuine materials (see *CD*, 821, and *DB*, So, 89b).

CD, 813, 1062. Spurious. This is a most interesting witness list and, if genuine, would give the most complete picture we have of royal household officers in the last days of Anglo-Saxon England, but unfortunately the designations are very likely, as Dr. Harmer has suggested, additions from the Norman period (*BJRL*, XXII, 342; cf. Goebel, *Felony and Misdemeanor*, p. 362). The list may have been based on a genuine list but as it stands it has some inadmissible names. Ælfweald, bishop of Sherborne, died in 1058. I know of no Ælfric bishop at this time. Two abbots by the name of Leofstan attest but I know of only one from this period, that of Bury St. Edmunds (1044–65). The names of several of the thegns do not admit of identification and seem to be fabricated.

CD, 815, 1065. Spurious. The charter purports to be made at Winchester on the Feast of St. Sylvester (Dec. 31) at the time when the Confessor lay at death's door. The witness list, not quite compatible with the date, is an unusual one, and Harold is styled *"dei gratia dux."* Tostig evidently returned from exile to sign it. On another copy, dated 1062, and also spurious, see *Vita Wulfstani*, p. xxvi.

CD, 816,* 1065. Doubtful. Kemble marked this charter spurious. It purports to

* The witness list to this charter is omitted by Kemble, but is printed in *The Calendar of the Manuscripts of the Dean and Chapter at Wells* (Hist. MSS. Comm., London, 1907), I, 428–9.

be written by Giso at the king's command on May 4, 1065, at Windsor. Yet it states that two years ago (*Cal. Mss. Dean and Chapter of Wells*, I, 428, says three years) the king sent Giso to Rome where he was consecrated by Pope Nicholas (1059–61), whereas Giso went to Rome in 1061 (*NC*, II, 302). The list of lands also looks suspicious. Yet the witness list is in every way compatible with the date of the charter. The titles used to designate some of the thegns have a Norman look, but the scribe may well have had a genuine list in front of him and added the designations. I would hesitate both to reject it entirely and also to accept it without question.

CD, 817, 1065. Doubtful. This, like *CD*, 816, is a charter confirming the rights of an abbey (this time Malmesbury) to a long list of lands. It is dated 1065 and purports to have been made by the Abbot Beorhtric. The witness list is unimpeachable as far as agreement with the date is concerned but it is not witnessed by any thegns. I doubt its authenticity. The date and the Indiction do not agree.

CD, 819, 1060–6. Genuine (cf. *DB*, L, 345b, 346; *Peter Chron*, p. 71).

CD, 824, 1065. Spurious. The Westminster forgery dated on the Feast of the Holy Innocents, 1065.

CD, 825, 1065. Spurious. A second Westminster forgery bearing the same date as the other one.

CD, 912, 1042–6. Spurious. The witness list contains the names of Bishop Lyfing and also Bishop Ealdred who succeeded him at Worcester. Again, the name of Bishop William of London is not reconcilable with the names of several other witnesses, e.g. those of the earls Swegen and Beorn.

CD, 914, 1042–66. Although this charter is witnessed I do not use it. It purports to be a grant to St. Michael of Rouen and is witnessed by eight men who all seem to be foreigners. St. Michael is not mentioned in *DB* as holding the land named in this document, which certainly does not stem from the witan of England.

CD, 916, 1043. Spurious. The charter speaks of Pope Alexander II (1061–73). The witness list is incompatible with this or any other date. Eadgyð signs as queen; Ealdred, who was not made bishop until 1046, signs as such; Tostig signs as earl. (On the charter see Tait, "An Alleged Charter of William the Conqueror," p. 162.)

CD, 1332, 1042. Genuine.

CD, 1335, 1046. Genuine.

FASM, II, Exeter xii, 1044. Genuine.

HLC, pp. 300–2, 1059. Genuine. Too little is known of the exact date of the death of Bishop Ælfweald of Sherborne (usually given as 1058) for me to brand the list spurious because his name appears on it.

II. Private Charters:

CD, 768, 1043–4. Genuine (cf. *ASC*, p. 433).

CD, 773, 1045. Genuine. A late endorsement dates this document 1044. The only name causing difficulty, if this is the true date, is that of Abbot Wulfric of St. Augustine (1045–61, cf. *ASC*, 436–7). It is likely, however, that the true date of the charter is 1045 (cf. *ASC*, 436, and *Encomium*, p. xlix). Dr. Harmer dates it between December 26, 1045, and 1047 (*Writs*, p. 547).

CD, 788, 1042–3. Genuine. The dorsal note has the date 1049 which is impossible. Alistair Campbell (*Encomium*, p. xlix) would date it 1043–4 during the period of Stigand's deposition from Elmham. I would date it a year earlier. Stigand signs as priest, so the charter was probably made before his elevation to the bishopric (cf. *ASW*, XXX and p. 189).

CD, 805, 1051–6. Genuine. The date is fixed by the signatures of Earl Ælfgar, whose earliest appointment to an earldom was about 1051 (*ASChr*, E 1048), and of Earl Odda, who died in 1056.

CD, 807, 1051–3. Genuine. The date is fixed by the signature of Archbishop Cynesige (1051–60) and that of Earl Godwin, who died in 1053.

CD, 818, 1042–66. Spurious. Both Siward and Tostig, who succeeded him, sign as earls. Also, it is impossible to reconcile the signature of Archbishop Ealdred with those of earls Leofric and Siward.

CD, 822, 1061–5. Genuine. The date is determined by the signatures of Archbishop Ealdred, Bishop Giso, and Abbot Æthelsige, all of whom received their offices in 1061, and that of Earl Tostig who was outlawed in 1065 (cf. *ASC*, pp. 469–70).

CD, 823, 1062–5. Doubtful. The name of Earl Leofric is not reconcilable with those of other witnesses. *DB* does not show this land in the possession of St. Mary at Worcester. The witness list ends "cum licentia Eaduuardi regis et Haroldi ducis."

CD, 923, 1051–2. Genuine. This, however, does not seem to have been made in the presence of the king. Only two abbots, both from Wo, and one earl, Leofric, attest along with fifteen thegns.

CD, 939, 1046–50. Spurious. The witness list is compatible with this date, but the body of the charter mentions Pope Alexander II (1061–73) and has other marks of spuriousness (cf. Tait, "An Alleged Charter of William the Conqueror," p. 164).

CD, 956, 1053–5. Genuine. The date is fixed by the signature of Bishop Leofwine, who was appointed to Lichfield in 1053, and that of Earl Siward, who died in 1055 (cf. *ASC*, 465–8, and F. E. Harmer, "*Chipping and Market*: A Lexicographical Investigation," pp. 358–60).

CD, 962, 1042–3. Doubtful. Although doubt has been cast on this charter by Miss Robertson (*ASC*, p. 417), I do not feel it possible to brand it spurious. It is true that the signature *Ælfgyfu imma* is suspicious, but this may here stem from a scribe copying an original which need not have contained the "imma." Campbell says it is probably a forgery (*Encomium*, p. 55). Of the lands mentioned in the document I have been able to identify only one, Abbots Langley, Ht, and this is shown in the possession of St. Albans in *DB*, Ht, 135b. The date of the charter is fixed by the signature of Swegen as a thegn. He received his earldom in 1043.

CD, 963, 1042–66. Spurious. It is impossible to reconcile the signature of Abbot Brand, who was appointed to Peterborough in 1066, with those of earls Ælfgar and Tostig. No thegns sign. *DB* does not show the land Daylesford, Wo, in the possession of Evesham.

CD, 964, 1042–66. Spurious. Evidently another Evesham fabrication. Both Ælfgar and his son sign as earls. It is not known that Eadwine held an earldom before the death of his father. The signature of Beorhtric, abbot of Malmesbury, also causes difficulty. The date of his appointment is usually given as 1063 but it may have been in 1062, for William of Malmesbury in reporting it says he held office for seven years before being removed by the Conqueror in, it would seem, 1070. *DB* does not show the land, Little Dorsington, Wo, in the possession of Evesham.

HLC, pp. 247–8, 1060. Genuine. The charter's date, 1058, cannot be accepted. The true date is fixed by the signature of Ealdred, who became archbishop in 1060, but signs here as bishop, and that of Abbot Eadmund, who was appointed to Pershore in 1060.

Suggested Provenance of the Genuine Charters

Wiltshire
CD, 1332

Winchester, Hampshire
CD, 768
768
774
775
776
780
781
783
1335

Worcester
CD, 797
805
807
HLC, pp. 247–8
pp. 300–2

Devon
CD, 791
FASM, II, Exeter xii

Cornwall
CD, 787

Essex
CD, 788

Kent
CD, 773

Rutland
CD, 784

Lincoln
CD, 806
808
819
956

Somerset
CD, 811
822

Occasions on Which the Confessor Consulted or May Have Consulted His Witan

	Place	Date	Business	Authorities
1.	London	June 9–10, 1042	Accession of Edward	*ASChr*, C 1042, E, F 1041; *FlWig*, 1042
2.	Winchester	April 3, 1043	Coronation of Edward	*ASChr*, C, D 1043; *FlWig*, 1043
3.	Gloucester	November 16, 1043	Despoiling of Emma and Stigand	*ASChr*, C, D 1043; *FlWig*, 1043
4.	London	August 10, 1044	Appointment of Manni to Evesham; outlawry of Gunnhild (?)	*FlWig*, 1044; *ASChr*, D 1045; *Chron Evesham*, p. 86
5.	Sandwich	1044	Gathering of the fleet	*ASChr*, C 1044
6.	?	January 23, 1045	Marriage of Edward	*Ibid.*
7.	?	Spring 1045	Appointment of Hereman to Ramsbury	*ASChr*, C 1045, D 1046, E 1043 *bis*; *FlWig*, 1045
8.	Sandwich	Summer 1045	Gathering of the fleet	*ASChr*, C 1045; *FlWig*, 1045
9.	?	Christmas 1045	Appointment of Wulfric to St. Augustine's	*ASChr*, E 1043 *bis*
10.	?	Easter 1046	Appointment of Leofric to Crediton and Ealdred to Worcester	*ASChr*, E 1044, D 1047; *FlWig*, 1046
11.	?	Christmas 1046	Outlawry of Osgod Clapa	*ASChr*, C 1046, E 1044, D 1047; *FlWig*, 1046
12.	?	Spring or Summer 1047	Sveinn's request for aid; appointment of Heca to Selsey	*ASChr*, D 1048, E 1045, C 1047; *FlWig*, 1047
13.	?	Autumn or Christmas 1047	Appointment of Stigand to Winchester	*ASChr*, C 1047, D 1048, E 1045; *FlWig*, 1047
14.	?	Summer 1048	Sveinn's request for aid; appointment of Spearhafoc to Abingdon	*ASChr*, D 1049, E 1046, *FlWig*, 1048
15.	?	1048	Appointment of Æthelric to Lindisfarne (Durham)	*FlWig*, 1048
16.	?	Spring 1049	Baldwin's revolt and the emperor's request for aid; mission of Dudoc, Wulfric, and Ælfwine to Rheims	*ASChr*, C 1049, D 1050, E, 1046; *FlWig*, 1049

Place	Date	Business	Authorities
17. Sandwich	Summer 1049	Gathering of the fleet; return of Swegen	*ASChr*, C 1049, D 1050, E 1046 *bis*; *FlWig*, 1049
18. London	Midlent 1050	Dismissal of nine ships; mission of Hereman and Ealdred to synod at Rome	*ASChr*, C 1049, E 1047
19. ?	Autumn 1050	In-lawing of Swegen; report of bishops from Rome	*ASChr*, C 1050, E 1047
20. Exeter	1050	Transfer of Crediton to Exeter	*CD*, 791
21. London	Midlent 1051	Appointment of Robert to Canterbury, of Spearhafoc to London, of Rotholf to Abingdon; *heregeld* abolished and all lithsmen dismissed	*ASChr*, C 1050, D 1052, E 1048; *FlWig*, 1050; *Chron Abingdon* I, 463
22. ?	*Ca.* June 30, 1051	Archbishop Robert's report on his return from Rome	*ASChr*, E 1048
23. Gloucester	August 1051	Visit of Eustace; proposal to punish men of Dover	*ASChr*, E 1048; GR, I, 241–2
24. Gloucester	September 8, 1051	Affair of Eustace	*ASChr*, E 1048, D 1052; *FlWig*, 1051
25. London	September 21–22, 1051	Outlawry of Godwin; appointment of William to London and of Odda and Ælfgar as earls	*ASChr*, E 1048, D 1052; *FlWig*, 1051
26. ?	Christmas (?) 1051	Visit of Duke William	*ASChr*, D 1052; *FlWig*, 1051
27. ?	Midlent 1052	Dispatch of fleet to Sandwich	*ASChr*, E 1052
28. London	September 14, 1052	Return of Godwin	*ASChr*, F 1051
29. London	September 15, 1052	In-lawing of Godwin; out-lawing of Frenchmen; Stigand's appointment to Canterbury and Leofric's to Peterborough	*ASChr*, E 1052, C 1052; *FlWig*, 1052
30. Gloucester	Christmas 1052	Welsh war	*ASChr*, D 1053; *FlWig*, 1053
31. Winchester	Easter 1053	Succession of Harold to Godwin's earldom, and of Ælfgar to Harold's	*ASChr*, C, D, E 1053; *FlWig*, 1053
32. ?	Christmas 1053	Appointment of Leofwine to Lichfield, of Æthelnoth to Glastonbury, and of Ealdred over Winchcombe	*ASChr*, C, D 1053; *FlWig*, 1053

	Place	Date	Business	Authorities
33.	?	Easter 1054	Expedition against Scots	*ASChr*, C, D 1054; *FlWig*, 1054
34.	?	Summer 1054	Mission of Ealdred to the emperor	*FlWig*, 1054; *ASChr*, C, D 1054
35.	?	Early in 1055	Appointment of Tostig as earl of Northumbria	*ASChr*, D, E 1055; *FlWig*, 1055
36.	London	March 20, 1055	Outlawry of Ælfgar	*ASChr*, C, D, E 1055; *FlWig*, 1055
37.	?	*Ca.* October 31, 1055	Welsh war	*ASChr*, C, D, E 1055; *FlWig*, 1055
38.	Gloucester	November–December 1055	In-lawing of Ælfgar; Hereman's request for Malmesbury	*FlWig*, 1055; *ASChr*, C, D 1055
39.	?	Midlent 1056	Appointment of Leofgar to Hereford	*ASChr*, C 1056; *FlWig*, 1056
40.	?	Autumn 1056	Welsh war	*ASChr*, C 1056; *FlWig*, 1056
41.	?	Autumn or Christmas 1057	Appointment of Ælfgar as earl of Mercia, and of Æthelric to Selsey	*ASChr*, D, E 1057; *FlWig*, 1057
42.	Gloucester	April 23, 1058	Outlawry of Ælfgar; consecration of Æthelwig to Evesham	*ASChr*, D 1058; *FlWig*, 1058; *Chron Evesham*, p. 88 (cf. *EHR*, XLVIII, 3)
43.	?	Summer 1058	Appointment of Siward to Rochester, of Wulfstan to St Peter's, Worcester, and of Hereman to Wilton	*FlWig*, 1058; *ASChr*, D, E 1058
44.	?	Autumn or Christmas 1058	In-lawing of Ælfgar	*FlWig*, 1058; *ASChr*, D 1058
45.	Gloucester	April 23, 1059	Consecration of abbot Æthelwig	*Chron Evesham*, pp. 87–88
46.	London	Whitsuntide 1059	Confirmation of Herewald; visit of Malcolm	Stubbs and Haddan, *Councils*, I, 292; *NC*, II, 293.
47.	Waltham	May 3, 1060	Consecration of Waltham	*De Inventione*, chap. 16
48.	?	Christmas 1060	Appointment of Ealdred to York, and of Walter to Hereford	*ASChr*, D, E 1060; *FlWig*, 1060
49.	?	Easter 1061	Appointment of Giso to Wells, and of Æthelsige to St. Augustine's	*ASChr*, E 1061
50.	Gloucester (?)	Easter 1062	Appointment of Wulfstan to Worcester	*FlWig*, 1062; *Vita Wulfstani*, pp. 74–75
51.	?	September 1062	Declaration of Ealdred that his consecration of Wulfstan set no precedent	*FlWig*, 1062
52.	Gloucester	Christmas 1062	Welsh war	*FlWig*, 1063

Place	Date	Business	Authorities
53. ?	*Ca.* May 1063	Welsh war	*FlWig*, 1063; *ASChr*, D 1063
54. ?	Autumn 1063	Welsh affairs	*ASChr*, D 1063
55. ?	August 1065	Welsh war; appointment of Baldwin to Bury St. Edmunds	*ASChr*, D 1065; *FlWig*, 1065; Liebermann, *Geschichtsquellen*, p. 245
56. Britford	*Ca.* October 25, 1065	Northumbrian revolt	*ASChr*, C 1065; *Vita Æduuardi*, p. 422
57. London	Christmas 1065	Hallowing of Westminster	*ASChr*, C, D 1065; *FlWig*, 1065
58. London	January 6, 1066	Election of Harold	*ASChr*, C, D 1065; *FlWig*, 1066

M

APPENDIX P

Classes of Witnesses on Royal Charters

I. Classes of Witnesses on Royal Charters (Genuine):

Date	1044	1044	1045	1045	1045	1046	1046	1049	1050	1044	1055–60	1060	1061	1060–6	1042	1046	1044	1059	Total
Charter	CD 774	CD 775	CD 776	CD 780	CD 781	CD 783	CD 784	CD 787	CD 791	CD 797	CD 806	CD 808	CD 811	CD 819	CD 1332	CD 1335	FASM, II, Exeter xii	HLC, pp. 300–2	
King	1	1	1	1	1	1	1	1	1	1	1	1	1	1	1	1	1	1	18
Queen			1	1	1	1						1		1		1			7
Queen Mother	1	1				1													3
Archbishop	2	2	2	2	2	2	2	2	2	1	2	2	1	2	1	2	2	2	33
Bishop	10	10	9	9	9	1	13	5	5	3	2	1	4	1	5	2	5	3	97
Abbot	6	6	5	5	3			3	2	4			2		2		5	2	45
Earl	4	4	4	4	6	2	5	5	5	4	2	2	4	1	3	2	4	5	66
Thegn	10	10	9	9	9	2		15	13		5		10	8	10	2	35	9	156
Priest									4										4
Dean										1									1
Monk										6**									6**
Reeve											1								1
Regis dapifer												2							2
Consiliarius													2						2
No title*												5							5
Total	34	34	31	31	31	10	21	31	32	20	13	14	24	14	22	10	52	22	446

* All would appear to be thegns.
** Four of these appear to be monks, but two are almost certainly thegns.

II. Classes of Witnesses on Royal Charters (Doubtful):

Date / Charter	1043 CD 767	1042–4 CD 769	1044 CD 770	1045 CD 778	1050 CD 792	1050 CD 793	1052 CD 796	1053 CD 798	1061 CD 810	1065 CD 816	1065 CD 817	Total
King	1	1	1	1	1	1	1	1	1	1	1	11
Queen	··	··	··	1	··	··	··	··	1	1	1	4
Queen Mother	1	··	··	··	··	··	··	··	··	··	··	1
Archbishop	2	2	2	2	1	1	1	··	2	2	2	17
Bishop	8	7	4	8	9	9	4	5	4	9	3	70
Abbot	4	7	··	8	3	3	3	··	6	3	6	43
Earl	3	3	4	5	5	5	5	··	6	6	4	46
Thegn	21	21	15	15	6	8	4	··	5	11	··	106
Priest	5	··	··	··	8	3	4	··	··	3	··	23
Reeve	4	··	··	··	1	5	1	··	··	··	··	11
Chancellor	··	··	··	··	··	··	··	··	1	··	··	1
Canon	··	··	··	··	··	··	··	··	1	··	··	1
Camerarius	··	··	··	··	··	··	··	··	1	··	··	1
Regis procurator aulae	··	··	··	··	··	··	··	··	··	4	··	4
Pincerna	··	··	··	··	··	··	··	··	··	2	··	2
Cubicularius	··	··	··	··	··	··	··	··	··	1	··	1
Total	49	41	26	40	34	35	23	6	28	43	17	342

III. Classes of Witnesses on Royal Charters (Spurious):

Date	1044	1044	1045	1047	1049	1044-50	1054	1055	1060	1062	1065	1066	1066	1042-66	1043	Total
Charter	CD 771	CD 772	CD 779	CD 785	CD 786	CD 794	CD 800	CD 801	CD 809	CD 813	CD 815	CD 824	CD 825	CD 912	CD 916	
King	1	1	1	1	1	1	1	1	1	1	1	1	1	1	1	15
Queen			1	1		1		1		1	1	1	1		1	9
Queen Mother	1		1											1		3
Archbishop	2	2	2	2	2	2	1	2	2	2	1	2	2	2	2	28
Bishop	12	7	8	4	3		7	6	3	11	3	8	9	8	9	98
Abbot	6	7	4	4			4	4	5	11		7	7	3	5	67
Earl	6	3	4	6	3		5	4	4	5	4	4	5	5	6	67
Thegn	11	7	5			3	10	6		14		6	12	6	11	88
Priest							6									6
Deacon															1	1
Reeve							2									2
Regis dapifer										2						2
Staller	2									2						4
Camerarius	1															1
Chancellor			1							1			2		1	5
Notarius									1			1	1			3
Cubicularius									1	2		1				4
Chaplain									1				2			3
Reginae dapifer										1						1
Procurator aulae regis										1						1
Regis pincerna										2						2
Regis aulicus										1						1
Regis palatinus										1						1
Regis consanguineus										2						2
No title*									3		8	4			1	16
Total	42	27	27	18	9	7	36	24	21	58	20	35	42	26	38	430

* Of these thirteen appear to be thegns, two chaplains, and one an earl (all three on CD, 815).

Classes of Witnesses on Private Charters

I. Classes of Witnesses on Private Charters (Genuine):

Date	1043–4	1045	1042–3	1051–6	1051–3	1061–5	1053–5	1060	Total
Charter	CD 768	CD 773	CD 788	CD 805	CD 807	CD 822	CD 956	HLC, pp. 247–8	
King	1	1	1	1	1	1	1	1	8
Queen	:	:	:	1	1	1	1	:	4
Queen Mother	1	1	1	:	:	:	:	:	3
Archbishop	2	:	2	:	1	1	2	:	8
Bishop	7	3	2	1	2	2	9	1	27
Abbot	:	4	:	:	2	4	6	3	19
Earl	4	2	2	3	2	2	4	:	19
Thegn	:	:	:	3	5	:	:	10	18
Staller	:	1	:	:	:	3	3	:	7
Dean	:	1	:	:	1	:	:	2	4
Priest	:	:	2	:	:	:	:	5	7
Sheriff	:	:	1	:	:	:	:	:	1
Monk	:	:	:	:	2	:	:	:	2
No title*	3	4	5	2	:	:	5	:	19
Total	18	17	16	11	17	14	31	22	146

* All the untitled names are almost certainly those of thegns except for the five on *CD*, 956, who are very likely lawmen of Lincoln and should probably be classified with the thegns.

II. Classes of Witnesses on Private Charters (Doubtful):

Date	1062–5	1042–3	Total
Charter	CD, 823	CD, 962	2
King	1	1	2
Queen	..	..	..
Queen Mother	..	1	1
Archbishop	1	..	1
Bishop	3	1	4
Abbot	3	..	3
Earl	2	2	4
Thegn	1	..	1
Priest	1	..	1
No title*	10	10	20
Total	22	15	37

* Of the untitled names, one (*CD*, 962) belongs to a bishop, the rest to thegns.

III. Classes of Witnesses on Private Charters (Spurious):

Date	No date	1046–50	No date	No date	Total
Charter	CD, 818	CD, 939	CD, 963	CD, 964	
King	1	1	1	1	4
Queen	..	..	1	1	2
Archbishop	1	1	2	2	6
Bishop	1	2	4	1	8
Abbot	..	3	3	6	12
Earl	4	3	4	3	14
Thegn	..	..	..	2	2
No title (thegns)	..	3	..	..	3
Total	7	13	15	16	51

The Anglo-Saxon Church

CONSIDERABLE work has been done in recent years on various aspects of the English church in the late Anglo-Saxon period though there is need for a full history. Rose Graham has made a valuable study, "The Intellectual Influence of English Monasticism between the Tenth and the Twelfth Centuries," *English Ecclesiastical Studies* (London, 1929). In this she writes (pp. 164–5): "The legislation of the Witan illustrated the powerful influence of the bishops. Their ideal was an independent theocratic State, a strong united kingdom. Within this state the power of the church should be more and more direct, the secular laws should be inspired by the ethical spirit of Christianity, the state should co-operate with the church in the appointment of bishops and abbots and in the making of ecclesiastical laws. It was a practical ideal and the laws of Edgar, Ethelred, and Canute show how far it was attained; but the close interdependence of Church and State involved the decline of the one with the other." Knowles, *The Monastic Order*, has much of great value. He states that simony "scarcely existed" in England (p. 93); Böhmer on the other hand, when speaking of the foreign and English parties in the church in the reign of Edward the Confessor, says that simony, nepotism, pluralism, and marriage characterized the English party (*Kirche und Staat*, p. 69), and that the English church was very corrupt and getting worse (pp. 70–72). He differs again from Professor Knowles on the question of the monasteries. The latter states: "We may say, then, that the monasteries of England, on the day when King Edward 'was alive and dead,' were as a body living and powerful. There is no trace of serious moral decadence, nor of that lay encroachment which in previous centuries had had such disastrous consequences both in England and abroad" (*The Monastic Order*, p. 81). Böhmer says the monasteries were in bad shape; the vow of poverty was grossly neglected; there were extravagance in dress and fondness for dice and worldly music; feasts, banquets, hunting and wild riding were common (pp. 73–79). Knowles does give some support to Böhmer's contentions (pp. 79–81 and 94), but the great difference between the two is that the former makes irregularities the exception, the latter makes them the rule. R. R. Darlington, "Ecclesiastical Reform in the Late Old English Period," pp. 385–428, takes a very favourable view of the church in the last years of the Anglo-Saxon state. He denies, for example, that simony and pluralism were rife (pp. 399–401, 403) and holds that relations between the English church and the papacy were close (pp. 417–21). F. M. Stenton inclines to a favourable view also (*ASEng*, p. 462). It is an interesting commentary on the rewriting of history by each successive generation that what seemed a cancer in the church (e.g., papal influence) to such men as Stubbs (*CH*, I, 267–8) and Freeman (*NC*, II, 82) seems a sign of health to Darlington and other contemporary scholars, e.g. Stenton (*ASEng*, p. 462). Reference may also be made to R. R. Darlington, "The Last Phase of Anglo-Saxon Society," pp. 1–13, and D. Knowles, *CHJ*, VII.

APPENDIX S

Military Matters

THERE is little trustworthy information about the military resources of the England of the Confessor. It would seem that such expeditions as those against Scotland and Wales consisted of local levies buttressed by the huscarles of the earls involved and, at times, those of the king. This seems clear from the account of Siward's invasion of Scotland in 1054 (*ASChr*, D 1054), for some of both his and the king's huscarles perished. The naval force must have been raised for the occasion. For the Welsh war of 1055 Earl Ralph at first gathered forces. Only after his defeat was a force gathered, under Harold, from almost all England (*ASChr*, C 1055). A national effort seems indicated also in 1063 (*ASChr*, E 1063).

How important the standing army—the *þingmannalið* or *here*—was is difficult to determine. By and large I accept Larson's views on this (*King's Household*, pp. 152–66). P. Vinogradoff distinguished sharply between the *þingmannalið* and the *here* (*English Society in the Eleventh Century*, pp. 20–21, 35–36), but it seems clear that during the reign of the Confessor the latter is the Anglo-Saxon term used to describe the standing army (*ASChr*, C 1049, E 1048, D 1052) which in Scandinavian works is called the *þingmannalið* (*Flateyjarbok*, III, 370; *Heimskringla*, p. 500). Modern historians seem generally agreed that the huscarles were an organized guild and an important element in eleventh-century England (*ASEng*, p. 406; Stenton, *First Century*, pp. 119–21; Steenstrup, *Danelag*, pp. 127–54, 271–3; Rolf Nordenstreng, *Vikingafärderna*, pp. 90–93). The laws governing the guild may have been similar to the Danish *Leges Castrenses* or *Viðrlög* (*Scriptores rerum Danicarum*, III, 139–64; these are summarized in Larson, *King's Household*, pp. 160–5, and Sir J. H. Ramsey, *The Foundations of England*, I, 413–14). There are several references, in addition to those already cited, to the force in Scandinavian literature (*Flateyjarbok*, I, 203, 205; *Heimskringla*, pp. 189, 500, 506; *Vallaljóts Saga*, p. 24; *Knytlinga Saga*, chap. 7). The *þingamenn* are mentioned as having been recipients of the Danegeld in the Laws of Henry I (*Ancient Laws and Institutes of England*, I, 526). There are also references to the *þingmannalið* on runic stones (Geo. Stephens, "Some Accounts of Scandinavian Runic Stones," pp. 115–17).

The *þingmannalið* is not a unique institution. Its origins may go back to the *Jómsvíkingar*, a Danish military association of the tenth century with headquarters on the island of Wollin (*Flateyjarbok*, I, 96–105, 153–203). The veracity of this saga and other authorities is examined by Jón Jónsson (*Víkingasaga*, pp. 234–5) who concludes his discussion: "Hvernig sem því [the origin of the *Jómsvíkingar*, ca. 960–70] hefir annars verið háttað, þá mun Jómsborg mestmegnis hafa verið skipuð handgengnum mönnum eða hirðmönnum Haralds Danakonungs, og hafa þeir haft lögbundið skipulag, sem hirðmönnum er títt." Jónsson sees the origin of the *þingmannalið* in the entry of the *Jómsvíkingur* Earl Þorkell into the service of Ethelred in 1012 (*Víkingasaga*, pp. 298–300). On the other hand Bjarni Aðalbjarnarson thinks that King Cnut established the force about 1018 and that it numbered some three to six thousand (*ÍF*, XXVII, 19; cf. *NC*, I, 297–8; 497–500).

A similar institution existed at this time in the force of mercenaries employed by the Byzantine emperors. Its members were known as *Væringjar* or Varangians. Guðni Jónsson writes (*ÍF*, VII, 271–2): "*Væringjar* voru nefndir Norðurlandabúar þeir, er gengu á mála hjá Miklagarðskeisara, og var slíkt algengt á 11. og 12 öld. Nafnið er dregið af *várar*: trygðir, heit, og þýðir því menn, sem bundizt hafa í félagsskap eða bræðralag eða svarizt undir sömu lög." (Cf. *ÍF*, V, 214.) Again he says (*ÍF*, VII, 273): "... Væringjar höfðu sín eigin lög í sínum borgarhluta og stóðu beint undir keisara sjálfum." References to their assemblies and virtual autonomy are to be found in *ÍF*, VII, 272–6 ("Þá váru þat lög þeira, at hverr sá, er mann dræpi, skyldi engu fyrir týna nema lífinu"), and in *Heimskringla*, p. 449 ("Hugða ek, at þat væri réttr Væringja hér . . . at þeir skulu vera sjálfráða ok frjálsir um alla hluti fyrir öllum mönnum, en vera konungi einum og drótningu þjónustu skyldir").

Another matter on which I am tempted to say something here is the dismissal of the lithsmen in 1049 and 1050 (*ASChr*, E 1047, C 1049, 1050). I am inclined to regard the dismissal of the permanent navy as being the work of Godwin, an attempt on his part to weaken the forces that might be arrayed against him, if a clash occurred between him and the king. If one knew whether the *butsecarls* (*ASChr*, C, D 1052) from Hastings, who joined Godwin in 1052, were sailors, as Plummer (*TSCP*, II, 239–40) and Professor Stenton (*ASEng*, p. 558), together with the majority of historians, hold, or the standing garrisons of Hastings and Sandwich, as Vinogradoff (*English Society*, pp. 20–21) argued, it would be easier to arrive at a conclusion, for it would hardly seem reasonable that men deprived of their employment by Godwin would join him. Probably no certainty is possible in this matter. I do not find Plummer's argument entirely convincing. The passage which he cites from Domesday Book speaks of expeditions "uel terra uel mari." The *butsecarls* mentioned are thus more likely to have been soldiers who could fight on either land or sea. The use of the word by Florence in 1066 would seem to clinch the argument, not for, but against, the interpretation of "sailor," for in speaking of the same event the *ASChr*, D 1066, uses the term *burhwaru*, which is usually translated "burgesses" or "townsmen," but possibly more properly "garrison." This word occurs in *CD*, 956, where it can only mean the townsmen or garrison of Lincoln. It may also be fairly asked: If *butsecarls* means the members of the permanent navy, i.e., the lithsmen (another double-edged term meaning, if AS, "sailors," if OIcel, "warriors"), how is their appearance in London in 1066 (sixteen years after the permanent navy was disbanded), in such numbers as to be influential, to be explained? It is true, as Plummer says, that the *ASChr*, E 1036, states that the lithsmen of London supported Harold, but it is by no means certain that the word here means "sailors" and not the "garrison and navy" or even the "húskarlalið" in London. However, even if in this instance it means "sailors" of the permanent navy, it should be remembered that in 1035 these would be of considerable importance, but non-existent or negligible in 1066. Vinogradoff's derivation of *butsecarls* from *boð* is quite acceptable, for the latter frequently has the meaning of a summons to the army or to a *þing*, e.g., Swedish *budsticka* (see Vigfússon, *Icelandic-English Dictionary*, s.v. *boð*), but a more likely derivation is from mediaeval Latin, *buza*, meaning a kind of galley or transport ship (see H. Shetelig and H. Falk, *Scandinavian Archaeology*, Oxford, 1937, p. 375). However, I see little possibility of a definite conclusion at present, and pursue the matter no further.

Itinerary of Edward the Confessor*

Date		Place
1042	June 9–10	London
	? Autumn	Wilts (*CD*, 1332)
1043	April 3	Winchester; *CD*, 768, may be from this date
	November 16	Gloucester, whence Edward went to Winchester to despoil his mother; *CD*, 773, testifies to his presence in Kent during the year
1044	Lammas	London; the king was also at Sandwich with the fleet, probably during the summer; he was also at Winchester during the year (*CD*, 774, 775) and likely in Devon (*FASM*, II, Exeter, xii); *CD*, 797, testifies to his presence in Worcester
1045	? Summer	At Sandwich with the fleet; *CD*, 776, 780, 781, testify to his presence at Winchester on two occasions during the year
1046	?	Rutland or Lincolnshire (*CD*, 784); Winchester (*CD*, 783, 1335); between 1046 and 1049 the king's movements cannot be traced
1049	? Summer	At Sandwich with the fleet; *CD*, 787 testifies to the king's presence in Cornwall
1050	? Midlent	London
	?	Exeter (*CD*, 791)
1051	Midlent	London
	August	Gloucester
	September 8	Gloucester
	September 21–22	London
1052	? Summer	The king may have been with the fleet at Sandwich
	September 14–15	London
	Christmas	Gloucester
1053	Easter	Winchester
1055	Midlent	London
	? November–December	Gloucester; there is no information about 1056 and 1057 unless, as Larson conjectures, the king was in London when the ætheling died
1058	Easter	Gloucester
1059	April 23	Gloucester
	May 23	London; *HLC*, pp. 300–2, shows the king at Worcester sometime during this year
1060	May 3	Waltham; if *HLC*, pp. 247–8, is from this year the king visited Worcester; *CD*, 808, shows the presence of the king in Lincoln

* The table of contents in *NC*, II, was helpful in the construction of this chart. Authorities not cited here will be found in Appendix O.

Date		Place
1061	?	Somerset (*CD*, 811)
1062	Easter	? Gloucester
	Christmas	Gloucester; Larson is wrong in interpreting *FlWig*, 1063, as saying that it was after Christmas 1063 that Harold left Gloucester; the reference is to Christmas 1062; there is no information for the years 1063 and 1064
1065	October 25	Britford
	December 28	London
1066	January 5	London

BIBLIOGRAPHY

Mediaeval Sources

(a) *Chronicles, Annals, Biographies, Sagas, etc.*

1. Adam of Bremen, *Gesta Hammaburgensis ecclesiae pontificum* (*PL*, CXLVI).
2. Ailred of Rievaulx, *Vita S. Edwardi regis et confessoris* (*PL*, CXCV).
3. *Anglia Sacra*, ed. H. Wharton, London, 1691 (2 vols.).
4. *The Anglo-Saxon Chronicle*, ed. B. Thorpe, London, 1861 (*RS*, 2 vols.).
5. *The Bayeux Tapestry*, ed. E. Maclagan, London, 1945.
6. *Beowulf and the Fight at Finnsburg*, ed. Fr. Klaeber, New York, 1928.
7. *Chronicon abbatiæ de Evesham*, ed. W. D. Macray, London, 1863 (*RS*).
8. *Chronicon abbatiæ Rameseiensis*, ed. W. D. Macray, London, 1886 (*RS*).
9. *Chronicon monasterii de Abingdon*, ed. J. Stevenson, London, 1858.
10. Eadmer, *Historia novorum*, ed. M. Rule, London, 1884 (*RS*).
11. *Encomium Emmae reginae*, ed. A. Campbell, London, 1949 (Camden 3rd series, LXXII).
12. *The First Nine Books of the Danish History of Saxo Grammaticus*, translated by O. Elton, London, 1894.
13. *Fjörutíu Íslendinga þættir*, ed. Þórleifr Jónsson, Reykjavík, 1904.
14. *Flateyjarbok*, Christiania, 1860–8 (3 vols.).
15. Florence of Worcester, *Florentii Wigorniensis monachi chronicon ex chronicis*, ed. B. Thorpe, London, 1848–9 (2 vols.). Also in *MHB*.
16. —— *The Chronicle of Florence of Worcester*, translated from the Latin by Thomas Forester, London, 1854.
17. *Foundation of Waltham Abbey: The Tract De inventione sanctæ crucis nostræ in Monte Acuto et de ductione ejusdem apud Waltham*, ed. W. Stubbs, Oxford, 1861.
18. Gaimar, Geoffrey, *L'Estorie des Engles*, ed. T. D. Hardy and C. T. Martin, London, 1888–9 (*RS*).
19. Giso of Wells, *The Autobiography of Giso of Wells: Ecclesiastical Documents*, I, *A Brief History of the Bishoprick of Somerset*, ed. J. Hunter, London, 1840 (Camden Old Series, VIII).
20. Henry of Huntingdon, *Historia Anglorum*, ed. T. Arnold, London, 1879 (*RS*).
21. *Historia et cartularium monasterii Sancti Petri Gloucestriæ*, ed. W. H. Hart, London, 1863, I (*RS*).
22. Hugh Candidus, *The Chronicle of Hugh Candidus*, ed. W. T. Mellows, London, 1949.
23. *Íslenzk fornrit*, Reykjavík, 1933 onwards.
24. *The King's Mirror (Speculum regale—Konungs skuggsja)*, translated from the Old Norwegian by L. M. Larson, New York, 1917.
25. *Knytlinga saga*, ed. Finnur Jónsson (*MGH*, SS, XXIX).
26. *Lives of Edward the Confessor*, ed. H. R. Luard, London, 1858 (*RS*).
27. Ordericus Vitalis, *Historia ecclesiastica* (*PL*, CLXXXVIII).
28. —— *Ecclesiastical History of England and Normandy*, translated by Thomas Forester, London, 1853–6 (4 vols.).
29. Roger of Hovedene, *Chronica magistri Rogeri de Houedene*, ed. W. Stubbs, London, 1868–71 (*RS*, 4 vols.).

30. *Saga hins heilaga Edvardar, Flateyjarbok*, III.
31. *Scriptores rerum Danicarum*, ed. J. Langebek and others, Köbenhavn, 1772–1878 (9 vols.).
32. *Scriptores X*, ed. R. Twysden, London, 1652.
33. Snorri Sturluson, *Heimskringla*, ed. Finnur Jónsson, Köbenhavn, 1911.
34. Symeon of Durham, *Opera omnia*, ed. T. Arnold, London, 1882–5 (*RS*, 2 vols.).
35. Thomas of Elmham, *Historia monasterii S. Augustini Cantuariensis*, ed. C. Hardwick, London, 1858 (*RS*).
36. *Two of the Saxon Chronicles Parallel*, ed. J. Earle and C. Plummer, Oxford, 1892–9 (2 vols.).
37. *Ungedruckte Anglo-Normannische Geschichtsquellen*, ed. F. Liebermann, Strassburg, 1879.
38. *Vallaljóts saga*, ed. Valdimar Ásmundarson, Reykjavík, 1898.
39. William of Jumièges, *Gesta Normannorum ducum*, ed. J. Marx, 1914 (Société de l'histoire de Normandie).
40. William of Malmesbury, *The Vita Wulfstani of William of Malmesbury*, ed. R. R. Darlington.
41. ―――― *Willelmi Malmesbiriensis de gestis pontificum Anglorum libri quinque*, ed. N. E. S. A. Hamilton, London, 1870 (*RS*).
42. ―――― *Willelmi Malmesbiriensis monachi de gestis regum Anglorum libri quinque*, ed. W. Stubbs, London, 1887–9 (*RS*, 2 vols.).
43. ―――― *William of Malmesbury's Life of St. Wulstan bishop of Worcester*, translated by J. H. F. Peile, Oxford, 1934.
44. William of Poitiers, *Gesta Wilhelmi Conquestoris* (*PL*, CXLIX).

(b) *Laws and Ecclesiastical Canons*

45. *Ancient Laws and Institutes of England*, ed. B. Thorpe, London, 1840 (2 vols.).
46. *Concilia magnae Britanniae et Hiberniae*, ed. D. Wilkins, London, 1737 (4 vols.).
47. *Councils and Ecclesiastical Documents Relating to Great Britain and Ireland*, ed. W. Stubbs and A. W. Haddan, Oxford, 1869–78 (3 vols.).
48. *Die Gesetze der Angelsachsen*, ed. F. Liebermann, Halle, 1903–16 (3 vols.).
49. *The Laws of the Kings of England from Edmund to Henry I*, ed. A. J. Robertson, Cambridge, 1925.
50. *The Leofric Missal*, ed. F. E. Warren, Oxford, 1883.

(c) *Landbooks, Wills, Writs, Fiscal Surveys, etc.*

51. *Anglo-Saxon Charters*, ed. A. J. Robertson, Cambridge, 1939.
52. *Anglo-Saxon Wills*, ed. D. Whitelock, Cambridge, 1930.
53. *Anglo-Saxon Writs*, ed. F. E. Harmer, Manchester, 1952.
54. *Cartularium monasterii de Rameseia*, ed. W. H. Hart and P. A. Lyons, London, 1884–93 (*RS*).
55. *Cartularium Saxonicum*, ed. W. de Gray Birch, London, 1885–93 (3 vols.).
56. *Codex diplomaticus aevi Saxonici*, ed. J. M. Kemble, London, 1839–48 (6 vols.).
57. *The Crawford Collection of Early Charters and Documents*, ed. A. S. Napier and W. H. Stevenson, Oxford, 1895 (Anecdota Oxoniensia, Mediaeval and Modern Series, VII).
58. *Diplomatarium Islandicum*, Kaupmannahöfn and Reykjavík, 1857 onwards.
59. *Documents Illustrative of the Social and Economic History of the Danelaw*, ed. F. M. Stenton, London, 1920 (The British Academy Records of the Social and Economic History of England and Wales, V).

60. *Domesday Book, seu liber censualis Willelmi Primi regis Angliæ*, ed. A. Farley and H. Ellis, London, 1783–1816 (4 vols.).
61. *Facsimiles of Ancient Charters in the British Museum*, London, 1873–8 (4 parts).
62. *Facsimiles of Anglo-Saxon Manuscripts*, ed. W. B. Sanders, Southampton, 1878–84 (Ordnance Survey, 3 parts).
63. *Feudal Documents from the Abbey of Bury St. Edmunds*, ed. D. C. Douglas, London, 1932 (The British Academy Records of the Social and Economic History of England and Wales, VIII).
64. *A Hand-Book to the Land-Charters and Other Saxonic Documents*, ed. J. Earle, Oxford, 1888.
65. *Hemingi chartularium ecclesiae Wigorniensis*, ed. T. Hearne, Oxford, 1723 (2 vols.).
66. *The Lincolnshire Domesday and the Lindsey Survey*, ed. C. W. Foster and Thos. Longley, Horncastle, 1924 (Lincoln Record Society, XIX).
67. *Monasticon Anglicanum*, ed. W. Dugdale; new enlarged edition by J. Caley, H. Ellis, and B. Bandinel, London, 1817–30 (6 vols. in 8).
68. *Regesta regum Anglo-Normannorum 1066–1154*, ed. H. W. C. Davis, Oxford, 1913.
69. *Select English Historical Documents*, ed. F. E. Harmer, Cambridge, 1914.
70. "Three Westminster Writs of King Edward the Confessor," ed. F. E. Harmer, *EHR*, LI.
71. *Transcripts of Charters Relating to the Gilbertine Houses of Sixle, Ormsby, Catley, Bullington and Alvingham*, ed. F. M. Stenton, Horncastle, 1922 (Lincoln Record Society, XVIII).
72. *Two Chartularies of the Priory of St. Peter at Bath*, ed. W. Hunt, London, 1893 (Somerset Record Society, VII).

Modern Works

73. Adams, G. B., *Constitutional History of England*, New York, 1925.
74. Amira, Karl von, "Recht," *Grundriss der Germanischen Philologie*, III, Strassburg, 1900.
75. Baldwin, J. F., *The King's Council in England during the Middle Ages*, Oxford, 1913.
76. Barraclough, G., *Mediaeval Germany 911–1250*, Oxford, 1948.
77. —— *The Origins of Modern Germany*, Oxford, 1949.
78. Bense, J. F., *Anglo-Dutch Relations from the Earliest Times to the Death of William the Third*, The Hague, 1925.
79. Bigelow, M. M., *History of Procedure in England*, London, 1880.
80. Bloch, Marc, "La Vie de S. Édouard le Confesseur par Osbert de Clare," *Analecta Bollandiana*, XLI (1923).
81. Böhmer, H., *Kirche und Staat in England und der Normandie im XI und XII Jahrhundert*, Leipzig, 1899.
82. Brandileone, F., "Early Anglo-Saxon Documents," *Illinois Law Review*, XIII (1918–19).
83. Breslau, H., *Handbuch der Urkundenlehre für Deutschland und Italien*, Leipzig, 1912–31 (2 vols.).
84. Brunner, H., *Deutsche Rechtsgeschichte*, Leipzig, 1906–28 (2 vols.).
85. Cam, Helen M., "Suitors and *Scabini*," *Speculum*, X (1935).
86. Chadwick, H. Munro, *Studies on Anglo-Saxon Institutions*, Cambridge, 1905.
87. —— *The Origin of the English Nation*, Cambridge, 1924.
88. —— *The Heroic Age*, Cambridge, 1926.

89. Chambers, R. W., *Beowulf,* Cambridge, 1932.
90. Chrimes, S. B., *An Introduction to the Administrative History of Mediaeval England,* Oxford, 1952.
91. Clarke, M. V., *Medieval Representation and Consent,* London, 1936.
92. Collingwood, W. G., *Scandinavian Britain,* London, 1908.
93. Coote, H. C., *The Romans of Britain,* London, 1878.
94. Craster, H. H. E., "Reconstruction of an Early Post-Conquest Chronicle," *EHR,* XL (1925).
95. Darlington, R. R., "Æthelwig, Abbot of Evesham," *EHR,* XLVIII (1933).
96. —— "Ecclesiastical Reform in the Late Old English Period," *EHR.* LI (1936).
97. —— "The Last Phase of Anglo-Saxon Society," *History,* XXII (1937–8).
98. Davis, H. W. C., "The Anglo-Saxon Laws," *EHR,* XXVIII (1913).
99. Deanesly, M., *History of the Medieval Church,* London, 1925.
100. —— "The Archdeacons of Canterbury under Archbishop Ceolnoth," *EHR,* XLII (1927).
101. —— "The Court of King Æthelberht of Kent," *CHJ,* VII (1942).
102. Dockhorn, Klaus, *Der deutsche Historismus in England,* Göttingen, 1950.
103. Dopsch, Alfons, *The Economic and Social Foundations of European Civilization,* London, 1937.
104. Douglas, D. C., "The Domesday Survey," *History,* XXI (1936–7).
105. Douglas, David, "Edward the Confessor, Duke William of Normandy, and the English Succession," *EHR,* LXVIII (1953).
106. Drögereit, R., "Gab es eine angelsächsische Königskanzlei?" *AfU,* XIII (1935).
107. Dúason, Jón, *Rjettarstaða Grænlands nýlendu Íslands,* Reykjavík, 1947.
108. Ekwall, E., *Oxford Dictionary of English Place Names,* Oxford, 1940.
109. —— *Scandinavians and Celts in the North-west of England,* Lund, 1918 (Lund Universitets årsskrift. N. F. Avd. I, Bd. 14, Nr. 27).
110. Ellis, H., *A General Introduction to Domesday Book,* London, 1833 (2 vols.).
111. Feiling, K., *A History of England,* London, 1950.
112. Feilitzen, O. von, *The Pre-Conquest Personal Names of Domesday Book,* Uppsala, 1937.
112a. Forsberg, R., *A Contribution to a Dictionary of English Place Names,* Uppsala, 1950.
113. Forssner, T., *Continental-Germanic Personal Names in England in Old and Middle English Times,* Uppsala, 1916.
114. Freeman, E. A., *The History of the Norman Conquest of England,* revised American edition, Oxford and New York, 1873–9 (6 vols.).
115. Galbraith, V. H., *Studies in the Public Records,* London, 1948.
116. —— "Literacy of the Medieval English Kings," *Proceedings of the British Academy 1935.*
117. —— "Monastic Foundation Charters of the Eleventh and Twelfth Centuries," *CHJ,* IV (1939).
118. Giry, A., *Manuel de diplomatique,* Paris, 1894 and 1925.
118a. Glover, R., "English Warfare in 1066," *EHR,* LXVII (1952).
119. Gneist, R., *The History of the English Constitution,* London, 1886 (2 vols.).
120. Goebel, J., *Felony and Misdemeanor,* New York, 1937.
121. Green, J. R., *The Making of England,* London, 1881.
122. —— *The Conquest of England,* London, 1883.

123. Grierson, P., "A Visit of Earl Harold to Flanders in 1056," *EHR*, LI (1936).
124. ———— "Election and Inheritance in Early Germanic Kingship," *CHJ*, VII (1942).
125. ———— "Les Livres de l'Abbé Seiwold de Bath," *RB*, LII (1940).
126. ———— "Relations between England and Flanders before the Norman Conquest," *TRHS*, XXIII (1941).
127. Hægstad, M., and Torp, Alf, *Gamalnorsk Ordbok med Nynorsk Tyding*, Kristiania, 1909.
128. Hall, Hubert, *Studies in English Official Historical Documents*, Cambridge, 1908.
129. Hardy, T. D., ed., *Descriptive Catalogue of Materials Relating to the History of Great Britain and Ireland*, London, 1862–71 (*RS*, 3 vols. in 4 parts).
130. Harmer, F. E., "Anglo-Saxon Charters and the Historian," *BJRL*, XXII (1938).
131. ———— *"Chipping* and *Market*: A Lexicographical Investigation," *The Early Cultures of North-west Europe*, ed. Sir Cyril Fox and Bruce Dickins, Cambridge, 1950.
132. Haskins, C. H., *Norman Institutions*, Cambridge, Mass., 1918.
133. Haskins, G. L., *The Growth of English Representative Government*, Philadelphia, 1948.
134. Heningham, Eleanor K., "The Genuineness of the *Vita Æduuardi Regis*," *Speculum*, XXI (1946).
135. Hodgkin, R. H., *History of the Anglo-Saxons*, Oxford, 1939 (2 vols.).
136. Hodgkin, T., *The History of England from the Earliest Times to the Norman Conquest*, London, 1906.
137. Holdsworth, W. S., *A History of English Law*, London, 1923 (7 vols.).
138. Hunt, W., *The English Church from its Foundation to the Norman Conquest*, London, 1899.
139. Jensen, O., *Der Englische Peterspfennig*, Heidelberg, 1903.
140. Jolliffe, J. E. A., *The Constitutional History of Medieval England*, London, 1937.
141. ———— "Northumbrian Institutions," *EHR*, XLI (1926).
142. ———— "English Book-right," *EHR*, L (1935).
143. Jónsson, Jón, *Víkingasaga um herferðir víkinga frá Norðurlöndum*, Reykjavík, 1915.
144. Keeney, Barnaby C., *Judgment by Peers*, Cambridge, Mass., 1949.
145. Kemble, J. M., *The Saxons in England*, London, 1876 (2 vols.).
146. Kendrick, T. D., *A History of the Vikings*, London, 1930.
147. Kern, Fritz, *Kingship and Law in the Middle Ages*, translated by S. B. Chrimes, Oxford, 1939.
148. Knowles, Dom David, *The Monastic Order in England*, Cambridge, 1940.
149. Kolsrud, O., "Den Norske Kirkes Erkebiskoper og Biskoper indtil Reformationen," *Diplomatarium Norvegicum*, XVII, pt. 1, Christiania, 1913.
150. Larson, L. M., *The King's Household in England before the Norman Conquest*, Madison, 1904 (Bulletin of the University of Wisconsin, 100).
151. ———— *Canute the Great*, New York, 1912.
152. ———— *A History of England and the British Commonwealth*, New York, 1932.
153. ———— "The Household of the Norwegian Kings in the Thirteenth Century," *AHR*, XIII (1907–8).
154. ———— "The Political Policies of Cnut as King of England," *AHR*, XV (1909–10).

155. Levison, W., *England and the Continent in the Eighth Century*, Oxford, 1946.
156. Liebermann, F., *The National Assembly in the Anglo-Saxon Period*, Halle, 1913.
157. Lingard, J., *The History of England from the First Invasion by the Romans to the Accession of William and Mary in 1688*, London, 1883 (10 vols.).
158. MacDonald, A. J., *Lanfranc: A Study of His Life, Work and Writing*, London, 1926.
159. Maitland, F. W. (*see also* Pollock), *Domesday Book and Beyond*, Cambridge, 1897.
160. —— *The Constitutional History of England*, Cambridge, 1919.
161. —— "Introduction to Memoranda de Parliamento," *Maitland Selected Essays*, ed. H. D. Hazeltine, G. Lapsley, P. H. Winfield, Cambridge, 1936.
162. McIlwain, C. H., *Constitutionalism Ancient and Modern*, New York, 1940.
163. McKisack, May, *The Parliamentary Representation of the English Boroughs during the Middle Ages*, Oxford, 1932.
164. —— "London and the Succession to the Crown during the Middle Ages," *Studies in Medieval History Presented to Frederick Maurice Powicke*, ed. R. W. Hunt, W. A. Pantin, R. W. Southern, Oxford, 1948.
165. Meister, Aloys, *Deutsche Verfassungsgeschichte von den Anfängen bis ins. 14. Jahrhundert*, Leipzig, 1913 (Grundriß der Geschichtswissenschaft, Reihe II, Abteilung 3).
166. Morris, W. A., *The Mediaeval English Sheriff to 1300*, Manchester, 1927.
167. —— *The Constitutional History of England to 1216*, New York, 1930.
168. —— "The Lesser *curia regis* under the First Two Norman Kings of England," *AHR*, XXXIV (1928–9).
169. Nordenstreng, R., *Vikingafärderne*, Stockholm, 1926.
170. Oman, Sir Charles, *England before the Norman Conquest*, London, 1937.
171. Palgrave, Sir Francis, *Collected Historical Works of Sir Francis Palgrave*, ed. Sir R. H. Inglis Palgrave, Cambridge, 1919–22 (10 vols.).
172. Parker, James, *The Early History of Oxford 727–1100*, Oxford, 1885.
173. Parsons, Mary Prescott, "Some Scribal Memoranda for Anglo-Saxon Charters of the 8th and 9th Centuries," *Mitteilungen des Österreichischen Instituts für Geschichtsforschung*, XIV, Erg.-Band (1939).
174. Pedler, E. H., *The Anglo-Saxon Episcopate of Cornwall: with Some Account of the Bishops of Crediton*, London, 1856.
175. Phillipps, Sir Thomas, "Three Old Charters," *Archaeologia*, XXVI (1836).
176. Plucknett, T. F. T., "Bookland and Folkland," *Economic History Review*, VI (1935–6).
177. —— "Deeds and Seals," *TRHS*, XXXII (1950).
178. Pollock, F., and Maitland, F. W., *History of English Law*, Cambridge, 1898 (2 vols.).
179. Poole, R. L., *The Exchequer in the Twelfth Century*, Oxford, 1912.
180. Purlitz, F., *König und Witenagemot bei den Angelsachsen*, Bremen, 1892.
181. Ramsey, Sir J. H., *The Foundations of England*, London, 1906 (2 vols.).
182. Robinson, J. A., *Flete's History of Westminster*, Cambridge, 1909.
183. —— *The Saxon Bishops of Wells*, London, 1918 (British Academy Supplementary Papers, IV).
184. —— *St. Oswald and the Church of Worcester*, London, 1919 (British Academy Supplementary Papers, V).
185. —— "The Church of Edward the Confessor at Westminster." *Archaeologia*, LXII (1910).

186. Round, J. H., *Geoffrey de Mandeville*, London, 1892.
187. —— *Feudal England*, London, 1895.
188. —— "The Officers of Edward the Confessor," *EHR*, XIX (1904).
189. *Safn til sögu Íslands*, Kaupmannahöfn and Reykjavík, 1856 onwards.
190. Sayles, G. O., *The Medieval Foundations of England*, London, 1948.
191. Schmitz-Kallenberg, L., *see* Thommen.
192. Schramm, P. E., *A History of the English Coronation*, Oxford, 1937.
193. Searle, W. G., *Onomasticon Anglo-Saxonicum*, Cambridge, 1897.
194. —— *Anglo-Saxon Bishops, Kings and Nobles*, Cambridge, 1899.
195. Southern, R. W., "The First Life of Edward the Confessor," *EHR*, LVIII (1943).
196. Steenstrup, J. C. H. R., *Danelag*, København, 1882 (*Normannerne*, IV).
197. —— *Normandiets Historie under de syv förste Hertuget 911–1066*, København, 1925 (K. Danske Videnskabernes Selskab, Skrifter, Hist-Fil. Avd., Række 7, 5:1).
198. Stenton, F. M., *William the Conqueror and the Rule of the Normans*, London, 1908.
199. —— *Types of Manorial Structure in the Northern Danelaw*, Oxford, 1910.
200. —— *The Early History of the Abbey of Abingdon*, Oxford, 1913.
201. —— *The First Century of English Feudalism*, Oxford, 1932.
202. —— *Anglo-Saxon England*, Oxford, 1943.
203. —— "The Danes in England." *Proceedings of the British Academy 1927.*
204. —— "The Foundations of English History," *TRHS*, IX (1927).
205. —— "The Historical Bearing of Place-Name Studies," *TRHS*, XXI–XXV (1939–43).
206. —— "English Families and the Norman Conquest," *TRHS*, XXVI (1944).
207. —— "Early English History," *TRHS*, XXVIII (1946).
208. —— "St Benet of Holme and the Norman Conquest," *EHR*, XXXVII (1922).
209. Stephens, Geo., "Some Account of Scandinavian Runic Stones which Speak of Knut the Great, King of All the North," *Archaeologia*, XLIII (1864).
210. Stephenson, C., "The Origin and Significance of Feudalism," *AHR*, XLVI (1940–1).
211. —— "Feudalism and Its Antecedents in England," *AHR*, XLVIII (1942–3).
212. Stevenson, W. H., "The Old English Charters to St Denis," *EHR*, VI (1891).
213. —— "An Old English Charter of William the Conqueror in Favour of St Martins-Le-Grand, London A.D. 1068," *EHR*, XI (1896).
214. —— "An Alleged Son of Harold Harefoot," *EHR*, XXVIII (1913).
215. Stubbs, W., *The Constitutional History of England*, Oxford, 1874–8 (3 vols.).
216. —— *Registrum sacrum Anglicanum*, Oxford, 1897.
217. Tait, James, "An Alleged Charter of William the Conqueror," *Essays in History Presented to Reginald Lane Poole*, ed. H. W. C. Davis, Oxford, 1927.
218. Taylor, H., *The Origin and Growth of the English Constitution*, New York, 1890.
219. Thierry, A., *History of the Conquest of England by the Normans*, translated by Wm. Hazlitt, London, 1847 (2 vols.).
220. Thommen, R., and Schmitz-Kallenberg, L., *Urkundenlehre*, Leipzig, 1913 (Grundriß der Geschichtswissenschaft, Band I, Abteilung 2).
221. Torp, Alf, *see* Hægstad.

222. Tout, T. F., *Chapters in the Administrative History of Mediaeval England*, Manchester, 1920–33 (6 vols.).

223. Turner, G. J., "Bookland and Folkland," *Historical Essays in Honour of James Tait*, ed. J. G. Edwards, V. H. Galbraith, and E. F. Jacob, Manchester, 1933.

224. Turner, Sharon, *The History of the Anglo-Saxons from the Earliest Period to the Norman Conquest*, London, 1828 (3 vols.).

225. *The Victoria History of the Counties of England*, London, 1900 onwards.

226. Vigfusson, G., *An Icelandic-English Dictionary*, Oxford, 1874.

227. Vinogradoff, P., *English Society in the Eleventh Century*, Oxford, 1908.

228. —— "Folkland," *EHR*, VIII (1893); reprinted in the *Collected Papers of Paul Vinogradoff*, Oxford, 1928, I.

229. White, A. B., *The Making of the English Constitution 449–1485*, New York, 1925.

230. —— "The Household of the Norman Kings," *TRHS*, XXX (1948).

231. Whitelock, D., "Wulfstan and the Laws of Cnut," *EHR*, LXIII (1948).

232. Wilkinson, B., "Freeman and the Crisis of 1051," *BJRL*, XXII (1938).

233. —— "Northumbrian Separatism in 1065 and 1066," *BJRL*, XXIII (1939).

234. Zinkeisen, F., "The Anglo-Saxon Courts of Law," *Political Science Quarterly*, X (1895).

Index

(Subjects and persons dealt with in the appendixes are not included in this Index except where they appear in the body of the book. Among abbreviations used are the following: abb., abbot(s); abp., archbishop(s); app., appointed, appointment; A-S, Anglo-Saxon; att., attestation(s); b., bishop; Cant., Canterbury; cha., charter(s); e., earl(s); emp., emperor; k., king; t., thegn(s); wg., witenagemot.)

ABBOTS: att. of, 51–52; deposition of, 92; importance of, as witan, 49, 51–52; method of app. of, 91–92; represent their houses, 67

Abingdon, att. of abb. of, 52

Administration, system of, 2

Ælfgar, e., 73; app., 94; att. of, 58; helped by Welsh, 79; outlawed, 3, 29, 108

Ælfgar, t., att. of, 56

Ælfgifu Emma, queen, 35; and accession of Confessor, 86; att. of, 48; opposes succession of Confessor and is despoiled, 2, 101–2; reconciled with the Confessor, 48

Ælfhere, e., 99

Ælfnoð, t., att. of, 57

Ælfred, brother of Confessor, 49

Ælfric, e., 99

Ælfric, monk, 3; elected abp. by monks at Cant., 91

Ælfstan, t., att. of, 56

Ælfweard, b. of London, dies, 27

Ælfwine, abb. of Ramsey, att. of, 52

Ælfwine, b. of Winchester, att. of, 50

Ælla, k., 84

Æthelnoð, t., 59

Æthelric Bigga, t., 46

Æthelstan, b. of Hereford, att. of, 51

Æthelwig, abb. of Evesham, app., 91

Æthelwig, t., 59

Æthelwine, b. of Durham, 91

Æthelwulf, k., disposes of kingdom, 84

"all", inexact use of, in mediaeval writings, 44

Alsherjarping, 23, 96

Anglo-Saxon Chronicle, information in, on witenagemots in reign of Confessor, 26–32

Appointment: of earls, 93–94; of prelates, 91–92

Archbishops, att. of, 50

Army, not equivalent to wg., 30

Áskell *Tokes sune*, t., att. of, 58

Assembly, *see* National assembly

Atsere, t., 99

Attestation, formulas of, 48

August, wg. in. 71, 72

Augustine, St., 67

Autumn, wg. in, 72

BALANCE OF FORCES, in A-S Eng., 69

Baldwin, abb. of Bury St. Edmunds, app., 92

Baldwin V, count of Flanders, 78

Baronage, hostility of Crown and, 63

Barraclough, G., on election of kings, 84, 85

Bath, cha. from abbey of, 47

Beorhtric, t. (1), att. of, 56

Beorhtric, t. (2), att. of, 56

Beorhtweald, b. of Ramsbury, 46

Beorn, e., 46, 107; and affair of Swegen, 102–4; att. of, 58

Beowulf, 85

Bishoprics: method of bestowal of, 75; number of, in A-S Eng., 50

Bishops: att. of, 50–51, 72–73; deposition of, 92; methods of app., 75–76, 91–92; represent their dioceses, 67

Blegent, k. of Wales, made k., 79, 94

Böhmer, H.: on churchmen as witan, 49; on personnel of wg., 12

Bondi, t., att. of, 58

Bookland, 38; nature of, 98; suits concerning, 100, 101

Brichtulf, t., 40

Britford, wg. at, 29–30, 70, 71

Bureaucracy, 61, 66, 112

Burgesses, 42

Burgraed, t., att. of, 59

Burhwaru, 88

CAMPBELL, A.: on election of Harold I, 84; on forged witness lists, 35–36

Carl, t., att. of, 56

Centralization, in reign of the Confessor, 65

PRINTED IN
GREAT BRITAIN
AT THE
UNIVERSITY PRESS
OXFORD
BY
CHARLES BATEY
PRINTER
TO THE
UNIVERSITY